Coups and Army Rule in Africa

Coups and Army Rule in Africa

Studies in Military Style

Samuel Decalo

New Haven and London   Yale University Press

1976

Designed by John O. C. McCrillis
and set in Times Roman type.
Printed in the United States of America by
The Colonial Press Inc., Clinton, Massachusetts.

Published in Great Britain, Europe, and Africa by
Yale University Press, Ltd., London.
Distributed in Latin America by Kaiman & Polon,
Inc., New York City; in Australasia by Book & Film
Services, Artarmon, N.S.W., Australia;
in Japan by John Weatherhill, Inc., Tokyo.

Contents

List of Tables, Diagrams, and Maps

DIAGRAMS

MAPS

Acknowledgments

Much of the fieldwork for this study took place during visits to ten African states in 1971 and 1972. In the process I conducted numerous interviews with local leaders, political observers, junior and senior military officers, and members of the diplomatic community, and I also had the opportunity to undertake extensive trips into the countryside. It would be impossible to acknowledge all those scores of individuals who so kindly gave of their time to assist me in my research into the sensitive topics of civil-military relations and the array of power in African armies. Most of my informants were refreshingly candid and open, though requesting anonymity; some (as the then head of Dahomey's *gendarmerie*) opted to have witnesses during our formal interviews; and a very few (all in Mali, but including President Jean Bodel Bokassa of the Central African Republic) would have nothing to do with me. I am deeply indebted to all those who shared with me their specialized knowledge. Though research in Uganda was at the time (and regretfully to this very day) inadvisable, and a visit to Brazzaville politically impossible, much valuable information was gleaned from a variety of sources in neighboring countries, especially Zaire, Gabon, and Kenya.

Of those whose assistance I can openly acknowledge I wish to thank in particular Mr. Finagnon Mathias Oke and Mr. Orou Gani, both of Dahomey's I.R.A.D., the former for his hospitality and assistance in ironing out the details of my initial visit, and the latter for assistance in the countryside in my research on mass-elite relations and attitudes toward political power and central author-ity. I also wish to thank Ms. Winifred Weislogel of the State Department and at the time Deputy Chief of Mission in Lomé, who provided me with valuable insights into Togolese politics. I am similarly indebted to Mr. Donald Easum and Mr. Robert Ander-son (at the time Ambassadors to Upper Volta and Dahomey respectively), Richard Pyle (at the time Councillor in Bangui),

Upper Volta's Minister of Finance Marc Tiémoko Garango and Dahomey's then-President Hubert Maga and Colonel Maurice Kouandété.

A number of colleagues read portions of earlier drafts of this book and I wish to thank them for their valuable comments. Among them are Claude Welch (SUNY/Buffalo), James Mittelman (Columbia University), William J. Foltz (Yale University), and Peter Schwab (SUNY/Purchase). My students at the Graduate Faculty of the New School for Social Research were, for better or for worse, sounding boards for many of the ideas I developed about the African military and I also wish to acknowledge an intellectual debt to Ruth First whose *Power in Africa* is, in my opinion, the best work to date on African civil-military relations. I also wish to thank my editors Ms. Marian Neal Ash and Charles Grench for tolerating as much as they did my stylistic idiosyncrasies in the process of preparing the text for publication.

I have drawn on data and research I have published previously: in particular chapter 1, which was originally presented as a paper at the African Studies Association 1973 meeting in Chicago and was later published in the Summer 1975 issue of the *Journal of African Studies.*

Finally, I wish to thank my research assistant and typist, Ms. Carol Levithan, for her unstinting help through the several drafts of the manuscript; and my wife, Roma, for her general encouragement and for expertly redrawing my originally crude country maps that appear in this volume. It is to her, and to my parents, that I dedicate this book.

New York City
December 1975

Introduction

In the past several years studies on coup d'états in Africa and the political role of African military structures have proliferated. Armies have been analyzed in terms of their social and ethnic composition, training, ideology, and socializing influences. Intense debate has focused on the overt and covert reasons for their intervention in the political arena. Simple and complex typologies of civil-military relations and of military coups have been constructed; statistical data—both hard and soft—have been marshaled and subjected to factor and regression analysis in order to validate general or middle-range theories of military intervention. And, once in power, the officer corps' performance has been examined for insights into its propensity to serve as a modernizing or developmental agent.

With nearly one half of the continent ruled at any particular moment by military elements or by military-civilian coalitions, the previously fashionable discourse on the merits of unipartyism, mass vis-à-vis elite parties, pan-Africanism, and African socialism in all its varieties has largely petered out, clearing the ground for the handful of qualitatively superior in-depth empirical case studies. The current intense interest in African military hierarchies may be equally ephemeral. For much of the contemporary outpouring takes place within a theoretical vacuum filled with mutually contradictory hypotheses, neither tested operationally nor grounded in solid empirical data. Striking indeed is the paucity of detailed case studies of African armies, coups, or military regimes based on field work and utilizing primary sources. Military intervention is practically always defined—a priori—as a dependent variable, with the focus shifting to the more easily analyzable systemic parameters for the "detection" of the particular catalysts that evoked intrusion into the political realm. This intellectual predisposition and analytic approach have resulted in a gross reification of African armies. They have resulted too in an uncritical acceptance of formal organization theory as the explanatory framework for military behavior and of official rationalizations for military intervention—all faults associated with the earlier facile examination of the party states in West Africa.

Needless to say, the study of civil-military relations in Africa is fraught with problems, not the least of which are the frequent lack of basic documentation and archival material and its nonreliability. There are difficulties in tracing and interviewing both key ex-colonial administrators and current African officers and defense officials. There is an understandable sensitivity—and sometimes suspicion—in government circles and in African command headquarters about this sort of analysis. Indeed, the more acute the polarization of the army on a multiplicity of planes (and hence perhaps the more interesting academically), the greater the likelihood that detailed information, if forthcoming, may be misleading. Even basic "noncontroversial" hard data varies according to the source; this may include the size of actual forces, the number of officers and their tribal breakdown, the military budget, and the ethnic configuration of the country being studied. And the methodological problems of constructing cross-cultural soft data indexes (for example, the degree of "modernization" of military elites, levels of socialization to Western military norms, class and/or occupational origin) are familiar to all. Needless to say, correlations linking sets of variables that are intrinsically unreliable can only be regarded with a great deal of caution. And the neglect of the idiosyncratic factor—the "personal element," which plays such an important role in syncretic and unstructured societies and which is of paramount importance for an understanding of military upheavals—tends to negate conclusions based on analysis of secondary sources or statistical data.

There are two other weaknesses connected with much of the literature on the military in Africa: it is frequently based on organization theory, which is largely inapplicable to African armies, and the theoretical utility of the research is greatly hampered by overconcentration on a few selected countries. The former point will be elaborated on at a later juncture; the latter criticism is attested to by the dearth of scholarly attention to much of French Africa. Africanists have, for a variety of reasons, preferred to study anglophone Africa and only a handful of other states. While continentally valid theories of military intervention and performance in political office are the goal of scholarly research, insights from anglophone examples alone are likely to lead to lopsided generalizations and conclusions that are inapplicable to such states as Congo/Brazzaville and Dahomey (now People's Republic of Congo and People's Republic of Benin, respectively). One need not belabor the equal theoretical importance of both the Ghanaian and Dahomean experiences with military coups for the purpose of formulating general theories of military intervention. Indeed, greater attention to French Africa's experience may well challenge certain current assumptions about military rule in Africa.

The purpose of this study is to shift attention away from the discipline's fixation upon the systemic weaknesses of African states and the organizational features of African armies as reasons for coups to the internal dynamics of African military hierarchies, their officer cliques, and corporate and personal ambitions. It is essentially here that the motivations for military upheavals can be found, with the fragmentation of power in society at large allowing, or even encouraging, their unfettered expression.

1 Military Coups and Military Regimes in Africa

The first military coup in West Africa occurred in Togo on January 13, 1963. Togolese soldiers, recently demobilized from the French colonial armies and facing functional unemployment as a result of the denial of their request to join the minuscule Togolese army, mounted an armed confrontation with President Sylvanus Olympio that led to his assassination. The new civilian regime, hastily set up by the inexperienced military junta, promptly capitulated to the insurgents' demands, tripled the size and budget of the army, and promoted the key NCOs to officer rank. Within three or four years they became the majors and colonels of the expanded army.

Africa's reaction to the coup in Lomé was immediate and sharp—marked by vociferous verbal attacks on the junta and international ostracism of the new government until it had legitimated itself through national elections. Though the vehement condemnation of the events in Lomé resulted in part from the grudging respect Olympio had gained in Africa (his more oppressive measures at home were not fully realized), the ostracism of Togo was to no small extent also intended as a lesson and a warning to other aspiring military commanders in Africa. For, with minor variations and few exceptions, most civilian regimes in Africa were equally susceptible to similar military upheavals. Though at the Organization of African Unity and elsewhere proposals were presented regarding measures to be taken to prevent the spread of coups or the legitimation of military regimes, no common policy was ever hammered out. Indeed, on January 13, 1967—exactly four years later—when the Togolese army seized power from the government it had set up, there was scarcely a ripple across the continent, jaded by then by the spectacle of continuous coups, attempted coups, and military mutinies.[1]

1. According to one tabulation sixty-four such upheavals had occurred in Africa by 1968. Kenneth W. Grundy, *Conflicting Images of the Military in Africa.*

In the interim the Congolese and Dahomean armies had presided over the overthrow of Fulbert Youlou in Brazzaville (August 1963) and Hubert Maga in Cotonou (October 1963), respectively, in both cases handing power to another set of civilian leaders. In early 1964 came the mutinies that rocked Kenya, Uganda, and Tanganyika; and in February 1964 the Gabonese army toppled Leon Mba's government only to have its coup reversed by French airborne troops sent to reinstate De Gaulle's faithful ally. The next spate of coups came in rapid succession as civilian regimes crumpled like houses of cards in Zaire (then Congo/Leopoldville) on November 25, 1965, Dahomey (November 29, 1965, and again on December 22, 1965), the Central African Republic (January 1, 1966), Upper Volta (January 3, 1966), Nigeria (January 15, 1966, and again on July 29, 1966), and Ghana (February 24, 1966). This contagion of coups produced the first African military juntas with no immediate intention of relinquishing power to civilian politicians. By 1975 twenty of the continent's forty-one states (or just under 50 percent) were led by military or civil-military cliques. Several of the remaining states also had records of predatory attacks by their military forces (see tables 1.1 and 1.2). On statistical grounds alone the coup d'état and military regime had become the most prevalent political phenomena in Africa.

Outside the continent the rash of political instability and military intervention was greeted with dismay but with little surprise. The first upheavals appeared to single out some of the weakest political entities—countries that were inherently economically unviable or beset by deep ethnic cleavages and that lacked either prolonged preparation for political independence or the alleged stabilizing influences of mass parties and charismatic leaders. It was only with the collapse of civil authority in the two political giants of Africa, Ghana and Nigeria (both of which suffered their first coups within six weeks), that the roots and causes of military intervention in Africa and the nature of military rule became the subjects of sustained and probing analysis.

Not only were the two British Commonwealth countries more important internationally, but they were also regarded as significantly more developed politically than the states that had previously succumbed to military rule. The spread of the coup d'état syndrome into anglophone Africa dashed myopic assumptions that the long period of tutelage had insulated the former British colonies from the instability of Gallic Africa. Ghana in particular possessed a more viable economy, a growing "modern" sector, higher per capita income and literacy rates, less intense ethnic cleavages, a British-trained army steeped in the principles of noninvolvement in, and supremacy of, civilian authority, a large mass party, and Africa's best-known charismatic leader—all ingredients hitherto regarded as sufficient to prevent the collapse of civilian authority. Nigeria, though lagging behind Ghana on most socioeconomic indicators and beset by intense regional-ethnic cleavages, had been viewed as politically the most sophisticated state in West Africa, embodying the best of the "Westminster model" and hence a pacesetter for the continent. With the twin coups in Ghana and Nigeria in 1966—to be later followed by another in each state—some of the more facile early explanations of military intervention in Africa were finally swept aside.

MILITARY INTERVENTION: MOTIVES AND RATIONALIZATIONS

There are essentially two schools of thought regarding the causes of military takeovers in developing nations and in Africa in particular. The first tends to stress societal and structural weaknesses—institutional fragility, systemic flaws, and low levels of political culture—which act as a sort of magnet to pull the armed forces into the power and legitimacy vacuum. Typical of this approach is some of the work of Samuel Huntington, who argues that "the most important causes of military intervention in politics are not military but political and reflect not the social and organizational characteristics of the military establishment but the political and institutional structure of society." [2] The second interpretation of military coups, which Huntington at one time adopted,[3] relies on organization theory in attributing to African

2. Samuel Huntington, *Political Order in Changing Societies*, p. 194. See also Samuel Finer, *The Man on Horseback*.

3. Samuel Huntington, *The Soldier and the States.* See also Morris Janowitz, *The Military in the Political Development of New Nations*; John J. Johnson, ed., *The Role of the Military in Underdeveloped Countries.*

TABLE 1.1
Sub-Saharan Africa: Military Data

Country	GNP		Armed forces		Military expenditures		
	In millions $	Per capita	In 100s	Per 10,000 population	As % GNP	As % budget	$ per soldier
Botswana	60	100	—	—	—	—	—
Burundi	170	50	10	3.0	0.7	6.9	1,190
Cameroun	785	140	35	6.4	2.7	19.5	6,055
Central African Republic	180	120	6	4.1	2.2	7.9	6,600
Chad	210	60	9	2.6	2.4	13.5	2,360
Congo/Brazzaville	207	230	18	20.9	4.7	8.9	5,405
Dahomey	208	80	18	7.2	2.5	12.0	2,888
Equatorial Guinea	72	240	—	—	—	—	—
Ethiopia	1,730	70	350	14.9	2.9	17.0	1,433
Gabon	155	310	8	16.9	1.7	7.6	3,293
Gambia	40	100	—	—	—	—	—
Ghana	1,445	170	160	19.6	2.0	7.4	1,806
Guinea	351	90	50	13.5	4.3	8.1	3,018
Ivory Coast	1,092	260	45	11.2	1.3	6.9	3,154
Kenya	1,405	130	48	4.8	1.4	6.9	4,097
Lesotho	72	80	—	—	—	—	—
Liberia	232	210	41	36.9	1.4	6.7	792

Country	GNP		Armed forces		Military expenditures		
	In millions $	Per capita	In 100s	Per 10,000 population	As % GNP	As % budget	$ per soldier
Malagasy	780	111	40	5.6	1.7	9.0	3,250
Malawi	220	50	9	2.2	0.8	3.3	1,955
Mali	432	90	35	7.4	3.5	21.2	4,320
Mauritania	200	180	10	9.1	3.4	17.9	6,800
Niger	274	70	13	3.7	2.4	10.8	5,058
Nigeria	3,973	70	500	8.1	1.6	9.9	1,033
Rwanda	246	70	25	7.6	2.3	9.7	2,263
Senegal	650	170	55	15.0	3.1	11.6	3,663
Sierra Leone	376	150	19	7.8	0.8	4.9	1,583
Somalia	163	60	95	35.7	5.0	18.1	858
Swaziland	130	301	—	—	—	—	—
Tanzania	1,033	80	50	1.6	1.0	3.8	2,066
Togo	182	100	15	8.7	1.8	13.5	2,184
Uganda	1,046	110	60	7.6	2.9	10.2	5,055
Upper Volta	261	50	15	3.0	1.9	14.1	3,306
Zaire	1,847	90	354	21.6	5.9	14.5	3,078
Zambia	881	220	30	7.6	2.4	5.7	7,048

Source: Donald G. Morrison et al., Black Africa.
Note: All figures are estimates circa 1967. Variations between sources are as high as 100 percent. Botswana, Equatorial Guinea, Lesotho, Gambia, and Swaziland do not have armies.

Table 1.2
Sub-Saharan Africa: Incidence of Coups

Country	Year of independence	Population (millions)	Number of coups	Dates of coups
Botswana	1966	0.6	0	
Burundi	1962	3.4	1	Nov. 28, 1966
Cameroun	1960	5.6	0	
Central African Republic	1960	1.5	1	Jan. 1, 1966
Chad	1960	3.5	1	Apr. 14, 1975
Congo/Brazzaville	1960	0.9	2	Aug. 15, 1963; Aug. 4, 1968
Dahomey	1960	2.6	6	Oct. 23, 1963; Nov. 29, 1965; Dec. 22, 1965; Dec. 17, 1967; Dec. 10, 1969; Oct. 26, 1972
Equatorial Guinea	1968	0.3	0	
Ethiopia	—	24.7	1	Sept. 12, 1974
Gabon	1960	0.5	0	
Gambia	1965	0.4	0	
Ghana	1957	8.5	2	Feb. 24, 1966; Jan. 13, 1972
Guinea	1958	3.9	0	
Ivory Coast	1960	4.2	0	
Kenya	1963	10.8	0	
Leosotho	1966	0.9	0	

Country	Year of independence	Population (millions)	Number of coups	Dates of coups
Liberia	1847	1.1	0	
Malagasy	1960	7.1	1	May 18, 1972
Malawi	1964	4.4	0	
Mali	1960	4.8	1	Nov. 19, 1968
Mauritania	1960	1.1	0	
Niger	1960	3.9	1	Apr. 15, 1974;
Nigeria	1960	56.7	3	Jan. 15, 1966; July 29, 1966; July 29, 1975
Rwanda	1962	3.5	1	July 5, 1973
Senegal	1960	3.8	0	
Sierra Leone	1961	2.5	3	Mar. 21, 1967; Mar. 23, 1967; Apr. 18, 1968
Somalia	1960	2.7	1	Oct. 21, 1969
Swaziland	1968	0.4	0	
Tanzania	1961	12.9	0	
Togo	1960	1.8	2	Jan. 13, 1963; Jan. 13, 1967
Uganda	1962	9.5	1	Jan. 25, 1971
Upper Volta	1960	5.2	2	Jan. 3, 1966; Feb. 8, 1974
Zaire	1960	20.5	2	Sept. 14, 1960; Nov. 25, 1965
Zambia	1964	4.0	0	

Source: Donald G. Morrison et al., *Black Africa*.

Note: All figures are estimates circa 1967. Variations between sources are as high as 100 percent. Botswana, Equatorial Guinea, Lesotho, Gambia, and Swaziland do not have armies.

military hierarchies certain characteristics of professionalism, nationalism, cohesion, and austerity that impel them to move into the political arena and to rescue the state from the grip of corrupt and self-seeking political elites.

In a sense both conceptualizations are two sides of the same coin, and when the analytic gunsights are trained at a specific coup the distinctions between the approaches tend to blur. Hence there is a consensus among most scholars about a broad syndrome of destabilizing strains and stresses in African societies that provoke the armed forces to overthrow civilian regimes. Military intervention in the political realm is viewed as a function of chronic systemic disequilibrium and of the alleged professional characteristics of armies, the precise dimensions of which (as well as their specific ingredients and "boiling points") may differ from country to country.[4]

The disequilibrium may be primarily economic in nature.[5] The army may feel compelled to intervene in order to implement unpopular austerity policies that political elites have been unable or unwilling to undertake or to correct politically or ideologically inspired fiscal imbalances that have led the economy to the brink of collapse. Instability may also be the highly disruptive consequence of overly ambitious social mobilization drives that unleash demands and unrest as populations are torn from traditional moorings.[6] Politicization of ethnic cleavages and intraelite strife in governmental structures may result in political and administrative paralysis;[7] corruption, nepotism, governmental inefficiency, and tribal favoritism may also tip the legitimacy pendulum away from discredited civilian elites to allegedly apolitical, untainted military

4. The fullest tabulation of structural deficiencies underlying instability in Africa is in Aristide Zolberg, "Military Intervention in the New States of Africa," and in Claude E. Welch, Jr., "Soldier and State in Africa," pp. 305–22.

5. "In every country, the issues which best account for the ease of military access to power relate to economic circumstances and their social consequences." See Dorothy Nelkin, "The Economic and Social Setting of Military Takeovers in Africa," p. 231.

6. Samuel Huntington, "Political Development and Political Decay"; James O'Connell, "The Inevitability of Instability," pp. 181–91.

7. "The Army coup d'état is plainly a short-circuit of power conflicts in a situation where arms do the deciding." Ruth First, *Power in Africa*, p. ix.

hierarchies that may be trusted to provide competent national leadership.[8] Moreover, viewed as corporate structures, armies may lash out at regimes that attempt to politicize them, tamper with established lines of command, or otherwise threaten their autonomy.[9] In recent studies, civil-military tensions have been conceptually linked to the burgeoning field of the social psychology of political violence, although no Africanist has fully pursued this line of analysis.[10]

A wide variety of other factors alleged to draw armed forces into the political scene can be culled from the extensive literature.[11] Yet the basic contention that coups occur as a result of systemic deficiencies grossly lacks in explanatory value, appealing as it may be to romanticize the "man on horseback" (or in the command car) as the heroic savior of nations from rapacious politicians. The core analytic flaw is the confusion of the very real and existing systemic tensions in African states (which are, however, the universal *backdrop* of all political life in the continent) with other factors— often the *prime* reasons for a military upheaval—lodged in the internal dynamics of the officer corps. It is both simplistic and empirically erroneous to relegate coups in Africa to the status of a dependent variable, a function of the political weakness and structural fragility of African states and the failings of African civilian elites.

As has been noted, the positive image of African militaries that underlies idealizations of motives for military coups is implicitly or explicitly anchored in formal organization theory. Briefly stated, African armies and officer corps are seen to have certain character-

8. Fred Riggs, "Bureaucrats and Political Development."

9. This interpretation is familiar to students of Latin America but is rather recent in African studies. See Claude E. Welch, Jr., "The Roots and Implications of Military Intervention," in *Soldier and State in Africa*, pp. 34–35, and Henry Bienen, "The Background to Contemporary Studies of Militaries and Modernization," p. 4.

10. For the general approach see Ted Gurr, "Psychological Factors in Civil Violence"; James Davies, "Towards a Theory of Revolution"; Betty Nesvold, "Scalogram Analysis of Political Violence"; Ivo and R. Feierabend, "Aggressive Behavior within Polities."

11. See, for example, Uma O. Eleazu, "The Role of the Army in African Politics," pp. 265–86. For an excellent review of some of the conceptual confusion in the literature see Robert E. Dowse, "The Military and Political Development."

istics related to their special skills and their training in staff colleges abroad. They are supposed to be molded into cohesive, nontribal, disciplined, and national units; as a result of their command of sophisticated weaponry and their membership in a complex hierarchical structure, African armies are viewed as the most modern, Westernized, and efficient organizations in their societies and the repositories of bureaucratic and managerial skills. They are believed to have internalized in military academies abroad the values of noninterference in political matters and the supremacy of civilian authority. Allegiance to these values is then severely tested on their return home, where they see corruption, mismanagement of resources, and interelite strife. Eventually unable to tolerate abuses of power the army intervenes to "tidy up the mess" and to create a new political order.

Empirical evidence suggests otherwise. African armies have rarely been cohesive, nontribal, Westernized, or even complex organizational structures. Neat hierarchical command charts camouflage deep cleavages—an extension of wider societal chasms shared by most African states. Differential recruitment and promotion patterns cause tensions that reinforce other lines of division based on rank, age, tribe, and education. These have been only superficially papered over by flimsy and brief training programs that metropolitan countries set up in the waning years of colonial rule. At independence many of the current top officers were rapidly promoted from the ranks or the officer corps in the drive to achieve Africanization of army commands. Their relative youth and spotty formal education, coupled with the limited number of senior positions in Africa's minuscule armies, created promotion bottlenecks for junior officers anxious to imitate their meteoric rise. Personal animosities and ambitions have also been rife in the officer corps. And whatever fragile organizational unity African armies may have originally possessed has usually been rapidly eroded by the politicization of their internal cleavages after independence and the sharpening of personal jealousies and power struggles. Indeed, many African armies bear little resemblance to a modern complex organization model and are instead a *coterie of distinct armed camps owing primary clientelist allegiance*[12] *to a*

12. "Where a society's impersonal legal guarantees of physical security, status, and wealth are relatively weak or nonexistent individuals often seek personal

handful of mutually competitive officers of different ranks seething with a variety of corporate, ethnic, and personal grievances. One direct corollary is that when the military assumes political power it is frequently not able to provide an efficient, nationally oriented, and stable administration, not only because of the immensity of the systemic loads assumed, but also as a result of its own internal cleavages and competitions. Where the latter are especially intense, military regimes may devote considerably more time and effort to consolidating and warding off alternate challenges to their authority than to providing the country with purposeful leadership.[13]

Students of civil-military relations in Africa have also often yielded to the temptation to accept official reasons for military takeovers, especially when it is obvious that the toppled civilian regime has been manifesting the weaknesses for which it has been attacked. Consequently other, covert motivations for a coup have not been detected or given sufficient weight. Motives are rarely simple, and proper assessment of their relative importance in a particular situation may be extremely difficult. Still, detailed empirical analysis and field work can reveal a variety of factors of much greater significance for an understanding of a military upheaval than the essentially static assumptions that clutter the literature.

Widespread government corruption provides a case in point, as this has been the most commonly cited complaint of army leaders moving against their civilian counterparts in political office. Yet as Dennis Austin has remarked, the charge of corruption is usually used ex post facto to justify intervention[14] by military forces that are often neither truly aggravated by it nor untainted themselves. The Ugandan army was probably even more corrupt before the 1971 coup than the regime it replaced, though government corruption was one of the prominent reasons cited for the assault on Milton Obote. In the Central African Republic the most

---

substitutes by attaching themselves to 'big men' capable of providing protection and even advancement." This general observation is also valid for subsystems. See Richard Sandbrook, "Patrons, Clients and Factions," p. 109.

13. This has certainly been true of many military regimes, particularly Mali, Dahomey, Congo/Brazzaville, and Sierra Leone.

14. Dennis Austin, "The Underlying Problem of the Army Coup d'Etat in Africa," pp. 65–72.

widespread complaint of junior officers and the rank and file was
not so much government corruption (though again, this was one of
the official reasons for the coup) as the unequal competition from
politicians, who were able among other things to corral the best
mistresses in Bangui.[15]

Nor was corruption in Modibo Keita's administration the true
reason for Lieutenant Moussa Traore's coup. And as Fisher has
pointed out, corruption was one of a succession of official
justifications for the second 1967 coup in Sierra Leone, which
suggests that the military itself was not sure what the official excuse
for intervention should be. The upheaval in that country was in
fact largely a result of major tensions within the officer corps
exacerbated during Brigadier Lansana's tenure as chief of staff.[16]

Even in cases of seemingly noncontroversial "umpire" coups—
where the army appears to be drawn reluctantly in, to mediating
between competing civilian cliques or presiding over a shift of
power from one group to another—motives may be murkier and
more convoluted than they appear at first sight. A good example of
this comes from Dahomey, which has suffered six coups since
independence. In 1965 General Soglo intervened in the clash
between President Apithy and Vice-President Ahomadégbé, each
of whom had mobilized his ethnic clientelist support in the
administration and in the urban centers, which led to extreme
tension in the country and complete government paralysis. While
Soglo's intervention is usually regarded as an "arbitrator" coup, the
background was somewhat more complicated than this simple
description implies. For within the tangled web of the dual power
gambit that was the background for the coup existed another factor
that throws more light on Soglo's motives: the personal element,
specifically, the long history of personal friction between Soglo and
Ahomadégbé (though both were of the same ethnic group) and the
latter's closer links with Soglo's immediate subordinate, Colonel
Aho, which Ahomadégbé tried to exploit when he tried to get the
army on his side on the eve of the coup. Moreover, Ahomadégbé
publicly humiliated his chief of staff the previous day, a fact

15. J. M. Lee, *African Armies and Civil Order*, p. 100.
16. Humphrey J. Fisher, "Elections and Coups in Sierra Leone 1967."

that must have had an effect on the state of Soglo's loyalties.[17]

Neither interethnic tension in the south, which was slowly abating, nor the government deadlock, which had been resolved with Ahomadégbé's "victory" in the party over Apithy, nor the poor performance of the regime—and indeed all regimes in Dahomey since independence—can fully account for the 1965 coup. In a very real sense Soglo's intervention can be seen to have stemmed at least to an equal extent from his anger and hurt pride; the political context allowed them unfettered expression in the form of a coup that would be acclaimed in two of Dahomey's three ethnic regions. Moreover, many of the army's high- and middle-level officers were also not averse to a military takeover for reasons of personal self-aggrandizement. The 1967 coup that later toppled Soglo himself was also not the result so much of the nepotism, vacillation, and corruption of his own regime as of the impatience of junior elements in the army for professional advancement. In 1966 they had forced Soglo to create a Military Vigilance Committee (to better supervise government activities), but even here they were allocated a very small share of the spoils and responsibilities.[18]

In like manner the 1965 coup in the Central African Republic occurred within the context of, not as a result of, a harsh budgetary crisis, corruption throughout the entire political hierarchy, and overt attempts to displace the wearied and disenchanted President David Dacko. The most important "cause" of the coup was the personal ambitions of Colonel Bokassa, the chief of staff, who had manifested his inclinations on numerous previous occasions, including the time when he had unilaterally taken over the War Ministry cabinet portfolio. Dacko's attempt to balance the army against the police was not so much a juggling of corporate interests as an unsuccessful effort to ward off the personal ambitions of Bokassa and Izamo, the chief of police, who lost out.[19]

The personal element in army coups in Africa is perhaps most clearly visible in General Idi Amin's takeover in Uganda in 1971. The failings of civilian leadership in that country—enumerated by

17. See Maurice A. Glélé, *Naissance d'un état noir.*
18. Samuel Decalo, "The Politics of Instability in Dahomey," pp. 5–32.
19. Pierre Kalck, *Central African Republic.*

Amin in his eighteen-point justification for the coup[20]—do not fully explain the military upheaval or its timing. These problems had afflicted Uganda even prior to independence. Interethnic strife and cleavages had been continuously denounced by President Obote, and the depressed economy appeared to be on the verge of an upward swing. Government corruption, moreover, had not been the sole preserve of the civilian regime, as the military (including Amin himself) shared in it to an even larger extent.

More cogent reasons for the coup were Amin's personal fears and ambitions combined with a deep malaise in the army, which had been in a state of convulsion even before the short-lived 1964 mutiny. Amin was correct in anticipating his imminent removal as commander of the army; indeed, according to one account, a few hours before the coup President Obote called from the Singapore Commonwealth Meeting to have him arrested.[21] In October 1970 Amin's powers had already been curtailed by the creation of two command positions parallel to his own. He was, moreover, involved in the death of at least one top officer, and a recent attorney general's report pointed to both misuse and embezzlement of defense funds.[22] Finally, the tacit Obote-Amin alliance of the mid-1960s had fallen apart; Amin's contempt for many of Obote's ideological pronouncements and his irritation over the large numbers of Acholi and Langi troops and officers in the army were well known in Kampala. All these considerations provided an overwhelming motive for a personal power grab that had little to do with the failings of civilian rule. Nor can the coup be seen as "class action" by the military against civilian authority, as one observer has recently argued.[23] Rather, the 1971 coup was a classic example of a takeover triggered by personal fears and ambitions. The existence of widespread civic malaise and an army rife with grievances did, however, facilitate the coup and assure it a measure of support. They also help to explain the intensity and brutality

20. Uganda, *The Birth of the Second Republic.*
21. Judith Listowel, *Amin,* pp. 69–71.
22. Ibid.
23. Michael Lofchie, "The Uganda Coup—Class Action by the Military," pp. 19–35.

with which personal and ethnic scores were settled following the takeover.

Personality differences, competing ambitions, and corporate grievances also played a role in both the 1966 and 1972 coups in Ghana. In the first instance Colonel Kotoka, one of the architects of the coup, was known not to get along with General Barwah and, like several other officers in the army, was doubtful about his professional advancement under the new commander. There was resentment throughout the officer corps over "political" promotions (Colonel Hassan) and retirements (Generals Otu and Ankrah), cutbacks in amenities and services for the armed forces, rumors regarding the possible dispatch of the army to fight in Rhodesia, attempts to indoctrinate it with Nkrumahist philosophy, and the direct threat to the army's professional autonomy and self-image from the increasingly powerful, better-equipped, and more trusted units of the President's Own Guard.[24] The timing of the coup was directly linked to this resentment, for the numerous failures and corruption of the Nkrumah regime had been manifest as far back as 1961. The existence of scores of other valid complaints against Nkrumah's abuse of power and the fact that the conspirators truly felt they were ridding Ghana of a pretentious authoritarian leader need not cloud the plain truth that the army did not move against civilian authority until personal and group interests appeared overwhelmingly threatened. This underscores Ruth First's observation that when the military stages a coup d'état "whatever its declarations of noble interest, [it] generally acts for Army reasons." [25] Though they may be predominant, secondary, or merely coincidental with civic unrest, corporate and personal motives are invariably present in coup situations and cannot be ignored.

Important grievances of this kind against both the Busia government and the senior hierarchy of the Ghanaian army precipitated the second coup in 1972. Indeed, many of the

24. See Jon Kraus, "Arms and Politics in Ghana"; Robert M. Price, "Military Officers and Political Leadership," pp. 361–79, and idem, "A Theoretical Approach to Military Rule in New States."

25. First, *Power in Africa*, p. 20.

complaints by Colonel Acheampong against the Busia civilian regime were reminiscent of the 1966 justifications: cutbacks in defense spending, officers' salaries, and fringe benefits, as well as discrimination in favor of those officers who had helped Busia come to power. Acheampong and other officers strongly resented being totally bypassed in the promotion scramble that followed the 1966 coup, with their chances for rapid professional advancement in the near future virtually frozen[26] while the coup leaders all attained the rank of General.

Nor can the 1967 overthrow of President Grunitzky in Togo be viewed solely in terms of the collapse of his alliance with his northern vice-president, Antoine Meatchi, and the general weakness of his government. Rather, the coup was a direct result of the threat to the position of Colonel Eyadema, the strong man of Togo. Against the background of the November 1966 southern (Ewe) demonstrations against Grunitzky in Lomé and the nonavailability of alternate and viable northern (Kabre) civilian leadership, Eyadema's choices were extremely limited. The option of a southern-dominated government was foreclosed by Ewe pledges that the arrest and trial of chief of staff Eyadema for the murder of Sylvanus Olympio in 1963 would be their first act once in power. Whatever the disadvantages were of thrusting the army into the center of the political arena at that time (though there was significant demand for such a course of action in the officer corps), Eyadema could not evade the fact that there was no possibility of setting up a civilian Kabre government, nor could he allow the Ewe leadership to assume power.[27]

Personal ambitions have also been an integral part of the long and turbulent history of civil-military relations and military rule in Congo/Brazzaville. Indeed, Major Marien Ngouabi's coup overthrowing Massemba-Debat and all attempted coups since then are best seen as personal attempts to seize power by different clientelist segments of the army within a textbook example of a praetorian

26. See Valerie P. Bennett's two articles, "The Military under the Busia Government," and "The Non-Politicians Take Over." Also *New York Times*, January 17 and 22, 1972.

27. Samuel Decalo, "The Politics of Military Rule in Togo."

system—with the much touted Left-Right ideological tug-of-war and the country's ethnic cleavages complicating rather than explaining the sequence of power grabs.[28]

Finally, the 1975 coup in Chad can hardly be seen as the army's reaction to the corrupt, oppressive, and inept rule of Ngarta Tombalbaye. Corruption had been rife in Chad since independence; major political purges had occurred regularly throughout Tombalbaye's reign; administrative ineptness, which had contributed so much to the outbreak of rebellion and civil war in the north, had been checked by the Administrative Reform Mission that France dispatched in 1969–70; and the rebellion had been more or less contained by 1973 with the assistance of French troops. Even the arrest of several of the Chad army's senior officers (for alleged sympathy for the rebel cause) had not triggered a coup in the early 1970s, since other officers stood to gain from the purges. While one need not doubt that many in the army's hierarchy shared the society's general weariness with Tombalbaye's rule, the fact still remains that the army moved only after rumors started to circulate of further purges of their officer corps. After the coup (and Tombalbaye's death) the military junta justified its intervention by citing abuses that had long been tolerated.

Hence detailed examination of motivations for coups reveals that the main weakness of attempts to explain them by pinpointing major areas of systemic stress is that insufficient weight is placed on the personal motives of ambitious or discontented officers, who have a great deal of freedom and scope for action in fragmented, unstructured, and unstable political systems. If armies intervene because of endemic failings of civilian regimes, then cross-national analysis ought to reveal key clusters of socioeconomic variables highly correlated with military intervention. It should be possible to differentiate between relatively stable and unstable civilian regimes on the assumption that political systems that suffer continuous takeovers by their armed forces (for example, Congo/Brazzaville, Dahomey, Sierra Leone) have more acute ethnic,

---

28. For an excellent critique of the relevance of the terms "Left" and "Right" in African politics see Immanuel Wallerstein, "Left and Right in Africa." See also Arthur H. House, "Brazzaville."

socioeconomic, and intraelite cleavages than countries that have not had such takeovers (such as Zambia, Equatorial Guinea, Kenya).

This hypothesis does not stand up to empirical examination. Cross-national multivariate analysis has been unable to account for the relative frequency of military takeovers in some political systems as opposed to others. Reducing the analytical distinction between the two groups of countries to the degree and intensity of internal weaknesses and failings of each state poses some very thorny problems of quantification. Yet quite apart from the difficulty of correctly measuring and comparing relative levels of government efficiency, corruption, ethnic cleavages, and intraelite strife, such analysis verges on being tautological. It can be taken as axiomatic that most African states are afflicted with all the systemic problems typical of fledgling economies, complex ethnic configurations, clientelist politics, and intraelite competition for the few high level positions and plums of office.[29] Similarly, most civilian regimes have had occasion to tamper with the internal hierarchies of their armed forces and to curb military budgets. As Zolberg has pointed out, "it is impossible to specify as a class countries where coups have occurred from others which have so far been spared." [30] And increasingly sophisticated attempts by scholars employing factor analysis on scores of societal and military variables (including both hard and soft data) continue to reveal statistically insignificant correlations with military intervention.[31] Needless to say, links between structural characteristics of political systems and the incidence of military takeovers will *not* appear if one of the key variables—the idosyncratic element, or personal ambitions of military officers—is not taken into account. Moreover, knowledge of the true motives of military officers in overthrowing civilian regimes can give us insights into the kinds of policies they are likely to follow once in office, while misjudgments of their motivations will lead us to uncalled for expectations of military rule.

29. Aristide Zolberg, *Creating Political Order.*

30. Zolberg, "Military Intervention," p. 71.

31. See, for example, Roberta Koplin Mapp, "Domestic Correlates of Military Intervention in African Politics"; Donald G. Morrison and H. M. Stevenson, "Political Instability in Independent Black Africa"; and Louis Terrell, "Societal Stress, Political Instability and Levels of Military Effort."

The Military as Rulers: Myth and Reality

Students of the Third World have had two conflicting images of military rule. The first, largely derived from the experience of Latin America, was one of incompetent, corrupt, and reactionary military regimes committed to the socioeconomic status quo.[32] The second, of more recent vintage, was of benevolent and progressive military regimes dedicated to rapid transformation of their societies and the purge of corrupt civilian autocracies.

Military regimes in Africa have usually been seen through the latter prism as examples of what Levy refers to, in a different context, "the most efficient type of organization for combining maximum rates of modernization with maximum levels of stability and control."[33] At the same time, the military's lack of a development ideology and its hierarchical conception of authority and political rule have been recognized as somewhat limiting factors.

Since the mid-1960s when this idealized image of African military rule first emerged, the academic pendulum has swung only marginally and slowly in the opposite direction. Much of the debate about the alleged modernizing propensities of African military regimes has taken place within an empirical vacuum; it has been hindered by the nonavailability or noncomparability of data on military performance in office and clouded by the kinds of erroneous underlying assumptions about motives that have been previously noted. While there is a growing awareness among Africanists that military rule does not necessarily lead to the policies of socioeconomic change suggested by the accepted theoretical frameworks, the discrepancy between theory and reality has tended to be explained away by the enormity of the problems faced by military regimes.[34]

It is certainly true that the small African armies, lacking in a number of skills, would have great difficulty reordering their

32. Lucian Pye, "Armies in the Process of Political Modernization," pp. 69–70; see also Pye, *Aspects of Political Development*, p. 182 inter alia.

33. Marion J. Levy, *Modernization and the Structure of Societies*, vol. 2, p. 603.

34. As in Claude Welch's works—see especially *Soldier and State*.

countries' priorities and initiating vast socioeconomic change, but this should not obscure the fact that the conceptual models of African armies as dedicated, nationalist, and cohesive hierarchies committed to change are simply not valid. Whether or not these military cliques are committed to modernization and change—and most do not differ on the whole in their orientations from the civilian regimes they replace[35]—is largely of secondary importance in light of their prime characteristic, which is overriding preoccupation with personal and corporate aggrandizement in a societal context of acute scarcity and intense competition from other elites (politicians, civil servants, unionists, students) for the same very limited rewards and benefits. Only from this conceptual viewpoint can one accommodate the empirical reality of military regimes that promote their own interests in disregard of the socioeconomic limitations of their states. Moreover, with this new conceptual approach one can better understand the frequent fragmentation of army discipline once a coup succeeds: a fragmentation that is only *indirectly* and *secondarily* along ethnic, class, or ideological lines and that is primarily a consequence of the eruption of competing personal ambitions (previously contained under the army's hierarchical umbrella) once a particular clique of officers has seized supreme civil power. Three of the four military regimes covered in this book—Dahomey, Congo/Brazzaville, and Uganda—illustrate this process. The fourth, Togo, may well be the exception that proves the rule, since the internal composition and dynamics of the Togolese military are unique.

One of the main charges made against toppled civilian regimes has been that they stultified economic growth through inappropriate policies and corrupt practices. The most universal pledge made by new military juntas is to provide honest and efficient administration in promoting economic development. Yet weak one-crop economies in traditional societies are usually affected by considera-

35. Though some inconclusive research indicates that the military cliques may be more conservative. Even if this can be substantiated cross-nationally more time must pass before it can be accepted as a valid generalization. Many leaders of the earlier wave of coups were older generation officers who might be expected to be more oriented toward the status quo, and the emerging pattern of the younger juntas is based on too few cases to allow valid generalization.

tions frequently extraneous to who holds power, and the "new" policies are administered on the local level by the very same civil service—often apathetic or corrupt—that served the preceding civilian government. The economic expansion of a few countries under military rule—usually cited as attesting to the abilities of a junta to spur economic growth—cannot be traced to any specific domestic or foreign policies espoused by military administrations. Intervening external variables need to be assessed (which has not been done rigorously) before correlations can be established between military rule and economic development. The sharp rise in world cocoa and diamond prices, for example, merely coincided with the advent of the military regimes of Ankrah, Eyadema, and Bokassa in Ghana, Togo, and the Central African Republic, respectively. The economic improvement in these countries at that time was really related to the upward fluctuation of world commodity prices. Likewise, elements of the Togolese economic "success story" under General Eyadema—expanding phosphate exports and German financial largesse to its former *Musterkolonie* (showcase colony)—were present long before the military came to power in 1967.[36] Had President Grunitzky managed to remain in power for one more year he might have been credited with the economic upturn. Zaire's economic potentials would have been exploited no matter what regime was in power (a start was made under Moise Tshombe) as long as it could assure social tranquility.

Public and private aid and investment, the sine qua non of any program of economic development, are usually attracted to Africa more by economic potential, expectation of profits, and political stability than by the existence of military cliques in power. Indeed, in several instances the emergence of military regimes has completely dried up the trickle of foreign investment or assistance, as in the cases of Amin in Uganda (though some alternate aid was secured from the Arab world), Micombero in Burundi, and Kouandété and Kerekou in Dahomey. Both Busia's civilian

36. See the analysis of Togo's economy in Samir Amin, *L'Afrique de l'ouest bloquée*, pp. 125–34, 148–49. On the other hand, Eyadema's decision to drastically cut taxes on imports and exports swiftly led to the greater prosperity of Lomé's market women and of smugglers working between Togo and Ghana, which greatly stabilized his regime.

government and the military regimes of Ankrah and Acheampong had extreme difficulty attracting foreign funds or developing Ghana's economy. Paradoxically, world cocoa prices rose once again after their decline during the Busia administration, a situation that was exploited by Acheampong. Neither President Dacko, favorably regarded by Paris, nor General Bokassa, who has been kept at arm's length, have had much success in developing the Central African Republic's vast untapped diamond and timber resources or in interesting anyone but shady financial consortiums in the country's immense tourist and economic possibilities. Nigeria's current economic boom, based largely on increased oil exports, can hardly be attributed to its military regime. The army's competent and dedicated administration of Upper Volta's wobbly economy and finances has not resulted in greater world confidence or development of its nonexistent economic potentialities. Neither has much changed in the Malian economy since Modibo Keita was toppled, while in Dahomey it was under the civilian Zinsou and second Maga administrations that a measure of economic development was noticeable.

The army's frequent inability to spur economic development while in power is further evidenced in a recent comparative study employing aggregate data analysis. Eric Nordlinger shows that if the economy improves it is often in spite of the military regime in power.[37] Increases in military budgets and salaries frequently wipe out any marginal increments in economic productivity that may result from the partial and temporary streamlining of administrative procedures. Only in economies that are naturally buoyant and have potential for internal and self-sustaining expansion—and there are very few of these in Africa—will economic development proceed under military auspices. Nordlinger's and other empirical studies of the performance of military regimes in the Third World cogently underscore the fact that examples of Ataturk-style socio-economic transformations of new nations are extremely rare.

Nor is there much evidence beyond rhetoric and pious declarations of any sincere desire by most of the military regimes in tropical Africa to bring about fundamental social change or a

37. Eric Nordlinger, "Soldier in Mufti."

rearray in the structure of power within African states. This is true of the so-called "radical" military juntas (Congo/Brazzaville), conservative military regimes (such as the Ankrah or Bokassa administrations in Ghana and the Central African Republic) and "populist" military autocracies (such as Amin's in Uganda).[38] As Ruth First so succinctly put it, "The coup as a method of change that changes little has become endemic to Africa's politics." [39] In the large majority of cases a change in political style, a redistribution of political and economic power among elites (with the army assuring itself of the lion's share), and the satisfaction of the personal and group grievances of the dominant officer clique are often the most significant outcomes of military rule.[40]

The change of political style has usually included a return to the apolitical rule characteristic of colonial administration. Strong links are established between the military rulers and the police and the civil service, which become vital control and administrative arms. Only a handful of officers are expendable for staffing political offices. With the imposition of a nonintegrative administrative grid, social mobilization and national integration policies are frequently deemphasized as costly and potentially disruptive, eroded traditional authority is resurrected, and a loose consensus of traditional and modern elites is pursued as the key to stability.[41] Where traditional values and personal idiosyncrasies favor it, an "imperial" style of personal rule may emerge as in Uganda and the Central African Republic.

If corruption was rife in the preceding civilian government, commissions of inquiry may be set up, but the purge will be largely illusory and limited, with the army consciously avoiding the implication of too many civil servants, its own personnel, or its allies in the coup. All too often the political elite, whose venality had been cited as a principal reason for the intervention, is treated with a magnanimity inconsistent with the impassioned accusations

38. A strong case can be made that Amin's regime is Black Africa's first fascist dictatorship. See chapter 5.

39. First, *Power in Africa*, p. 22.

40. See also Anton Bebler, "Military Rule in Africa."

41. Edward Feit, "Military Coups and Political Development," and "The Rule of the Iron Surgeons."

previously leveled against it. In Dahomey's 1963 coup, for example, General Soglo did not even consider at first detaining President Maga and some of his more corrupt ministers, nor was Chabi Mama—the power broker behind Maga—arrested until he had started to foment opposition to the new government in his northern fiefdom.[42] And while the young putschists of 1967 initiated a purge of some of the more corrupt officers involved in Soglo's 1965 administration this was in the nature of a settling of personal scores following an internal rearrangement of power within the military.

In Ghana General Ankrah's widely heralded, sweeping inquiries into corruption during the Nkrumah era left intact the bulk of the civil service and the army and hardly touched the police—one of the most corruption-ridden structures in the country. The same holds true for investigations in Sierra Leone, Mali, Nigeria, and the Central African Republic following their coups. In Upper Volta former President Maurice Yameogo was brought to trial for embezzlement (as was Maga in Dahomey) only after strong pressure from Ouagadougou's trade unionists and junior officers in General Lamizana's army. The Central African Republic's former President Dacko (not particularly corrupt by Bangui standards) is not likely even to be brought to trial in light of the damaging things he might reveal in public about the current military clique.[43]

If it is not already present, corruption tends to seep into military regimes as if to prove that greed and avarice know no distinction between soldier and civilian. Contrary to the pseudotheoretical literature about its austerity and puritan tastes, the officer corps does not differ markedly in its bourgeois tastes from other elites; traditional African cultural values do not usually place a high premium on ascetic lifestyles. There are apparently few saints in situations of acute economic scarcity, especially in cultural systems where the rise to eminence of one individual triggers an obligation to provide for the welfare of an entire kinship group.[44]

Though exceptions exist—Upper Volta is a good example—military regimes have tended not to be significantly freer of corruption

42. Decalo, "Politics of Instability in Dahomey," pp. 18–19.
43. From interviews in Bangui (June 1972).
44. See Stanislav Andreski, *The African Predicament*, especially chapter 7.

or nepotism than the civilian governments they replaced. Police corruption continued unabated in Ghana during the Ankrah military regime, and it was common knowledge in Accra that many officers had profited financially from the coup; General Ankrah himself had to resign from the army when it was discovered that he had been soliciting funds in anticipation of his civilian presidential candidacy. Actually, Ankrah had been involved in several shady deals even before he assumed power in 1966. And in 1970 former Chief of Staff Brigadier Kattah was placed on trial on a five-year-old charge of theft. General Amin's involvement in the 1964–65 Congolese ivory and gold affair were only minor precedents for his extravagances following the coup that toppled his former ally, Obote, while the army as a whole grew more brazenly open in its extortionist practices with the wild promotions of several of Amin's self-seeking cronies to high officer rank. General Bokassa's imperial manners in Bangui include treating state coffers as his own personal preserve;[45] the same process is visible in Zaire since General Mobutu seized power, though in this case the treasury can better afford presidential splurges.

The more modest commercial activities of Major Adewui and a few of his army colleagues in Togo, petty corruption (and occasional grand larceny) in the Nigerian armed forces,[46] and the almost routine participation of Dahomean, Togolese, Ghanaian, and Nigerian border patrol officers in the active smuggling across their states' borders are only a few further examples of the pervasiveness of a non-Spartan ethic in African armed forces. At official border crossing points in Nigeria, as in several other states, payment of a "gift" is virtually a precondition for entry, while military patrols in the interior exact similar "tolls" on commerce and other traffic. Fully one-third of Togo's exports, especially of coffee and cocoa, come from across the Ghanaian border. And if Togo's imports of cigarettes, liquor, watches, and soap are taken at

45. The dispatch of a mission to Viet Nam to search for his illegitimate daughter, the pomp of the wedding of the "two Martines," the distribution of diamonds at diplomatic receptions, the airfield built in his home village (only forty-five miles from Bangui), etc.

46. Such as the embezzlement of 10 percent of the navy's budget in 1966 by three officers.

face value the country's per capita consumption of these items is the highest in Africa: actually as much as 50 percent of these imports are destined for immediate "reexport" across the porous Togo-Ghana frontier with the active connivance of military officers on both sides.

Military juntas have also been as prone to favor certain ethnic groups as the civilian regimes they replace. In Congo/Brazzaville the rise to power of Major Marien Ngouabi resulted in a policy to pack the police and promote in the army Mbochi and other northern elements. Every time a northern group percolates to power after an upheaval in Dahomey it has tried to purge the army's senior Fon and Yoruba officers; in Togo the overwhelmingly Kabre and Moba army has pushed northern elements into high-level political and administrative positions. In both Burundi and Uganda widespread massacres and "disappearances" accompanied the shift of power from one group of officers to another, and these brutal purges have been extended in both countries to eliminate broad cross sections of the opposing ethnic group's intellectuals and educated personnel.

In the rearray of political and economic power that accompanies the overthrow of civilian authority the military, police, and civil service are the net gainers, the masses in the countryside and development plans, the prime losers. African armies, and their officer corps in particular, are very small and, except for Burundi and Uganda, do not normally use excessive force or terror to remain in power. The stability of military regimes is therefore contingent upon close cooperation with the civil service, much as civilian regimes have discovered in the past. Since civil service salaries already consume 55–80 percent of government budgets, the satisfaction of the interests of the army, police, and civil service can only be achieved through reductions in expenditures in the countryside.

Nowhere has this been more visible than in Ghana under both the 1966 Ankrah and 1972 Acheampong military administrations— the former having been regarded abroad as an example of progressive, enlightened, and self-sacrificing military rule in Africa. An analysis of Ankrah's budgets reveals a very different picture.

Despite the austerity policies necessary to pull Ghana from the economic mire bequeathed it by Nkrumah, army allocations went up by an annual 22 percent, and the police and civil service similarly received salary adjustments and increases. Social services in the countryside, however, declined drastically by 28 percent and 78 percent.[47] Whatever the failings of the succeeding Busia civilian government, Colonel Acheampong's 1972 intervention was very much an "officers' amenities coup"—at least in terms of its motives. The overthrow of Busia was unaccompanied by any attempt to camouflage the new clique's desire to redress both personal and military grievances. High on the official list of reasons for the coup were Busia's tinkering with the defense budget, the removal of many army and civil service fringe benefits, and the erosion of the purchasing power of military salaries through draconian devaluation of the *cedi*.[48] On a personal level, Acheampong and the officers on his National Redemption Council had been bypassed in the promotion and patronage scramble following Ankrah's 1966 coup and were eager to redress the balance and settle scores. Once again as in Ankrah's time there were cuts in social and infrastructure-building allocations, increases in defense expenditures, and a major overhaul of the austerity measures Busia had imposed on the civil service and military officials. Since the economic picture was equally bleak, this was achieved in part by renunciation of several of Nkrumah's international debts and unilateral postponement of repayment of the rest.

The same bias in favor of army, police, and civil service salaries and fringe benefits can be observed in practically every military regime in Africa. Indeed this should not be surprising; whenever an elite group (civil or military) acquires power its own interests tend to be satisfied and protected above all. In Congo/Brazzaville pay increases of 20–40 percent were announced for the army and civil service following the Ngouabi coup. Libya's Colonel Qaddafi consolidated his control over the army and the urban elements by

47. See, for example, Price, "Theoretical Approach to Military Rule," p. 471.

48. Bennett, "Military under the Busia Government" and "Non-Politicians Take Over"; Dennis Austin, "The Army and Politics in Ghana"; *The London Times*, January 22, 1972.

doubling army salaries (probably the highest in the world), increasing civil service wages, and decreeing a 30 percent cut in all rents.[49] In Uganda widespread military corruption and embezzlement of funds coupled with unlimited budget allocations to the armed forces led the country practically to financial bankruptcy until it was temporarily bailed out with Libyan and Saudi Arabian funds.[50]

Occasionally, of course, acute financial pressures and/or empty state coffers preclude such a course of action. A good example is the experience of Upper Volta. There General Lamizana's natural inclination after the coup led him to abolish most of President Yameogo's austerity cuts, which had sparked the massive union demonstrations preceding his fall. Yet the very same cuts along with other austerity measures were reimposed on the civil service as the army grew to realize the precariousness of the economy; when the unions tried to repeat their show of force, many of their rights were curtailed. Even here, however, the Voltaic officer corps—though more conscientious in office than its counterparts elsewhere in Africa—exempted its own salaries from the austerity measures. And in Dahomey, where the financial picture was only slightly less bleak, the 1965 Soglo regime maintained, and even increased, the squeeze on civil service salaries inherited from the civilian regime even as it declared customs exemptions for officers wishing to import private vehicles. It was essentially left to President Zinsou to enact the more draconian measures necessary for budgetary equilibrium, and his efforts, which caused considerable unrest in the urban areas, were cut short by Colonel Kouandété's 1970 coup. Hence, there is little empirical validity to contentions that most African military regimes even aim at radical socioeconomic change, the reduction of corruption, or economic development. In essence, with some variations as noted above, their conduct in office does not differ significantly from that of their civilian predecessors, except that with control of the purse strings they tend

49. *New York Times*, June 4, 1970.

50. *Africa*, June 1972, pp. 55–56, notes that government borrowing from the Bank of Uganda went up from 103 million shillings at the time of the coup to one billion shillings by the end of 1971.

to find greater justification for increased "defense" allocations. One may also recollect that the withdrawal of the military from the Ghanaian political scene in 1969 was accompanied by "gratuities" given to them by the state.

Similarly, military administrations rarely aim at political development, the exceptions of Nigeria (still to be substantiated), Ghana (Ankrah's regime), and Upper Volta notwithstanding. Insofar as political development is defined in terms of political institutionalization—that is, the development and legitimation over time of stable, complex political structures and procedures with a degree of subsystem autonomy[51]—most military regimes can be regarded as dysfunctional. Indeed, a pattern of political coups in any specific country (such as Dahomey, Congo/Brazzaville, Sierra Leone, and Ghana) attests on the contrary to political decay and the development of the praetorian syndrome.[52] African officers have usually had both an intense contempt for the political process and an even more intense desire to perpetuate themselves in power; hence, rarely have they been inclined to begin building a new political order. While most military juntas have integrated civilians into their decision-making structures, set up civil-military consultative organs, and established general policy guidelines or operational procedures for bureaucracies, few have considered either a return to civilian rule or the setting up of viable political structures.

The occasional creation under military auspices of national "political" parties is evidence, however, that the army is sometimes aware of its quasi isolation from the bulk of the population and seeks the legitimation that might be gained through such structures. On the other hand, fearful that any such "liberalization" might snowball into a demand by their own "parties" that they step down from power, military juntas have seen to it that the political organs created to date have either been paper structures or under their tight control. Hence Zaire's MPR, Congo/Brazzaville's PCT, Burundi's UPRONA, and the Central African Republic's MESAN

51. Huntington, "Political Development and Political Decay."
52. See David C. Rapoport, "A Comparative Theory of Military and Political Types"; Amos Perlmutter, "The Praetorian State and the Praetorian Army"; and Claude Welch, Jr., "Praetorianism in Commonwealth West Africa."

cannot be considered as even modest attempts at political institutionalization, though Togo's RPT may still turn out to be a deviant example.[53] The creation of even these hollow structures, with their limited opportunities for upward mobility and political patronage, has, however, somewhat consolidated military rule, especially in Togo and Zaire.

Military regimes have not proven more nationalistic than their civilian counterparts, as current theories claim. The acute poverty of most of these countries and the relative nonexistence of easily exploitable natural resources practically force them to remain tied to the financial apron strings of the metropolitan countries and the West, creating a neocolonial relationship. This precludes a great deal of nationalistic maneuverability for most African governments, civilian and military alike. While some military juntas may adopt radical international or domestic postures, these tend to affect their relationship with the metropolitan country very little, and it does not usually imply anything beyond the adoption of empty slogans—a manifestation of convictions and long-run expectations, perhaps, but devoid of immediate practical import.

Congo/Brazzaville illustrates this point to the ultimate degree. The Ngouabi military regime has acquired most of the outward trappings and symbols of a Marxist state: a red flag, a revolutionary anthem, a nonenforced decree on the wearing of Chinese-style tunics,[54] talk of a "cultural revolution," state industries, the nationalization of service sectors and a few marginal enterprises, a "vanguard" party, Marxist-Leninist jargon, extensive relations with other "progressive" states, and sharp, periodic internal power struggles whose ideological justifications resemble the Left-Right struggles in early Stalinist Russia. Yet all this has not prevented the regime from anxiously and jealously reinforcing its ties with France, encouraging French public and private investment, and adopting a non-nationalist yielding posture with respect to French expatriate interests in the country.[55]

53. Decalo, "Politics of Military Rule in Togo."
54. Enacted largely in order to subsidize the Chinese-built and government-owned textile factory.
55. See Wallerstein, "Left and Right in Africa," and House, "Brazzaville."

Even military regimes in control of more developed economies have not tended to adopt radical nationalist policies. Robert Price has demonstrated the extent to which several top Ghanaian officers had internalized British values regarding noninterference in the private sector of the economy and relied upon the West for the development of Ghana. Such an orientation on the part of the Ankrah regime led to the strongly pro-West foreign and domestic policies of Ghana that at times tended even to discriminate against indigenous entrepreneurs.[56] (This was also undoubtedly a reaction to the opposite policy of the Nkrumah government, which had just been toppled.)

The Nigerian and Zaire military regimes have also, on only partly justifiable economic grounds, adopted non-nationalist postures regarding their national resources and foreign economic policies, though this is less true for Zaire than for Nigeria. Even General Amin's pseudo-nationalist and extremely popular policies (for example, expulsion of Uganda's Asian minorities, appropriation of British and other expatriate commercial and plantation enterprises, rejection of British and Israeli military assistance) are less a result of his nationalist credentials than of a variety of other factors including personal idiosyncrasies and his urgent need to popularize himself with the masses.[57] Moreover, by means of these unilateral decrees Amin has been able to annul international debts (thirty million dollars to Israel alone),[58] attract alternate financial aid, and expropriate without compensation vast plantations, commercial enterprises, and choice urban sites—all vitally needed to replenish state coffers drained by financial anarchy and increased military spending and corruption since the 1971 takeover.

Finally, stability—the ultimate justification for military rule—is not a necessary outcome of the replacement of bickering and plotting civilian leaders by a military junta, though here the record is somewhat more mixed. Sources of opposition to military rule have rarely emerged from the masses in the countryside. Nor has

56. Price, "Theoretical Approach to Military Rule."
57. Intellectually inferior to many of his colleagues and ethnically from one of Uganda's smaller and less developed tribes (Kakwa), Amin combines in his "policies" earthy shrewdness and emotion.
58. *New York Times*, January 12, 1973.

opposition usually stemmed from modern or traditional elites, which have been "bought off" in ways that have already been noted, though the occasional eruption of union or student demonstrations is not uncommon. Rather, military hierarchies often carry within them the seeds of their own destruction or instability. Most of them have been rocked by internal power struggles, factionalism, decay of cohesion and discipline, personal power gambits, and successful or attempted countercoups (Dahomey, Congo/Brazzaville, Sierra Leone, Uganda, and Mali); in others the intensity and frequency of such disturbances have been low or moderate (Ghana, Nigeria, Somalia, Zaire). Only in three states has military rule been relatively free of such tensions: Upper Volta, Togo, and the Central African Republic. In Togo and Upper Volta competing personal ambitions in the army have either been balanced or are nonexistent, and factional group interests have been satisfied. In the Central African Republic's minuscule army the few contenders for the politico-military throne have either been eliminated (Colonel Banza) or strategically dispersed to remote outposts, though the 1975 conspiracy suggests that ultimate power still has its fearless seekers. Such manipulations are not easily executed everywhere and coupled with more significant internal personalist power formations account for either the immobility of military juntas (as in Dahomey, Mali, and Sierra Leone) or their acute susceptibility to internal power grabs and instability (Dahomey, Congo/Brazzaville).

Hence a detailed comparative analysis of the features and characteristics of army rule in sub-Saharan Africa confirms the statistical correlations slowly being established by several scholars and validates a negative image of military elites in office. The specific army faction that initiates the coup, and the officer corps in general, is neither more cohesive, nationalist, progressive, nor self-denying than the civilian clique being toppled. While there is no reason to doubt the sincerity and good intentions of some military leaders (especially in the earlier phase of coups) their motives for intervention have always been complex and included personal considerations. Systemic problems have been exaggerated and personal or corporate motives camouflaged. Once in power military leaders have not been able to resolve the socioeconomic and political issues facing them: many are linked to external factors outside their control; others are either intractable or not amenable to simple solutions; and still others require social and fiscal policies contrary to the army's inclinations or incompatible with stable military rule.

The case studies that follow explore the specific societal and military factors that helped propel officer cliques into the center of the political vortex in four African states and the different methods by which military leaders have attempted to cope with the developmental tasks of their states. The concluding chapter will compare the major systemic features of military rule in these countries and suggest a tentative typology in which they may be placed for comparative purposes.

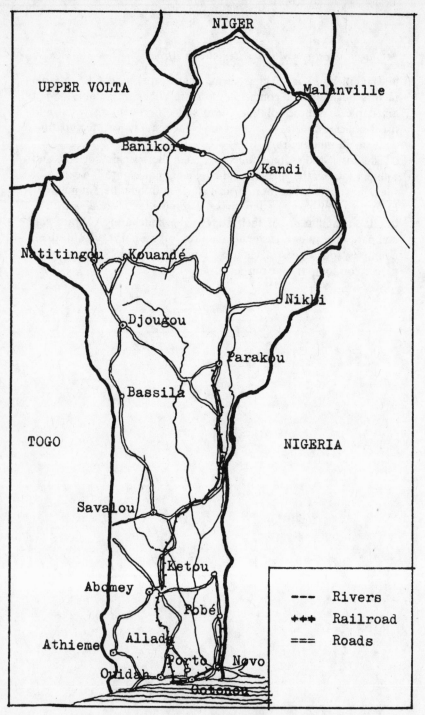

PEOPLE'S REPUBLIC OF BENIN (DAHOMEY)

2 The Army in a Praetorian State: Dahomey

Dahomey holds the unenviable African record of having the largest number of military coups since it became independent on August 1, 1960. Six times in just nine years (1963–72) the army, or factions of it, successfully toppled civilian authority, and there has also been a high incidence of attempted coups, military mutinies, and internal army strife. Since independence Dahomey has had five different constitutions and ten civilian or military presidents. Its political institutions have been manipulated, subverted, demoralized, and pulverized by civilian and military rule alike as the country moved from its alleged golden era of political cohesion in 1946 through the intense power struggles of its towering patrimonial rulers[1] to the development of a classical praetorian system where ultimate power stems from the barrel of the gun. If there was any doubt during Dahomey's first half-decade of independence about the army's destabilizing role in the political and economic evolution of the country, there is little now; since 1965 the army has been the final arbiter of political power, and over and beyond Dahomey's severe systemic problems, military dissension and factionalism have set the tone for the country's pattern of instability.

REGIONALISM AND PATRON-CLIENT RELATIONSHIPS

Dahomey's social and political life has been marked by fragmentation, mass-elite gaps, patron-clientelist relationships, and strong regional cleavages. The regional schisms arise out of the fractured nature of the social system and are one consequence of the compression of many ethnic groups into the territorial unit established by treaties between France, England, and Germany at the outset of the colonial era. Within the boundaries of Dahomey

1. G. Roth, "Personal Rulership, Patrimonialism and Empire-Building," pp. 194–206.

are the cultural successors of the two traditionally hostile kingdoms of Danhomé and Porto Novo in the center and the south and a mosaic of isolated, unintegrated, and less developed ethnic groups in the north. These ethnic-regional divisions, which involve different languages, rites, histories, life-styles, expectations, and even external linkages,[2] have diminished little over the years.[3] Indeed, at the outset of colonial rule they were aggravated by the French policy of administratively differentiating between the less developed northern region and the southern populations that were more open to modern, Western influences. With the advent of indigenous political life in the 1940s, appeals for ethnic solidarity and electoral support by ambitious elites politicized existing cleavages and gave them yet another dimension.[4]

In the south the Fon of Abomey, one of the more powerful and expansionist precolonial states, and the Yoruba of Porto Novo had been locked in a state of semipermanent warfare that only ended with the final invasion of French troops in 1892.[5] Though royal and chiefly authority was greatly curtailed (and Abomey's King Behanzin exiled to Algeria) it was not until 1913 that the last of the southern thrones became vacant and monarchy was abolished.

2. The Yoruba and Nagot of the Porto Novo region have always been linked to their compatriots in western Nigeria, who in the eighteenth and nineteenth centuries were at war with the Fon of Danhomé. (In order to better differentiate between the country as a whole and the former Danhomé kingdom the latter will be referred to as Abomey, after its capital.) Likewise, the Mina and Ewe in the western coastal areas have tended to gravitate much more toward Togo, and the northern populations were also pulled in different directions. See Robert Cornevin, *Histoire du Dahomey*, or his shorter, *Le Dahomey*.

3. Decalo, "Politics of Instability in Dahomey."

4. Dov Ronen, "Preliminary Notes on the Concept of Regionalism in Dahomey" and Finagnon M. Oke, "Survivance tribale ou problematique nationale en Afrique noire."

5. Resistance to this intrusion continued after the two bitter clashes that shattered Abomey's military hegemony in the region. See K. P. Moseley, "Rural Resistance in Southern Dahomey 1900–1919"; David Ross, "Dahomey"; I. M. Kouandété, *Kaba: Un Aspect de l'insurrection nationaliste au Dahomey*. For a few works on the precolonial social and political scene in the south see Melville J. Herskovits, *Dahomey*; W. J. Argyle, *The Fon of Dahomey*; I. A. Akinjogbin, *Dahomey and Its Neighbors*, as well as the two bibliographies published in *Etudes Dahoméennes*.

Recognizing the popularity and traditional authority of the royal lineages, however, the French selected from their ranks the cantonal chiefs needed for the administration of the colony. This practice gave a measure of modern authority to elements of the traditional ruling class and provided loci for the coalescence of ethnic-regionalist sentiments and, later, electoral power.

TABLE 2.1
Dahomey: Demographic Data

Department	Rural	Urban Population	Total	Area in km²	Population density/km²
Ouémé	419,720	68,560	488,280	4,700	103.9
Atlantique	226,930	119,140	346,070	3,222	107.4
Mono	307,560	—	307,560	3,800	80.9
Zou	422,660	31,650	454,310	18,700	24.3
Borgou	304,110	16,800	320,710	51,000	6.2
Atakora	313,820	11,110	324,930	31,200	10.4
Total	1,994,800	247,060	2,241,860	112,622	19.9

Source: Reorganization of data in p. 10 of M. Glélé, *La République du Dahomey* (Paris: Berger Levrault, 1969).

Paralleling the sharp fissure between the two dominant ethnic groups in the south is the cleavage that separates both of them from the northern populations. No centralized protostates had emerged among the Bariba, Pila Pila, and other groups, though small power formations existed in Nikki, Kouandé, Djougou, and Kandi—see table 2.1.[6] The region had been in a state of chronic, dry season, intervillage warfare and had had little contact (except for the Mahi) with Abomey, whose traditional ambitions had been to the southeast and west. Isolated, undeveloped, and relatively neglected by the French, the north also resisted the inroads of outside influences and remained quite traditional in its socioeconomic orientations. On most developmental scales the region still trails badly behind the southern areas; indeed, statistics from the north

6. For a thorough study of the Bariba, the most important northern group, see Jacques Lombard, *Structures du type "feodal" en Afrique noire.*

and south resemble figures assembled from different countries. In education, for example, southerners avidly sought facilities that would make them upwardly mobile within a Western framework. By the 1930s southern Dahomey had become a prime exporter of educated and trained personnel to France's other colonies at a time when educational facilities in the north were still extremely rudimentary and shunned by the more traditional chiefs and population. The gap between the regions never truly narrowed: in 1967, while Dahomey's overall school attendance stood at 30 percent, the spread was from 90 percent in Cotonou to 13 percent in Tanguieta in the northwest.[7]

The wide disparities between the regions sparked deeper animosities, since administrative positions in the north were staffed by southern cadres whose distaste at their posting to the "savage" north was apparent. Northern feelings of exploitation were further exacerbated when their first delegates to the Territorial Assembly became more fully aware of the discrepancies in the colony's budgetary and developmental allocations. As Thompson put it, the developing regionalist sentiments in northern Dahomey were characterized "by withdrawal on the part of a mosaic of peoples with few bonds between them except a collective sense of inferiority vis-à-vis the south," while regionalism in the south "reflects a kind of corporate jealousy between equals, each proud of its distinctive culture and progress."[8] Following independence the overtly regionalist policies of each successive political group to capture national power have further deepened these mutual resentments and strained the territorial integrity of the state.

While regional animosities set the stage for a three-cornered struggle for political supremacy, the unviability of the economy has tended to intensify the conflict. Well endowed in the quality of its human resources, Dahomey possesses one of the weakest economies in francophone Africa. Except for the recent discovery of offshore oil shales which, if exploited, might change the financial outlook, Dahomey has few mineral resources of sufficient richness or easy access. Until recently the agricultural sector, where

7. *L'Aube Nouvelle* (Porto Novo), December 17, 1967.
8. Virginia Thompson, "Dahomey," p. 170.

improvements are possible, has been stagnant—see table 2.2.[9] Its 1.4 percent annual rate of growth for 1957–65 was one of the lowest in Africa, and some of the increased exports of the past few years (see table 2.3) are in actuality commodities smuggled in from Nigeria. The balance of trade has been unfavorable since 1924, eroding dramatically with independence. The median coverage of imports by exports for the period 1960–72 has been 44.8 percent, with the ratio as low as 31.2 percent in 1966 and 1967.

The country has also suffered from chronic budget deficits despite French subsidies. (See table 2.4.) Only a trickle of foreign investment has reached Dahomey, though in recent years there has been a modest increase in loans and grants from the European Economic Community and United Nations agencies. Within these fiscal constraints economic development can only proceed at a snail's pace, outstripped by the country's high rate of population growth. Short- or long-range planning is very much a juggling of guesstimates, day-to-day administration a hand-to-mouth experience, and assembling the money for civil service salaries the fortnightly nightmare of treasury officials. The extreme dependence of the government on French largesse and the semiannual, hat-in-hand pilgrimage of Dahomean officials to Paris and other world capitals has fostered deep resentments among the more militant and proud intellectuals and students, leading to periodic antiestablishment riots and demonstrations.[10]

The weakness of the Dahomean economy has its most unsettling effect on the salaried class in the urban centers. The glut in educated and upwardly mobile Dahomeans had already developed in the mid-1930s. It was absorbed by France—one of the first instances of a "brain drain" from developing to developed countries[11]—and especially by the neighboring French colonies. There Dahomeans rapidly seeped into many sectors of the administration, educational services, and trade. With the independence of most of these countries Dahomeans were among the first to

9. Amin, *L'Afrique de l'ouest bloquée*, pp. 134–50, 235–38.

10. Samuel Decalo, "Regionalism, Politics and the Military in Dahomey," pp. 456–57.

11. There are more Dahomean M.D.s in Paris alone than in all of Dahomey.

TABLE 2.2

Dahomey: Principal Commodities Exported, 1961–73

(in tons)

Product	1961	1962	1963	1964	1965	1966	1967	1968	1969	1970	1971	1972	1973
Palm oil	11,051	9,293	9,256	12,707	13,257	9,907	8,515	10,526	12,370	15,981	18,369	6,952	5,399
Palm kernels	48,482	43,901	50,558	56,159	16,743	5,762	3,971	7,153	8,500	9,753	10,501	4,950	—
Palm kernel oil	—	—	—	—	16,691	11,698	16,890	22,715	24,598	18,550	27,142	17,769	8,499
Palm kernel cakes	—	—	—	—	16,120	11,737	21,730	23,516	23,503	18,103	22,021	22,219	16,466
Peanuts	12,522	4,303	6,593	3,984	2,268	3,284	5,492	8,029	5,675	5,544	3,658	6,770	3,311
Karite	2,891	2,572	953	7,398	4,964	2,796	6,440	8,133	5,712	5,498	9,179	11,758	3,158
Copra	265	314	577	1,525	1,731	1,061	597	700	1,416	1,824	675	120	156
Coffee	2,189	1,728	1,002	1,065	891	1,041	1,086	511	2,268	1,940	2,173	2,624	1,341
Cotton	1,330	655	1,425	1,056	1,275	2,295	2,590	4,771	6,435	10,758	13,611	15,767	14,896

Sources: 1969–73 data from Banque Centrale des Etats de l'Afrique de l'Ouest, *Indicateurs économiques dahoméens*, April 1975, p. 6. Data from 1961–68 from several previous issues of ibid.

TABLE 2.3
Dahomey: Imports/Exports, 1960–73
(in millions CFA francs)

	Imports	Exports	Balance of trade	Exports as % of imports
1960	7,643	4,513	− 3,130	59.0
1961	6,275	3,579	− 2,696	57.0
1962	6,627	2,699	− 3,928	40.6
1963	8,249	3,155	− 5,094	38.3
1964	7,762	3,254	− 4,508	42.0
1965	8,491	3,367	− 5,124	39.8
1966	8,270	2,585	− 5,685	31.2
1967	11,983	3,750	− 8,233	31.2
1968	12,211	5,505	− 6,706	45.0
1969	14,129	6,693	− 7,436	47.3
1970	17,660	9,062	− 8,598	51.3
1971	21,202	11,648	− 9,554	54.9
1972	23,510	9,189	− 14,321	39.0
1973	26,568	10,018	− 16,550	37.7

Sources: Banque Centrale des Etats de l'Afrique de l'Ouest, *L'Économie Dahoméenne en 1964* and *Indicateurs économiques dahoméens*, February 1973.

be affected by the indigenization drives. Fully 17,000 had to be repatriated from Ivory Coast alone in October 1958.[12] Back home they have either joined the ranks of the educated unemployed or have been integrated into Dahomey's already severely bloated administration. Since the private sector of the economy is small and equally glutted by the rural exodus that has produced a 25 percent unemployment rate, a civil service position is literally a matter of survival for many. The result has been an immense and irresistible pressure on all governments for an ever-expanding bureaucracy. Allocations for civil service salaries have consumed upward of 65 percent of the budget, even though it has been estimated that fully 40 percent of the personnel could be discharged without any serious decline in the quality of state services.

Just over 3 percent of Dahomey's adult population is integrated into the modern wage economy. Though few in numbers and until

12. Amin, *L'Afrique de l'ouest bloquée*, p. 138.

TABLE 2.4
Dahomey: Budgets, 1960–75
(in millions CFA francs)

	Receipts	Expenditures	Deficit	% deficit
1960	5,280.0	5,550.0	1,170.0	21.0
1961	4,610.0	5,775.0	1,622.0	28.0
1962	5,486.0	6,077.0	1,591.0	26.0
1963	6,481.0	6,722.0	1,453.0	21.6
1964	6,206.0	6,809.0	1,353.0	19.8
1965	6,494.0	7,762.0	2,022.0	26.0
1966	6,381.0	7,282.0	1,751.0	24.0
1967	6,583.0	6,885.0	802.0	11.6
1968	6,905.3	7,675.9	770.6	10.0
1969	7,347.2	8,706.6	1,359.4	15.6
1970	10,103.1	9,673.8	+429.3	+4.4
1971	10,859.9	10,248.5	+611.4	+5.9
1972	10,441.9	11,916.4	1,474.5	12.3
1973	12,390.5	13,191.7	801.2	6.0
1974	12,485.0	13,572.0	1,087.0	8.0
1975	13,737.9	14,478.7	740.7	5.1

Sources: Banque Centrale des Etats de l'Afrique de l'Ouest, *Indicateurs économiques dahoméens*, July 1970, February 1973, and April 1975.
Note: Percentages calculated by author. Figures for 1974 and 1975 are estimates.

1972 dispersed among several trade unions of the public and private sectors, labor has played a major destabilizing role in Dahomey's political life. Its strategic position at the nerve centers of the modern economy (the cities) and frequent government attempts both to control the unions and to nibble at salaries and fringe benefits has created the perennial labor-government tug-of-war that has distinguished recent Dahomean history. Very much an elite in terms of social status and standards of living compared to most of the population, the civil service and upper echelon in the private sector have internalized expatriate values and expectations that are not easily fulfilled in an economically weak state. On the other hand, most maintain large families as well as other dependents from their home villages at a time when inflation has slowly eroded purchasing power. Attempts by fiscally hard-pressed governments to effect significant economies by lopping off civil service salaries and fringe benefits have usually been the last segment in the vicious circle, leading to sharp retaliations from organized labor, which has been fiercely jealous of its existing privileges and pay scales. The strong corporate autonomy and progressive radicalization of Dahomean labor distinguishes it from its counterparts in neighboring states, especially Togo and Upper Volta. Yet, while most Dahomean governments have collapsed or compromised when confronted with paralyzing strikes mounted by the unions, the losses to the economy from the strikes themselves have further exacerbated the fiscal dilemma, leading to yet another wave of austerity policies. Since practically the only area for budgetary economies and increased revenues has been the taxation of salaries and elimination of fringe benefits—and to be of use the cuts must be large in light of the small base—the seeds of the next union-government confrontation are sown with the compromise of the previous one.

Parties, Politics, and Patrimonial Leaders

Political power in Dahomey has traditionally revolved around a small elite whose authority stems from patron-clientelist formations[13] they have established in their respective regions with the aid of political brokers (chiefs, notables). During the colonial period, when the franchise was very limited, social and economic status in the urban areas was of greater importance and allowed a handful of "Brazilians" (former slaves returning from abroad) to dominate the political scene. However, since they rarely had roots or traditional power bases in the countryside, the extension of the franchise practically eliminated them as a major political force. The new political leadership that emerged, though modern in outlook and training, had roots and extensive social networks in

13. A large amount of literature has accumulated over the past five years on these kinds of relationships. See especially René Lemarchand, "Political Clientelism and Ethnicity in Tropical Africa"; René Lemarchand and Keith Legg, "Political Clientelism and Development"; John D. Powell, "Peasant Society and Clientelist Politics"; Roth, "Personal Rulership."

the traditional sector that allowed them to garner the solidly ethnic electoral vote.[14]

A political triumvirate emerged in the early 1950s that has since dominated Dahomean politics through tight electoral strangleholds over their regional fiefdoms. All three, as well as many of their lieutenants, have wielded traditional status with modern power. Justin Ahomadégbé's power base in Abomey and the Fon areas in south and central Dahomey stems from his direct descent from the Abomey royal house. A prince of the Aglongo branch, he attended the prestigious Ecole William Ponty in Dakar, the finishing school for budding African leaders. A dentist by profession (he was at medical school with Ivory Coast's President Houphouët-Boigny), he broke off from the single "national" party established by Zinsou, Apithy, and Hazoumé in 1946 to set up his own regional party, becoming first mayor of Abomey and a trade union leader in Cotonou. With the grant of universal franchise, Ahomadégbé's royal credentials, political patronage outlets, and union power base in Cotonou made him the uncontested leader of the Fon.[15]

In like manner Sourou-Migan Apithy was to capture the Nagot-Yoruba allegiance of the Porto Novo area. Though he was of modest background, the "migan" in his name denotes descent from the chief ministers of the Porto Novo kingdom. A political protégé of Father Aupiais[16] and supported by French interests, Apithy acquired national prominence when he became Dahomey's deputy to Paris. Despite his ineptitude and other character faults he was able to forge a powerful network of traditional power brokers that made him the undisputed leader of the Yoruba of the southeast.

Hubert Maga, "the man from the north," was a schoolteacher for twenty years in Natitingou before he acquired the urge for politics. A student under Zinsou's father in Parakou, he too attended

14. For the early phase of Dahomean politics, see in particular Glélé, *Naissance d'un état noir*, and Finagnon M. Oke, "Des comités electoraux aux partis dahomeens."

15. For biographical data on Ahomadégbé and other Dahomean leaders, see Samuel Decalo, *Historical Dictionary of Dahomey* (Metuchen, New Jersey: The Scarecrow Press, 1976).

16. See Georges Hardy, *Le Reverend Père F. F. Aupiais.*

William Ponty. Born of a Bariba mother and Voltaic father (and married to a Fon from Ouidah), he possessed relatively low traditional status with only weak family connections with the Borgou kingdom. Encouraged by the French[17]—who had by this time lost confidence in Apithy—and aided by wealthy Bariba merchants in Djougou, Maga organized the first political grouping of the north in 1951. Originally a member of the "national" party in the early days of elite unity, he too broke off from it over the discrimination of the north. Without overly strong traditional credentials he had to rely more than his two competitors in the south on support from lieutenants with greater traditional status and prestige. Two of these have been Faustin Gbaguidi (to become his *chef du cabinet*), who delivered him the Savalou vote in 1956, and Chabi Mama, a blue-blooded prince of Parakou and Nikki, the true power wielder in Borgou and Maga's right-hand man.

Other secondary political figures exemplify this union of high traditional status and modern power: Paul Darboux, a scion of the Djougou mercantile class, of noble birth, and the one who has rallied the Dendi and Bariba of Djougou behind Maga; Michel Ahouanmenou, an Apithy political broker in the Porto Novo region; Valentin Aplogan, an early Apithy man of the royal family of Allada; Oké Assogba, Maga broker from the Ouémé district; Tahirou Congacou, Speaker of the House and Interim President in 1965, a Dendi of the royal family of Djougou; and Paul Hazoumé, one of Dahomey's most prominent authors and a longtime politician descended from Porto Novo dignitaries. Even within the army traditional status or royal descent have played an important role, interfering with the impersonal bureaucratic hierarchy of rank.

For most of the population in the countryside, national identity and allegiance are in many respects empty terms; they are meaningful only to urban elements and even then only precariously superimposed on tribal identity and allegiance. Local loyalty is bestowed upon patrimonial leaders who have the strongest links or claims to traditional authority. Such allegiances are hard to sever for "those steeped in traditional values are conditioned to accept

17. According to Glélé (p. 120) Maga was "created" by Peperthy, the French colonial administrator in Borgou.

the permanence of a man in his office" and "the initial loyalty of the masses to their traditionally conceived *first leader* cannot be destroyed." [18] This explains to a large extent the permanence of the power base of the triumvirate despite revelations of corruption (Maga), ineptitude and opportunism (Apithy), or arrogance and authoritarianism (Ahomadégbé). It also clarifies somewhat the nature of their powerful remote control over their fiefdoms when despite two years of exile in Paris (after the 1965 coup) they were able to torpedo the elections, in which they were barred from participating, by a call for electoral abstention.[19]

The collapse of the 1946 political coalition of the most important ethnic leaders in Dahomey heralded the beginning of the three-cornered struggle for power and the politicization and mobilization of the regional and ethnic camps[20] behind each of the contenders. Given the pattern of interregional suspicions and animosities and the permanence of traditional values and clientelist politics, existing cleavages were frozen—indeed, imbedded—deeper in the country's political culture. The political history of Dahomey since that brief early moment of elite cohesion has been the chronicle of the power struggles of the country's three political giants. Efforts to create interregional or ideological parties and electoral campaigns by aspirants lacking an ethnic-regional base have failed miserably in Dahomey. Indeed, in the 1970 presidential elections veteran politician and former President and Foreign Minister Emile Derlin Zinsou ran against the triumvirate as the nontribal, nonregional alternative and obtained only 3 percent of the vote; the rest of the electorate split along predictable lines with the percentage of the vote each of the trio polled equalling *exactly* that cast for their parties in 1960! [21] Zinsou even failed to carry his hometown,

18. Dov Ronen, "The Two Dahomeys," p. 56.

19. Seventy-three percent of the electorate stayed away from the polls; most of those who went voted for Ahomadégbé's candidate. *Dakar-Matin* (Dakar), May 8, 1968.

20. These resemble the vertical cleavages *(verzuiling)* of Lijphart except that stability is eluded since interelite compromise has been impossible. See Val R. Lorwin, "Segmented Pluralism"; Arend Lijphart, *The Politics of Accommodation*, and "Consociational Democracy."

21. For the 1960 elections see Cornevin, *Dahomey*, p. 76. For the 1970 results see *Afrique Contemporaine*, May-June 1970.

Ouidah, which was effectively delivered to Ahomadégbé by its power brokers.

In like manner all attempts to recreate elite consensus and establish a one-party system in Dahomey, though "successful" on paper, only provided a structural umbrella of artificial unity underneath which the tripartite struggle for ultimate hegemony continued unabated. As Zolberg has noted, "the latent tendencies of the societies in which these political processes occur militate against the one-party state." [22] Persistent infighting at the apex of power, competitive ethnic pyramids of personal allegiances, and the keen struggle for control of patronage in conditions of acute scarcity and immense pressures from below have plagued all attempts to establish interregional coalitions. The internal fissiparous tendencies have rapidly caused both the collapse of the superficial and opportunistic alliances and the reemergence from their ruins of the true power-building blocs—the regional networks. Essentially the only change in Dahomey's party structure since 1951 has been the party nomenclature, which has added to the epistemological confusion on the Dahomean scene.[23] The highly personalist regional power formations have remained the same; their leaders largely intact at the apex of their ethnic pyramids.

Because of these reasons as well as personality differences neither a Maga-Apithy (1960 and 1960–63), a Maga-Ahomadégbé (1960, linking the most compatible leaders), nor an Apithy-Ahomadégbé (1963–65, uniting the south against the north) alliance succeeded. By 1965, when the army established Dahomey's first military government, virtually every possible civilian coalition (including a brief tripartite one in 1960) had been tried and found wanting. Though the specific factors that combined to erode each alliance were different, mutual jockeying for sole power by each one of Dahomey's triumvirate was a common ingredient.

22. Zolberg, *Creating Political Order*, p. 36. See also Samuel E. Finer, "The One Party Systems in Africa."

23. An excellent schematic guide to the intricacies of Dahomey's party nomenclature is contained in the addenda of Oké, "Des Comités electoraux." See also the excellent two-part article on Dahomey's early political evolution, Martin Staniland, "The Three-Party System in Dahomey," *Journal of African History* 14, nos. 2 and 3 (1973), pp. 291–312, 491–504.

A detailed analysis of Dahomey's convoluted political history would be outside the scope of this study and has already been traced elsewhere.[24] A brief overview, however, may be helpful. Dahomey's First Republic[25] collapsed on October 28, 1963, when, following a week of union strikes and massive demonstrations in the coastal areas, the army moved in to preside over a rearray of power which eclipsed Maga and promoted Apithy and Ahomadégbé to the presidency and vice-presidency, respectively.[26] The immediate cause of Maga's downfall was government corruption and misallocation of resources (for the costly Presidential Palace) while unionists were being asked to bear the brunt of the concomitant austerity policies in salaries and fringe benefits. The new constitution provided for a bicephalous executive, which proved unworkable in light of the natural inclinations and incompatibilities of the two political leaders who were asked to share power. The Second Republic survived until November 29, 1965, when feuding between the two factions and leaders reached an apogee and paralyzed day-to-day administration. As demonstrations erupted in the coastal areas in support of one or the other camp, General Soglo intervened again and handed interim power to Tahirou Congacou, Speaker of the House. The latter's inability to resolve the constitutional impasse and strong opposition within the army itself to a return to civilian politics led Soglo to intervene a third time, on December 22, 1965, banning politics, elected bodies, and political parties and setting up the country's first military regime. Though the country was to experience two further periods of civilian rule (Zinsou's 1968–69 army-sponsored government and the triumvirate's rotating Presidential Council, 1970–72) the 1965 coups actually marked the end of Dahomey's brief exposure to constitutional government and the emergence of the army as *the* dominant factor in Dahomean politics. Though the

24. See the articles by Decalo, "Politics of Instability in Dahomey," and "Military in Dahomey."

25. Following French practice each major constitutional change since independence is given a number.

26. A good account of the 1963 upheaval is contained in Emmanuel Terray, "Les Revolutions congolaise et dahomeenne."

process of political decay[27] started much earlier with Maga's rigging of elections in 1960 (some may even point out that Dahomey was France's most unmanageable colony, devouring the energies of twenty-one governors during the colonial era), the assumption of executive power by Dahomey's highly factionalized army was to accelerate the process. To understand the reasons why this small and lovely state was to become the continent's enfant terrible and the classic example of a praetorian system, it is necessary to analyze the internal dynamics and the motives of the army in 1965 and the course of military rule and army disintegration since.

FACTIONS AND PERSONAL CLIQUES

Dahomey's armed forces had traditionally been the least cohesive in francophone Africa. Though quite small even by African standards—1,800 soldiers and roughly 1,200 *gendarmes*[28]—their compact size and training by French officers did little to cement the internal fissures. The organizational complexity of the armed forces was rather low and their operational capabilities limited. Moreover, the troops were mostly stationed in the coastal areas (for example, Cotonou and Ouidah) with few military duties and fewer opportunities to conduct maneuvers—a result of budgetary limitations and the nonexistence of extraterritorial threats. The army's limited *military* role expectations, its physical proximity to the major urban centers, the compact nature of the modern and political sectors of the state, and the diffuseness of civil-military boundaries all facilitated the rapid politicization of the military hierarchy. The process was further aided by personal linkages that were established between military personnel and the three regional political leaders and by residual allegiances of the rank and file to their ethnic power formations. Since the triumvirate's agents were continuously canvassing it to drum up support, the army was transformed into a patchwork of conflicting political allegiances.

The military budget, though small in absolute terms, took a

27. For theoretical background see Huntington, "Political Development and Political Decay."

28. David Wood, *The Armed Forces of African States*, p. 8. There were, at that date, also 1,000 civilian police.

significant bite out of Dahomey's limited resources. The country spent two and three times as much on defense as on education and public health respectively, with military allocations standing at 2.5 percent of the GNP and 12 percent of the national budget.[29] These figures placed Dahomey in twelfth and eleventh rank among thirty-two sub-Saharan states in terms of allocations to the armed forces.[30] Military hardware and other materiel was also regularly supplied by France under treaty provisions. For all practical purposes the army was an elite corps with limited societal or military functions except when called upon in times of civic unrest to act as a superpolice.[31] Without clearly defined garrison and defense duties and responsibilities, the very briefly ingrained colonial tradition of the army as "grand muette"—the silent apolitical prop of legitimate political authority—became transformed into the concept of the military as arbiters of political power and, later still, the *source* of political legitimacy.

Officers' salaries were quite high and were linked to French pay scales: personnel of intermediate rank frequently were paid at par with cabinet ministers, and in addition they had a variety of fringe benefits. Many also engaged in petty smuggling across the Togolese border, at times with the active cooperation of their counterparts in Togo. Several ranking officers amassed small fortunes while others were involved in a variety of commercial transactions or enterprises. The best example is General Soglo, the chief of staff, who owned valuable real estate in Cotonou, including the buildings that housed the U.S. Embassy and the U.S. Cultural Center. That high rank appeared to correlate with personal wealth was not lost on the junior officers and constituted one of their gripes.

When Soglo assumed power in 1965 in the name of the army, the military had already experienced at least one unpublicized mutiny, and its hierarchy of command was strained by internal factional tensions. As long as the army stayed in its barracks the internal

29. United States, Arms Control and Disarmament Agency, *World Military Expenditures 1970*, p. 12.

30. Donald G. Morrison et al., *Black Africa*, pp. 118 and 119.

31. Indeed, the paracommando unit which spearheaded the 1967 Kouandété and 1972 Kerekou takeovers was designed as a highly mobile force to be used to suppress civil disorders whenever they occurred.

conflict tended to be over petty issues—promotion, professional advancement, posting; when the army moved into the center of the political arena the stakes became much bigger. The banning of formal political activities for the duration of the military regime inevitably made the army itself the arena for competing political views. Officers with dormant political ambitions saw an opportunity to play a greater role in public affairs. Consequently a variety of new fissures developed after the decision to stake the army's reputation on the success of the Soglo experiment.

One of the earliest cleavages separated the officer corps, preponderantly Fon with a minority of Yoruba and northerners,[32] from the rank and file, mostly from the north. Partly due to conscious French policy in recruiting personnel from allegedly "militaristic" ethnic groups, the predominance of Fon officers was a result of the educational advantages they had over the northern populations. The lower percentage of Yoruba in the officer corps was a consequence of the greater inclination of upwardly mobile youth from Porto Novo to move into the commercial spheres. Though Maga tried to redress this balance during his first presidency (1960–63) there were few northern recruits with the requisite educational qualifications, and any new intake of officer cadets would have required an expansion of the army since all command positions were either filled or already committed. Aware of his unpopularity in the south where the major army bases were located, Maga directed his efforts at packing the *gendarmerie* with Bariba recruits who tended to regard themselves as his personal militia. The tension that arose between the two forces led to dangerous confrontations on several occasions and was only resolved when the army appointed one of its own officers—Major Benoit Sinzogan, a Fon—as commander of the *gendarmerie*. The internal ethnic power balance in the officer corps did not, however, appreciably change until the junior officers' coup of 1967 and subsequent upheavals. The purges, demotions, and other personnel shifts that followed finally dislodged the senior Fon hierarchy, promoted several middle-ranking northern officers to top positions, and created openings for new junior officers, several of whom have been northerners.

32. In 1966 only fourteen of the army's ninety officers were from the north.

The ethnic composition of the armed forces was only one source of tension within the officer corps. The balance of power was much more fluid than a simple array of southerners vis-à-vis northerners. Within each group and at times cutting across both, cliques formed around the more popular, ambitious, or powerful officers. These cliques at times were stable but often were not, reflecting the relative power shifts within the officer corps and underscoring the extent to which they were mutual advancement groups rather than purely ethnic or ideological. Rank, seniority, and de facto power were not always the criteria that determined leadership of these factions. The erosion of Soglo's authority over the army after 1965, for example, was largely due to the fact that he relied solely upon his formal power base as chief of staff. Colonel Sinzogan, in spite of his high rank and series of top command responsibilities especially since 1967, was never one of a core of power wielders in the army largely because he tended to be too stolid and cautious.

Within the Fon group informal power and leadership revolved around Colonel Philippe Aho and Major Benoit Adandejan (descendants of Abomey kings Glélé and Ghézo, respectively) who commanded somewhat more respect from their subordinates than Soglo himself, though personality variables also played a role. Their separate power bases were not badly eroded, at least at the outset, when Soglo demoted them both to less sensitive positions in 1967, though they were easily forced into retirement following the 1967 junior officers' coup. In like manner Lieutenant Colonel Alphonse Alley, Soglo's chief of staff, though a Basila from the north central region had a significant personal following in the armed forces that cut across the ethnic and generational camps. Even when purged in 1969 by his rival, Colonel Kouandété, Alley's power base in the army remained largely intact and much of the internal military strife during 1969–70 was a result of this. Yet though still popular after his full rehabilitation early in 1971 he was shunted aside as more junior elements scrambled for leadership.

Colonel Maurice Kouandété, who became the leader of a group of northern and junior officers in 1967 and played such a dominant role in Dahomean politics up to 1970, also saw his position erode rapidly once he was removed from operational command. The leadership of his faction was assumed by his former protégé Major

Mathieu Kerekou, also a northerner, who led the junior personnel in the 1972 assault against the political and military establishment. Even lower in the hierarchy, fluid cliques coalesced around captains, lieutenants and NCOs, which vividly attests to the erosion of the prime prerequisite of a modern army—a hierarchical structure of formal authority—and the shift to personalist power formations.

Generational differences and different commissioning practices also played an important role in sharpening the polarization of the factions in the officer corps. The senior officers (Colonels Soglo, Aho, and, to some extent, Alley), who had received their commissions after varying periods of service in the ranks, felt threatened by the "young upstarts" who had vaulted to officer rank via brief training courses in France. The latter "professionals" likewise bore a deep resentment against their commanding officers, whom they felt were both inferior to them in education and professional qualifications and overly politicized through their contacts with the political elites. The resentment was sharpened by the promotion blocks that developed at all levels following the rapid Africanization of the officer corps within a few years after independence. The prospects of prolonged promotion freezes following their relatively rapid rise in the earlier years was intolerable to many junior officers, especially after General Soglo assumed political power without granting them a share in the administrative or decision-making powers of the state.

The Soglo Regime

The feuding between Ahomadégbé and Apithy for political supremacy (Maga was jailed after the 1963 coup) reached its climax in November 1965. Day-to-day administration halted as factions within the bureaucracy undermined each other or opted for the safest course of action, inactivity. The showdown between the two regional leaders rose over the issue of which part of the bifurcated executive held the appointive powers to the Supreme Court.[33] The matter was of no small consequence in light of the

33. See Philippe Decraene's analysis of the different interpretations of the Constitution. *Le Monde*, November 26, 1965.

constitutional role of the Court in any succession crisis. When
Apithy refused to ratify his rival's appointees the struggle burst into
the open. The deeply divided single party established in 1964,
tightly under Ahomadégbé's control, voted to depose Apithy from
the presidency. Carefully staged demonstrations and rallies in
Cotonou and Abomey called upon him to step down, while
Ahomadégbé released Maga from jail to swing the north to his side.
In Porto Novo huge crowds gathered to support their regional
leader, and their numbers were augmented by unionists demonstrating against the regime's austerity policies and, especially, the
recently imposed "solidarity tax" on their salaries. Once again, as
in 1963, the call "The army to power" went out as unrest spread
throughout the coastal areas.

It was in this tense situation that Deputy Chief of Staff Major
Aho received orders from Ahomadégbé to disperse the Porto Novo
crowds, with force if necessary. The order bypassed Aho's superior,
Soglo, who had not been on good terms with Ahomadégbé. This
seemed to substantiate the rumor that Soglo was shortly to be
replaced by his deputy. In any case the troops in Porto Novo did
not fire at the crowds and Soglo, who rushed to the site, personally
countermanded Ahomadégbé's orders. A heated exchange followed as Ahomadégbé publicly rebuked the chief of staff in the
presence of several of his officers.[34] Boiling over this humiliation
and the manner in which his authority had previously been
bypassed, Soglo immediately convened his staff officers in Cotonou
and ordered Ahomadégbé's arrest for constituting "a public
menace." [35] Cooler tempers prevailed, but it was decided to topple
the president the next morning. A belated effort by Ahomadégbé
(alerted by supporters in the army) to placate Soglo was to no avail.
On November 29 the army moved in and empowered the president
of the National Assembly, Tahirou Congacou, to resolve the
constitutional crisis. Three weeks later, on December 22, when it
was obvious Congacou had failed to find a solution, Soglo assumed
executive power. He was nudged in this direction by Lieutenant

34. Glélé, *Naissance d'un état noir*, p. 181, and W. A. E. Skurnik, "The Military
and Politics," p. 79.
35. Skurnik, "The Military and Politics," p. 79, n. 17.

Colonel Alley and was fully supported by many officers who were anxious to move into the political spotlight.

With the triumvirate sent packing to Paris—where amidst considerable joviality they made up in front of the press—Soglo set up his first cabinet, the most competent one to that date.[36] Only three of its thirteen members were officers and most of the civilians were young "technocrats" uncommitted to any of the regional power formations. In order to preserve a modicum of civil-military dialogue a National Renovation Committee was created to supplant the defunct National Assembly. A cross section of society, it had thirty-five members, only three of whom were officers, and the majority was "elected" by a specially convened assembly of Dahomey's most prominent civic personalities and the ranking army officers.

According to Soglo, Dahomey's history of political instability was a direct result of the economy's frailty: "no matter how skillful the African leaders are, the masses remain dissatisfied. . . . Strong healthy finances are essential to the political stability of the State." [37] His paramount concern, therefore, was to arrest the progressive deterioration of Dahomey's budgetary situation and trade balance—a necessary precursor to any new plea for increased French developmental aid. Adopting a rigid fiscal posture, Soglo's preponderantly southern government immediately attempted to tackle the economic morass. A deluge of austerity decrees started to flow from the cabinet. The solidarity tax, inherited from Ahomadégbé, was ruthlessly increased to 25 percent and extended to the private sector as well; consumer taxes went up, family allowances were halved, and several embassies were shut down. There was also an attempt to trim the fat from the civil service with compulsory "retirements," a freeze on replacements, and an unsuccessful drive spearheaded by Soglo himself ·to redeploy redundant personnel in the hinterland and stem the rural-urban exodus.[38] Through these and several other fiscal economies (including turning off air conditioners in the Presidential Palace) the

36. *Le Monde*, June 30, 1966.
37. *Afrique Nouvelle*, April 21, 1966.
38. "Back to the Land."

budgetary deficit was more than halved,[39] but at the cost of thoroughly alienating the unions that had been at the outset favorably disposed to the new government. As one trade union declared, "the situation of the workers has never been so bad. The military-technocrats regime of General Soglo . . . has surpassed [previous governments] in cynicism." [40]

Along with the austerity drive, the government formulated a modest Five-Year Plan for economic recovery stressing rural development and the diversification and mechanization of agriculture. Roughly three quarters of the envisaged expenditure of $141 million was to be channeled into agrarian or agrarian-related fields, the majority of the funds to be obtained from France or the European Economic Community. The plan never really had a chance to prove its merits, for Soglo was to be ousted in 1967; indeed, his period in office coincided with the nadir of Dahomey's trade imbalances, though some of the country's subsequent economic recovery is traceable to funds invested during his presidency.

As labor in the coastal areas started to agitate for relief from the onerous solidarity tax the Soglo regime slowly started to come apart. The discovery of plots spawned by agents of the exiled triumvirate and the growth of union militancy adversely affected the dynamism with which the government had tackled Dahomey's problems. Subtle overtures were made for the support of the ethnic regional power brokers, and late in 1966 several "political" appointees were brought into the government. Later, in 1967, both Soglo and Alley initiated contacts with the "Big Three" in Paris to sound them out regarding a possible role for them in a future government. This inevitably led to the disgusted resignation of several of the more militant technocrats in Soglo's first cabinet. Slowly Soglo's more "representative" government became afflicted with the symptoms of the preceding administrations: creeping corruption, vacillations, political compromises, and indecisiveness. To a similar extent Soglo started losing his grip over the army and

39. From 1.3 billion CFAF in 1965 and 501 million in 1966 to 372 million in 1967—a reduction of 71 percent in two years.

40. *Afrique Nouvelle*, September 14, 1967.

with it his ultimate source of legitimacy. The more his administration resembled previous ones, the more the rationale for a military regime faded. The same criteria that had been used to evaluate and condemn the leadership of Maga and Apithy-Ahomadégbé appeared valid in Soglo's case.

The tensions within the officer corps had been greatly exacerbated with Soglo's assumption of power and his elevation of several senior Fon officers to cabinet rank. Colonel Philippe Aho's appointment was particularly resented by the junior ranks. Aho, the sublimely proud and self-confident descendant of Abomey's King Glélé, flagrantly misused his position as Minister of Defense and Interior to further his own and Fon interests. A growing embarrassment to the hard-pressed Soglo, he was finally removed from the cabinet and later retired from the army by the young junta that came to power. The more militant junior officers were also aggravated by Soglo's relaxed and unrefined political style,[41] the "fumblings, hesitation, and delay" [42] of his government, and his informal circle of advisers, which included his cousin and his unpopular French wife. Soglo's inability to either unite the nation or give it a sense of direction was apparent to all; this especially galled younger army cadres that had a highly idealized image of Mobutu-style military rule and were frustrated at being kept from important positions in the regime. Their growing disenchantment with their leaders was matched by the growing unpopularity of the regime among the masses, who did not distinguish between the officers-turned-politicians and the army as a whole. In more ways than one the professional pride and integrity of the military was tied to, and consequently eroded by, the floundering Soglo leadership.

Under pressure from the junior officer cliques a Military Vigilance Committee (CVM), the most important of several such institutions set up since 1965, was created in April 1967. With Major Sinzogan as its first chairman, and against Soglo's wishes, the CVM was essentially a watchdog committee with supervisory

41. See the portrait of Soglo in Paulin Joachim, "Le General Soglo, ou le provisoire qui dure."

42. *West Africa*, December 30, 1967.

powers over governmental activities. Its very creation was a victory for the lower ranks in the officer corps. It signaled a general tightening of military control over civilian life and a curb on Soglo's autonomy and powers. Composed of fifteen middle and junior rank officers and NCO's the CVM was the end product of a long tug-of-war to make General Soglo personally accountable and responsible to a quasi parliament of the military; its egalitarian composition was a result of the smallness of the officer corps itself and in the long run demolished rank distinctions. Yet even the CVM was not fully satisfactory to the junior officers. Its powers were limited, its composition and leadership reflected the continuing hegemony of the senior Fon establishment (nine of its members were southerners), and Soglo never took it very seriously. As the young December 1967 putschists were later to argue, "major decisions affecting the country's future . . . were made within the family circle" [43] of Soglo's informal advisers and the Fon senior clique.

The CVM, like the armed forces it was supposed to represent, rapidly became torn by factionalism, as cliques clashed over its limited powers, patronage, and possibilities for graft. The dominant group was composed of Majors Adandejan and Sinzogan and Captain Hachemé, the core of the informal "Abomey" faction. Adandejan and Hachemé were particularly disliked by the northern officers: Hachemé for his rough quelling of civil disorders in the northern town of Parakou in 1964 and Adandejan (tracing his lineage to King Ghézo), who was referred to as the Beria of Dahomey[44] after he served as head of the Security Services prior to his demotion by Soglo.[45] Sinzogan was relatively meek and could not control the unruliness that crept into the CVM's deliberations, which were dominated increasingly by Adandejan. The most important other faction was the one that coalesced around the mercurial Major Maurice Kouandété, the vice-chairman. A Somba

43. *L'Aube Nouvelle*, December 24, 1967.

44. See René Lemarchand, "Dahomey."

45. The rapid turnover of officers in that critical position more than anything reflected the tumult in the armed forces. In less than three years (1966–69) six officers headed the Security Services, practically every one demoted after utilizing the appointment to promote personal and clique interests.

from the northern Gaba region (his hometown was Natitingou), Kouandété was a graduate of St. Cyr and the Ecole Militaire and was very conscious of his "professional" credentials. Arrogant, self-confident, and highly ambitious, Kouandété had no patience for the political machinations of his superiors. His style was direct, even abrupt, and his conception of military rule harsh and uncompromising. As *chef du cabinet* to Soglo and head of the palace guard and the Security Services he had continuously tried to discredit the Abomey group and promote his own position. Caught falsifying intelligence reports, he was detached from his previous duties and made *chef du cabinet* to Colonel Alley, Soglo's chief of staff, where he polarized the staff officers into opposing camps. Within the CVM he was the most uncompromising and militant supporter of direct control over the policies of the regime. In this he was supported by northern officers like Captain Mathieu Kerekou and Lieutenant Arcade Kitoy and several militant Fon and Yoruba junior officers from the strategic Ouidah garrison. Moreover, as deputy commander of the paracommando company he had operational control over Dahomey's crack mobile unit—a fact he was to put to good use in December 1967.

The creation of the CVM was preceded by the demise of the consultative civil-military National Renovation Committee (CRN) about ten months earlier. The CRN, which had also become faction-ridden, had arrogated to itself quasi-legislative powers and had been slapped down in January 1966; it was finally disbanded in June 1966. The elimination of the last formal civil-military channel of communication increased the gap between rulers and ruled in Dahomey and in the eroded state of public confidence highlighted the struggle for power going on in the military. In the midst of the tumult stood Colonel Alphonse Alley with one foot in each camp. Though promoted from the ranks, Alley was also a graduate of the Ecole d'Etat Major and Saint Maxient's. Born in Bassila in the central north (though raised in the south), he was popular among most cliques in the army and, more importantly, trusted by the unionists in the coastal areas. Critical of many of Soglo's political maneuvers as chief of staff, he tried to preserve the army's hierarchy of command. Nudged several times to depose General Soglo he refused out of loyalty to his former commander and was thus considered part of the Abomey clique. He was not overly ambitious ("wine, women, and song Alley," he was referred to in diplomatic circles), and a government under his aegis would probably not have been markedly different from Soglo's, though it might have soothed tempers in the south.

The trade union strikes of December 1967 and Soglo's reactions to them were the incidents that finally broke the tenuous allegiance of the junior officers to their superiors. In typical manner Soglo temporized in the face of a general strike which had paralyzed the south, first waving the stick by issuing Decree 36 that banned all union activities, and then dangling the carrot and capitulating on all fronts by repealing the decree and promising unionists an alleviation of their tax burden. On December 16 the CVM was summoned to a meeting in which an Alley-Sinzogan negotiated truce with the unions was to be explained. Kouandété and his most intimate supporters did not show up. Instead, next morning at the head of sixty soldiers of the paracommando company, Kouandété stormed the Presidential Palace and drove Soglo to refuge in the French Embassy, while all senior officers were placed under house arrest.[46]

A Military Revolutionary Committee (CMR) was promptly set up composed of the less important junior ranks (three captains, eight lieutenants, and three NCOs) under the chairmanship of the Fon Captain Jean-Baptiste Hachemé, who would shortly be purged. (Apart from his 1964 brutality he became involved in a clumsy power gambit.) Kouandété and some of his confidantes moved into the government, which was ethnically balanced and composed of three majors, three captains, and three lieutenants. The army promised a new constitution, national elections, and the withdrawal of the military to their barracks within six months.[47] Despite these noble goals and the outraged puritanism that came through Kouandété's speech to the nation, the coup signaled the beginning of the era of praetorianism in Dahomey. Not many in

46. For excellent documentation of the coup see the reports in *West Africa*, December 23 and 30, 1967.

47. For Kouandété's address to the nation announcing his reasons for the coup and his original cabinet, see *L'Aube Nouvelle*, December 24, 1967, and Robert Cornevin, "Les Militaires au Dahomey et au Togo."

his faction desired a total renunciation of political power; most, including Kouandété himself, wished a civilian regime controlled by the army and beholden to it. But once arms had been used by a specific faction to make or break a government the process of coup and countercoup would not be arrested.

MILITARY PRAETORIANISM AND CONSTITUTIONAL EXPERIMENTS 1967–73

The Zinsou Interregnum

Overthrowing Soglo's regime was far easier than resolving the civic and military cleavages that had led to its demise. Kouandété's young putschists were themselves completely divided about their future course of action. A few wanted a total withdrawal of the army from politics; others, including Kouandété, aspired to political power or control over a subsequent regime; still others were ardent supporters of one or the other of the old guard. The coup that temporarily displaced the active senior Fon military leadership was not popular among the masses. The unions in particular were very uneasy, since they were quite aware of the triggering cause of the upheaval and Kouandété's rigid, dim view of the validity of their demands. Intellectuals, merchants, and the resident European and Asian communities also feared him, for he was a political unknown and might move in any direction. As late as 1973, few in Cotonou could evaluate his political inclinations beyond his personal ambitions and social rigidity.[48] Despite its failings the Soglo regime—which came to power with a measure of popular support—was not regarded by many as a serious deviation from constitutional legality. The 1967 coup, however, was essentially an internal reshuffling of power within the military, sanctioned by force alone and resulting in a takeover by northern elements. Thus the coup was greeted with uneasiness in Dahomey and with open distaste in Paris, where De Gaulle had just hosted General Soglo.

48. From interviews with Kouandété in 1971 it appeared that he had no specific political programs beyond his conviction of the need for a "strong" military government such as Mobutu's in Zaire.

The fact that France icily ignored the coup and stopped its subsidies to Dahomey was the major reason for the reshuffling of power that occurred several days after the coup.[49] On December 20 Kouandété declared at great cost to his pride, "We still consider Colonels Aho, Alley, and Major Sinzogan as our leaders," [50] and ceded to Alley his positions as head of state and chief of staff, while Sinzogan was included in the new government as foreign minister. The strong northern overrepresentation continued, however, and the interim cabinet was preponderantly military. Investigations into the corruption of Soglo's regime displaced several top administrators and resulted in the purge of three more southern officers (Major Chasme and Captains Hachemé and Johnson), which further tilted the military balance in favor of a young northern-dominated clique. After a series of heated discussions at Camp Guezo, in which civilian elements participated, the military leadership announced that it would withdraw from the political arena after the promulgation of a constitution and the holding of presidential elections.

The new constitution was approved by 76 percent of the registered voters, but the junta's decision to disqualify the presidential candidacies of all former officeholders led to a stunning electoral fiasco in May 1968. The military haughtily overrode the Supreme Court's objections that the unilateral decision to disqualify candidates was patently illegal under the newly ratified constitution. The disqualification of the triumvirate opened yet another fissure in the badly split officer corps. It was rammed through by the Kouandété group, which desired the election of an untarnished figure and one whom they could control more easily than Dahomey's established patrimonial rulers. With most of the true power wielders in the country barred from running, the election was essentially a low-keyed, five-cornered race between political hopefuls who had little mass support and no regional power bases. ("Fantasy-candidates," according to L'Aube Nouvelle.)[51] The elec-

---

49. A payroll of 350 million CFAF was due at the end of the month while the state coffers had only 50 million CFAF.

50. Cornevin, "Les Militaires."

51. Cited in West Africa, April 27, 1968. See also Afrique Nouvelle, April 18 and 25 and May 2, 1968.

torate heeded the call for abstention from Maga and Apithy and when the polls were closed fully 73 percent had shunned the election.[52] The "victory" of Dr. Basile Adjou, who was endorsed by Ahomadégbé and captured the latter's vote in the Fon strongholds, was promptly annulled by the army, whose leaders retired in a dangerous mood to Camp Guezo to ponder their future course of action. For several weeks factions clashed bitterly within the quasi-parliamentary body of ninety officers, NCOs, and common soldiers that constituted the ultimate decision-making organ of the army. Personal ambitions surfaced rapidly; several power gambits and at least one attempted putsch (by Alley who favored the return of the old guard) were later revealed to have taken place. Only strong unionist and intellectual opposition prevented the establishment at this stage of a Kouandété-led fully military regime. The decision was finally reached in a highly charged vote, which once again underscored the emergence of Kouandété as Dahomey's new strong man, to appoint Emile Derlin Zinsou as president for five years.

Though Kouandété's "candidate," Zinsou's appointment was very much a compromise between the various factions in the army that were exhausted by their inability to agree on anything substantive. Still, it was a surprising selection, since Zinsou was not much liked by any particular faction. A strong antimilitarist, he regarded the Kouandété coup as treason and had refused to join the provisional government. A political figure whose roots went back to the 1940s Zinsou had participated in various administrations but had kept independent of any of the regional formations. Nor was he tarnished by any of the scandals of the previous regimes he had served in, usually as foreign minister. Forthright and impeccably honest, Zinsou had excellent contacts in Paris and in the West—probably his major assets to the junta in 1968—though at home his conservative foreign policies had not endeared him either to the unions or to the more militant students and intellectuals. Finally, while Zinsou had some support in his hometown, Ouidah, as a "Brazilian" he did not have a traditional

52. For the results see *Dakar-matin* (Dakar), May 8, 1968, and Gilbert Comte, "Dahomey."

political network, a fact that grossly misled Kouandété to assume
that he could be manipulated.

Zinsou's nomination as president was ratified by the popular
plebiscite that he demanded and that the army, fearful of yet
another fiasco that might totally discredit it, only reluctantly
agreed to. Amidst rumors of an imminent return of the old guard to
reclaim their thrones—rumors that caused serious jitters in the
army—and a renewed appeal by the triumvirate for a boycott of
the plebiscite, Zinsou scored a personal victory when he was
affirmed by 55 percent of the registered voters.[53] He was rapidly
inaugurated as the army finally withdrew to its barracks.

Zinsou's seventeen months in power were marked by three
linked processes: a significant improvement in Dahomey's fiscal
and trade imbalances, the erosion of his support in the country,
and the virtual disintegration of the military. The fiscal policies that
Zinsou espoused immediately brought him into a collision course
with the unions. The constant pruning of the budget, new taxes on
cars, gasoline, and luxury commodities for the urban elites, major
cuts in family and child allowances, and the first serious crackdown
on the widespread smuggling and tax evasion of the powerful Porto
Novo and Cotonou merchants alienated him from the very groups
that might have sustained his regime.[54] More than anything else his
harsh and uncompromising line vis-à-vis the frequent student
strikes and demonstrations (over educational grievances and Dahomey's conservative foreign policy) drove a wedge between him and
the urban middle class by threatening their children's educational
and employment prospects.

An astute administrator who did not flinch from the execution of
unpopular policies, Zinsou's fiscal orthodoxy brought about a
semblance of budgetary balance by late 1969. The import-export
gap similarly improved until exports covered 45 percent of
imports—a ratio unattained since 1961. Playing on Dahomeans'
long-suffering national pride he stressed the slogans of "fiscal
independence" and "a balanced budget by 1970." Actually these

53. *Afrique Nouvelle*, August 1, 1968.
54. For a detailed analysis see Samuel Decalo, "Full Circle in Dahomey," and E.
Makedonsky, "Nouvelle Tentatives de creation d'un parti unique au Dahomey."

were economic imperatives, since French subsidies were scheduled to end shortly. He tried to placate the unions by frequently consulting them and by reducing the solidarity tax to 20 percent; yet his cuts in their ample fringe benefits took more than he gave and earned him their wrath. Thus despite Zinsou's strong leadership (though by late 1969 he too had started to compromise in the face of widespread civil unrest) and largely honest administration, his days in office were numbered. He had fallen afoul of the unions (which mounted several furious strikes quelled only by Kouandété's paracommandos), the urban middle class, and the merchants, and he was also progressively alienating his ultimate "patron," Kouandété.

From the moment the military withdrew to their barracks they collapsed in convulsions. Finally out of the national spotlight a major settling of personal grievances commenced that reflected the new internal balance of power and the emergence of Kouandété as the strong man of Dahomey.[55] Alley, who had been reduced to the status of Kouandété's mouthpiece because of his role in the attempted June putsch, was promptly ordered to Washington as Dahomey's military attaché, a position expressly created for him. When he refused to be eliminated from the power hierarchy in this manner he was cashiered from the army and Kouandété became chief of staff. Colonel Aho and Major Adandejan had already been retired in 1967 and General Soglo was in exile in Paris. Colonel Sinzogan was shunted to head the *gendarmerie* in Porto Novo, an important position but devoid of operational control over troops. The sweep of the Abomey faction included Major Chasme, who had been found guilty of gross corruption by the anticorruption tribunal he himself had proposed, set up, and chaired for one day before his arrest. In like manner Majors Jean-Baptiste Hachemé and Ferdinand Johnson, both Fon, were demoted to nonoperational duties, as Kouandété's faction (including several young militant southern officers) consolidated itself in power.

The purge of the Abomey clique and especially the expulsion of Alley from the army only exacerbated existing tensions by creating

55. "Dahomey: Reglement des comptes entre officiers superieurs." See also S. Olatundji, "Pourquoi le president Zinsou à ecarté Alley de l'État-major."

yet another major divisive issue that was to preoccupy the officer corps but did not succeed in diminishing Alley's personal popularity. Despite the purges, the army command was still top-heavy with southerners who resented Kouandété's meteoric rise. Their new chief of staff's active cultivation of the allegiance of junior officers and the rank and file threatened their positions in the hierarchy of command and their control over their personnel. Many resented Kouandété's gruff and cocky style while others were uneasy about their chances of promotion and advancement under his command. Thus while the internal military rearray of power could not be legitimately blocked (Alley and the purged officers were patently guilty of the offenses they were charged with), a significant element in the officer corps was biding its time, waiting for Kouandété to stumble before pouncing on him. In the meantime, plotting and intriguing reached new heights and military discipline decayed as officers, NCOs, and ordinary soldiers coalesced into informal, highly fluid, competitive cliques.

The decay in the army's chain of command became overtly manifested in the series of armed assaults that punctuated Zinsou's presidency. On the night of July 11, 1969, a clumsy attempt was mounted by pro-Alley supporters to kidnap or coerce Kouandété. Despite an open trial, the true intentions of the plotters are still not fully known. The prosecution claimed the assassination of Zinsou, Kouandété, and Sinzogan was intended; the defense maintained the aborted plot stemmed from the professional insecurity of many in the army who merely wished to question their chief of staff about a reported file of blacklisted personnel in his possession.[56] Though Alley and several other defendants were imprisoned for their role in the conspiracy, the nature of the trial and the composition of the court drove a deep wedge between Zinsou and his chief of staff. The latter had demanded a military trial for the defendants, which Zinsou rejected because of its patent illegality (Alley was then a private citizen) and probable verdict (the death sentence). Zinsou's compromise, a special Security Court that would include two military officers was successfully challenged by the defense, and the

56. *Afrique Nouvelle*, September 25 and October 9, 1969; *West Africa*, October 4, 1969.

civilian court that tried the case issued what Kouandété felt were ridiculously low sentences.[57]

In the following few months several other attempts were reported on Kouandété's life: in two of these automatic weapons were used, suggesting military elements were involved in a spillover of the army's internal strife into the streets of Cotonou. Rumors spread that the assaults were actually engineered by Kouandété himself in order to prepare a background of crisis prior to a personal takeover. Whatever the merits of these contradictory interpretations, the breakdown of law and order was one of the prime arguments used by Kouandété when he moved to topple his own choice for the presidency. The roots of their falling out are directly traceable to Kouandété's midjudgment of Zinsou's personal integrity and potential maleability—a surprising error in judgment since Zinsou had proven on numerous occasions during his long history of political activities that while willing to bend to reason he was no puppet. Zinsou felt beholden to no one, having obtained his mandate in the plebiscite he had demanded for this very reason. Aware of his chief of staff's ambitions and impatience he tried to tame him by acquiescing in Alley's retirement and by granting Kouandété an extraordinary promotion to lieutenant colonel in October 1969. These gestures were not sufficient to bridge the gap between the two men. Zinsou's concern for legality in the Alley trial, his belief in an apolitical army, and his "insensitivity" to the policy suggestions of his military "patron" incensed Kouandété, who felt he had elevated Zinsou from obscurity and "as arbiter of power, what he gave he could take away." [58] As relations between the two deteriorated it appeared that Zinsou was finally preparing to disencumber himself of his increasingly predatory chief of staff or at least bring in the rest of the high command to reassert his own supremacy.[59] However that may be, Kouandété struck first. On the morning of December 10, 1969, the presidential vehicle was accosted and sprayed with bullets by a unit led by Kouandété's

57. Ten years' imprisonment for the two main defendants, Alley and a former Soglo aide-de-camp, Lieutenant Bouraima.

58. *West Africa*, December 20, 1969.

59. See Claude Garin's dispatch to *Africa Report*.

loyal protégé Lieutenant Arcade Kitoy, and Zinsou was escorted under armed guard to Natitingou, the chief of staff's hometown.

The Return of the Old Guard

The hastily summoned officer corps met that afternoon to hear Kouandété justify the coup on the grounds of Zinsou's failure to secure law and order, unite the nation, or carry out the directives left by the army prior to its withdrawal from the political arena in 1968.[60] Tense meetings continued for three full days, and it was obvious that Kouandété had overplayed his hand in relying on his de facto control of the armed forces but ignoring the informal balance of power against him. His motives were highly suspect and there was resentment that he had not consulted his senior colleagues prior to his assault on Zinsou. The outcome of the coup could not be reversed though Zinsou, who was promptly released, demanded his immediate reinstatement and Kouandété's arrest on the ground of gross insubordination. Above all else the army wished to protect whatever shreds of corporate dignity it still retained. Zinsou's reinstatement (apart from the fact that he was still not popular among the officers) would have laid bare the Army's total disunity and made it the national laughingstock while risking an armed revolt of Kouandété's faction. On the other hand, the latter's increasingly independent actions had to be restrained.

Kouandété's bid for appointment as provisional president was rejected. Instead a Military Directorate was set up, responsible to the Supreme Council of the Armed Forces (the officer corps). The directorate was composed of the three colonels heading the army (Kouandété), the *gendarmerie* (Sinzogan), and the Department of National Defense (Paul-Emile de Souza, Zinsou's *chef du cabinet*). Colonel de Souza was appointed chairman of the directorate by virtue of seniority and hemmed in by the two Fon officers, Kouandété's powers were severely restricted. When Zinsou's loyal cabinet refused to serve in an interim capacity without their head, the portfolios were divided among the directorate, with the least sensitive allocated to Kouandété.

60. *Le Monde*, December 11–17, 1969 (weekly edition).

The 1970 coup brought about the neutralization of Kouandété's power network in the army and a reassertion of Fon hegemony. Alley was promptly released from prison, reinstated in the army with his rank and decorations, promoted to full colonel and appointed Director General of National Defense, a position originally promised to him in the Zinsou government. His "crime" had, after all, been to fail in the kind of conspiracy that Kouandété had just succeeded in. Kouandété also had to observe the rehabilitation of several Fon officers purged under his leadership, especially Majors Hachemé and Chasme (who became director of the Security Services). Later Kouandété himself was purged for a crude and haughty attempt to liberate a friend from prison. Stripped of his command, he was finally reinstated in the army as Alley's deputy, yet another striking manifestation of how the clock had been turned back to the pre-1967 power structure.

After prolonged and stormy sessions the army decided to invite back the only true power brokers, the triumvirate. This was the most cogent possible admission that the badly divided army was throwing in the towel—that it could no longer agree about, let alone dictate, the future course of political life in the country. One condition was imposed on the trio: that they agree among themselves to back only one candidate in the scheduled presidential elections. The promise was rapidly disregarded by the old guard after their return to Dahomey. Reunited with their political lieutenants, who had been shut out of power since 1963 or 1965, no one was in any mood to share potential political spoils. As it became clear that the old bickering of the past was becoming part of the present, the army narrowly escaped a violent armed confrontation when Sinzogan and Kouandété clashed in a dual power gambit in support of Apithy and Maga, respectively. This potentially fratricidal military convulsion was reportedly quelled in a tense meeting of the army command during which each faction stationed its fully armed personnel outside the conference room.[61]

Though a formal vote had been taken to withdraw from the political arena,[62] the army was no longer cohesive enough to abide

61. *Africa Report*, April 1970, p. 6.
62. According to one military source it was a three to two decision.

by the majority decision and no officer, least of all Colonel de Souza, was willing to risk the widespread mutinies and interfactional shootouts enforcing discipline would have entailed. As all four ex-presidents (including Zinsou) presented their candidacies to the electorate they were actively supported by various military factions. Allegations of intimidation, bribery, and illegal distribution (and nondistribution) of electoral cards were rife as the long dormant but still powerful regional political brokers strained to deliver the ethnic vote to the candidates.

Zinsou, the one candidate without an ethnic power base and the modern, "national" alternative to the big three, was humiliatingly crushed, obtaining less than 3 percent of the vote. The results once again attested to the regional division of power in Dahomey, unchanged despite the five-year exile of the triumvirate. Apithy, who found his regional apparatus rent by divisions, finished second after Ahomadégbé, while Maga, trailing the two southerners, was about to obtain the overwhelming endorsement of the northwestern Atakora district, which would have catapulted him to victory, when the elections were stopped and then annulled by De Souza on the grounds of mounting violence (see table 2.5).[63] The political crisis that developed after what amounted to the denial of the presidency to Maga was the severest Dahomey had ever faced. As the army command reconvened in an ugly mood Maga retreated to his headquarters in Parakou amidst rumors of an imminent secession of northern Dahomey. To lend credence to this threat an Assembly of the Northern Populations was created. The opportunistic Apithy joined the bandwagon by letting his lieutenants talk of a possible secession of Porto Novo to Nigeria even as he was trying to exploit the army's divisions in favor of a mixed civil-military

63. There was a great deal of friction in Atakora in particular, where a small groundswell of support had surprisingly emerged for Ahomadégbé, but reports of violence were exaggerated. The main weakness of the election was that it was conducted region by region (in theory to allow the *gendarmerie* to prevent electoral abuses), a practice that resembled the election of regional leaders rather than a national president and tended to heighten and prolong the tension throughout the country. The 1970 results (minus Atakora) gave 200,092 votes to Ahomadégbé, 176,828 to Apithy, 152,551 to Maga (only 24,000 votes from the entire south), and 17,653 to Zinsou. See *Afrique Contemporaine*, May-June 1970.

TABLE 2.5
Dahomey: 1970 Presidential Election

Date	Region	No. of registered voters	No. of voters	% voting	Ahomadégbé	Apithy	Maga	Zinsou
March 9	Ouémé	234,664	112,729	47.7	8,679	92,295	6,129	4,104
March 13	Atlantique	229,309	109,278	47.7	56,843	38,009	6,100	5,724
March 17	Mono	144,197	73,613	51.0	31,961	19,725	5,705	4,074
March 21	Zou	221,137	137,024	62.0	99,592	26,511	6,211	3,494
March 25	Borgou	167,919	132,703	78.9	3,017	288	128,406	257
March 29	Atakora	190,000	—	—	—	—	—	—
Total	—	—	565,347	—	200,092	176,828	152,551	17,653

Source: *Afrique Contemporaine*, May-June 1970, p. 7.
Note: The elections were suspended prior to the vote in Atakora.

regime (a la Upper Volta) with himself as prime minister.[64] Threats of violence and dissidence poured in from all parts of Dahomey and there was a minor exodus of southerners from the north as fear spread that civil war was about to erupt.

It is somewhat difficult to explain why the military did not fully disintegrate at this stage. There was certainly a great deal of factional maneuvering as personalist cliques prepared for a take-over. No military leader had sufficient authority to impose even nominal cohesion on what was at this point a swirling cauldron of highly fluid and competitive cliques whose only allegiance was to their key officers. From hindsight, however, it appears that a new center of gravity was emerging in the officer corps around a "third-generation" clique of junior lieutenants and captains (many of them Yoruba and Fon) from the Ouidah artillery camp.[65] Not powerful enough yet to initiate a power play and dissatisfied with the stale machinations of the old guard politicians, they were also unwilling to see any other faction seize power, a gambit that might have ushered in a civil war. Certainly the experience of neighboring Nigeria was a powerful constraint on any precipitous action by various cliques in the Dahomean army. This "centrist" position also neutralized any hopes for a quick putsch by reducing a clique's chances of acquiring support from the rest of the corps after the seizure of power. These junior officers were to emerge into the national spotlight in the subsequent military eruptions and in the 1972 coup, whose prime characteristic was the total demolition of the entire senior army establishment, northern as well as southern.

The 1970 political crisis finally abated when the triumvirate hammered out a unique constitutional formula under which a Presidential Council was set up with each one of the troika in power for two years and all patronage (especially cabinet positions) divided equally. Maga, as the potential victor of the annulled elections, became its first chairman to be followed by Ahomadégbé and Apithy. Paradoxically, the arrangement—greeted with extreme skepticism at home and abroad—did not collapse despite its flaws and inconsistencies: indeed in May 1972 Dahomey was to witness

64. Zinsou did not participate in any of the subsequent negotiations with Maga, which were initiated by Ahomadégbé and later joined by Apithy.

65. From interviews in Dahomey (July 1972).

its first peaceful transfer of political power as Maga stepped down as chairman and was succeeded by Ahomadégbé. Aware of the dangerous mood of the military and that they themselves might not survive another spell in exile, the three leaders endeavored to maintain at least a facade of unity even though their petty rivalries continued unabated.

Maga's chairmanship of the Presidential Council (1970–72) was marked by an informal alliance with Ahomadégbé that all but squeezed out Apithy, and in the few months prior to the 1972 coup it was apparent that Maga had linked himself with Apithy to sabotage Ahomadégbé's chairmanship.[66] Despite these opportunistic political maneuverings, the economic picture, benefiting from some of the policies initiated by Zinsou, brightened markedly. Budget surpluses were recorded for the first time and the poor export-import ratio improved.[67] Potentially exploitable offshore oil shales were discovered by Union Oil of California and other explorations continued for what may still turn out to be a much needed pot of gold at the end of a very long rainbow. In the meantime, through sharp reductions in some expenditures, continuation of French aid beyond the 1970 deadline, and increased revenues from goods smuggled in from Nigeria, the Maga government was able to eliminate one major source of social unrest in the south—the solidarity tax. This reduced the intensity of the perennial union-government tug-of-war. On the other hand, elements shut out of the tripartite alliance of the regional bosses tended to penetrate the increasingly politicized and radicalized student associations, utilizing them to create widespread disturbances such as occurred late in 1971 and again in 1972.[68] Other ideologically militant groups (for example, the intellectuals) also

66. For some of these internal rifts see *West Africa*, December 12, 1970, and *Afrique Nouvelle*, March 25, 1971.

67. Some of the boom in exports was a result of increased smuggling from Nigeria. Dahomey exported 800 tons of cocoa in 1970–71, although it did not grow this crop. Indigenous textile production tripled, and the cotton crop in the north was higher than expected. The situation is still not stabilized, however, and is subject to sharp fluctuations. *Le Monde*, February 2, 1971, and *West Africa*, February 11, 1972.

68. *West Africa*, November 19, 1971, December 17, 1971; *Afrique Nouvelle*, December 16, 1971.

expressed their dissatisfaction with the social and political status quo policies of the Presidential Council. For all practical purposes, however, the major threats to the stability of the council came from the military.

A reorganization of the armed forces in July 1970 confirmed De Souza's largely apolitical leadership while consolidating the positions of the Fon top-echelon officers.[69] With some of the major military figures of the past either retired or "promoted" to nonoperational duties (Alley, Kouandété) it was hoped that the dissidence in the armed forces might slowly abate. This was a patently unrealistic expectation, for praetorian patterns are not easily broken up. Throughout 1971 and 1972 a series of incidents erupted that further underscored the extent to which discipline had eroded in the armed forces. In March 1971 a small mutiny broke out in the Ouidah artillery base and in May military elements tried to assassinate co-President Ahomadégbé in an ambush on the main road to Abomey.[70] A more extensive mutiny rocked the Ouidah base on January 28, 1972, when the troops "deposed" the base commander, Major Rodriguez, "elected" an NCO as his replacement, and demanded the resignation of Colonel de Souza, the chief of staff.[71] In both instances the mutiny leaders went unpunished after order was restored.

The Ouidah mutiny was quelled (it was hardly even announced in the press) after the presidency dispatched Kerekou to talk to the troops, but on February 23 (several weeks before Maga was scheduled to step down) military elements tried to assassinate De Souza and seize power in an aborted coup. Twenty officers and soldiers and several civilians were arrested for their role in what were essentially two different conspiracies with two sets of goals and motivations rolled into one. The first plot was a straightforward attempt by Kouandété to seize power through erstwhile colleagues who were in operational control of troops (Captain Glélé, Lieutenant Kitoy, and Captain Boni, a medical officer). They pretended to go along with Kouandété only until De Souza

69. *Afrique Nouvelle*, August 6, 1970.
70. *West Africa*, December 3, 1971.
71. *Afrique Nouvelle*, February 28, 1972.

was assassinated, at which time they intended to eliminate Kouandété as well and seize power in the name of Zinsou.[72]

As one observer pointed out, this was the first time in Dahomey that assassination was tried as a method of capturing power.[73] Amidst stringent security precautions a seven-man military court presided over by Lieutenant Colonel Chasme (who had been personally purged by Kouandété in 1968) decreed six death sentences for the main defendants, to be executed within twenty-four hours. Government efforts to have the accused tried by civilian magistrates and defended by Cotonou advocates were frustrated by the complete disengagement of Dahomey's legal hierarchy from the case. Nothing in Dahomey's checkered political history better attests to the total decay of institutions than the flat refusal of Dahomey's magistrates to try the defendants. Their argument was simple and poignant—since past experience had indicated that whatever verdict they might reach would not be executed anyway and the defendants were likely in typical Dahomean style to emerge later as the country's leaders, trying them for capital offenses would simply place the magistrates in jeopardy.[74] Their timidity was quite justified: neither the military court that passed the death sentence nor the Presidential Council that ratified it dared to execute the prisoners, who were eventually released when the army again came to power in October.

Major Mathieu Kerekou's October 26, 1972, coup d'état essentially signaled the coming-of-age ("coup-wise") of the third-generation officers, the young militants of the Ouidah base who maintained they had not seized power but merely "collected it back." [75]

72. *West Africa*, March 10 and 17, 1972, and April 21, 1972. Zinsou, according to all accounts, knew nothing of the ploy. Glélé had been his *chef du cabinet* and had forewarned him of Kouandété's forthcoming 1970 coup. Kitoy was Kouandété's faithful protégé until the double plot and had been at his side at practically every important juncture since 1967. Boni was a former Maga supporter who had threatened the secession of the north after the 1970 elections were annulled. An incredible variety of personnel, allegiances, viewpoints, and ideologies coalesced in planning the aborted 1972 coup.

73. Ibid.

74. *Afrique Nouvelle*, April 10 and 30, 1972.

75. "The ousted civilian leadership held its power from the Army. The Army has taken back what it gave," *West Africa*, November 20, 1972. See also *West Africa*,

The upheaval probably also brought to an end the political careers of Maga, Ahomadégbé, and Apithy and resulted in the complete eclipse of the entire upper echelon of the military establishment. The army's seven colonels were shunted into civilian administrative positions. Alley, for example, was appointed government commissioner (a prestige title) of the National Company of Oil Mills. Sinzogan was placed in charge of the state agency dealing with forestry products, De Souza became commissioner of the Agricultural and Marketing Credit Company while Hachemé was allocated the humiliating (for him) leadership of the state Ceramic Crafts Company. Not surprisingly, several of the purged officers (Alley, Hachemé, Chabi) attempted a comeback in January 1973 for which they were tried and sentenced to twenty years' imprisonment.

Kerekou's all-military cabinet included three majors (he promoted himself shortly to lieutenant colonel), seven captains, and one adjutant intendant. Among the key appointments were those of two young Fon militants, Captains Janvier Assogba (minister of finance) and Michel Aikpé (minister of interior and security), both of whom had played important, if secondary roles in previous upheavals and military administrations.[76] Kouandété, though promptly released from prison together with the other plotters of 1972, was deftly shunted aside by the new military hierarchy.

Among the central institutions set up by the new administration were a Military Committee for the Revolution (MCR) and a National Consultative Committee (NCC). The MCR was created as an all-military watchdog committee to supervise the "morals" of the administration and provide it with advice and criticism. The NCC [77] eventually became a "representative," deliberative organ of one hundred people divided into three sections charged with financial and economic issues, social and cultural matters, and

---

November 6, 1972, and the excellent coverage of this takeover in *West Africa*, February 12 and 19, 1973.

76. For the full list of the initial appointments see *West Africa*, November 20, 1972.

77. The respective acronyms in French are CMR and CNC. The precise names of these and several other structures also established by Kerekou (as well as their membership and functions) has changed slightly since they were announced.

general policy guidelines. All segments, vocations, and religions in Dahomean society are represented. In most structural and functional respects the NCC resembled the National Consultative Assembly established a few months before the 1972 coup.

The most striking feature to date of the present regime in Cotonou is its increasingly radical ideological tone. For the first time one hears of the Marxist-Leninist "alternative," the application of socialism in Dahomey, and even of "Dahomean Socialism." The regime has pledged the radical transformation of society and the economy on more "equitable" lines. An administrative reorganization of the country was decreed in 1974 in an effort to decentralize the decision-making process, grant local units a greater degree of autonomy, and promote peasant involvement in socioeconomic development. Local "revolutionary" committees have been established to spearhead this societal transformation. Yet, as observers have pointed out, much of this preoccupation with structural reorganization is still either largely paper or rhetoric, while the imagination of the countryside has not been greatly captured by the projected visions of a better society and economy.[78] Just as the structural reorganizations have turned out to be merely changes in nomenclature, so too have many of the widely heralded nationalizations, especially of education and the petroleum distribution network. The latter is so minute in Dahomey that its nationalization can only be seen as symbolic, and the announced state takeover of the large number of Catholic (that is, private) schools, accompanied as it was by a plea that existing personnel remain in their posts, may also turn out to be only nationalist rhetoric that does not affect the substance of the educational system.

Assisted by several radical ideologues (some of whom are protégés of Guinea's Sekou Touré), the new junta in Dahomey decreed several other nationalizations during 1975. In most instances the nationalized industries were placed under the supervision of the kind of state organs that have in the past proved to be notoriously inefficient and corruption-ridden. Cotonou's delightful

78. See, for example, Michael Wolfers, "Letter from Cotonou," *West Africa*, December 16, 1974.

waterfront Hotel de la Plage was also expropriated, allegedly because the efficient service it provided tourists hurt the more casually run state-owned hotel. The regime also decreed earlier closing hours for bars and dancehalls (regarded as "hotbeds of reactionary forces") and specified the proper manner in which all correspondence to and from state organs should conclude ("Kindly accept the assurance of my revolutionary commitment"). These and other policies recently announced in Cotonou have resulted in a minor exodus of Dahomean intellectuals and civil servants; in mid-1975 the government announced that exit permits would not be granted to civil servants wishing to travel abroad on nonofficial trips. At the same time an opposition Liberation Front for the Rehabilitation of Dahomey, aimed at reversing the policies of the military junta, was formed both abroad and in Porto Novo.

Internationally, the government has also adopted a radical posture. Relations with China were reopened, a break with Israel was initiated early, Libyan, Saudi, and other Arab fiscal aid was solicited, formal demands were made in Paris for a revision of the treaties signed at independence,[79] and Dahomey's Permanent Representative to the United Nations replied sharply to United States Ambassador Daniel Moynihan's criticism of General Idi Amin's address to the General Assembly. Yet these militant international postures have not brought about a shift in Dahomey's dependence on France, just as the recent domestic decrees have not altered much in the country's economy. Rhetoric aside, what has been created domestically is a larger array of bureaucratic state organs that might prove to be powerless without adequate financing (currently nonexistent) and greater "control" over sectors of the economy that in reality are beyond the control of any Dahomean government. There can be little doubt that several of the junior officers now in positions of power are sincerely committed to radical socioeconomic change even though the realities of Dahomey's situation prevent any concrete and immediate actualization of their aspirations. For most of them, however, sweeping changes in nomenclature and meaningless structural reorganizations are

79. *West Africa*, February 19, 1973.

confused with real societal change, while to some their new ideological garb is the socially accepted contemporary cloak for personal advancement.[80] Hence, despite the superficially sharp divergence of Kerekou's policies from those of previous leaders, civilian and military, the concrete domestic reality is systemically similar.

Nor is the current administration free of cleavages and tensions or necessarily more secure in office. It is true that the purge of the army's senior officers after the 1972 coup eliminated some key and perennial personal competitions in the officer corps. The latter is no longer divided by professional qualifications: practically all officers are graduates of some foreign military academy. Most of them are also of roughly the same generation (none are over forty-three years old and Kerekou himself is only thirty-six) and not overly beholden or attached to either the old political triumvirate or regional power brokers. Yet these elements of cohesion have not been sufficient to paper over personality tensions and ambitions or ethnic competitions in the army. And though most of the junior officers are still political unknowns outside their barracks (even in their own country) they appear to have become polarized on yet another plane that hitherto had not been so important in Dahomey—the ideological. The combination of new and old tensions has already produced a number of sharp clashes between competing military personalities and their power pyramids,[81] as well as

80. A few of the officers who rose to power as a result of the 1972 coup and who are currently regarded as ideologically militant did not exhibit such orientations when interviewed in July-August 1971, nor were they regarded in knowledgeable Dahomean circles as especially radical. Among the current militant officers one can note Captains Béhéton, Badjogoumé, and Azonhiho. Kerekou is regarded as a moderate struggling to juggle the diverse ideological-personalist strains in his cabinet and command hierarchy.

81. The most serious of which pitched the then minister of posts and telecommunications, Captain Nestor Béhéton, against Cotonou Port Authority commissioner, Major Richard Rodriguez. (The latter had been relieved of his Ouidah command because of his unpopularity with the troops.) The two clashed continuously, with Béhéton encouraging a strike by the dockworkers against Rodriguez. In August 1973 the crisis came to a head and both officers were removed from their respective offices.

demotions and cabinet reshufflings. On January 21, 1975, came the first publicized attempted coup when the minister of public function, Captain Assogba (recently demoted in the cabinet) drove his Ouidah-based troops into Cotonou, where the attempt mysteriously fizzled.[82] Several months later Captain Aikpé, one of the strong men in the regime, who was rumored to be preparing a power grab, was killed (or murdered, depending upon the version) during an alleged assignation with Kerekou's wife. Aikpé's elimination sparked major union strikes in the south that did not abate for some time despite a government curfew and threats of instant dismissal of those refusing to appear for work. By the end of 1975 the regime was "governing" Dahomey from a command post in Cotonou; the MCR had not been convened for several months due to its "unreliability";[83] and Kerekou was seen to be relying more and more on Captain Dohou Azonhiho, Aikpé's successor and a former political unknown.

Thus, from the systemic point of view, the current military junta appears little different—Marxist-Leninist jargon aside—from all previous military administrations that have tried to rule via a combination of symbolic decrees and lifeless structural innovations. The new radical pronouncements emanating from Cotonou attest, however, to the coming-of-age of a new political class more attuned to the militancy in other parts of the Third World. Probably the most significant aspect of Dahomey's long and sad history of civil-military relations is its dramatic illustration of the progressive decay of civil and military structures that commences when a cleavage-ridden army, permeated with competitive cliques, takes over political power. But Dahomey is not a unique example of the development of a praetorian syndrome in Africa. Both Congo/Brazzaville and Sudan share the same tendencies, while a number of other countries may also be moving in the same direction. Once armed force is employed to bring about a rearray of political power—no matter how justified or popular the initial intervention may be—guns become trumps and every officer is transformed into a potential political broker. Whether or not a bid

---

82. *West Africa*, February 3, 1975.
83. Ibid., September 15, 1975.

is placed at the winner-take-all game seems to depend largely on the personal and corporate ambitions in the officer corps. Dahomey, which has produced so many of Africa's distinguished intellectuals, administrators, and professionals, has also produced many avid players of coupmanship.

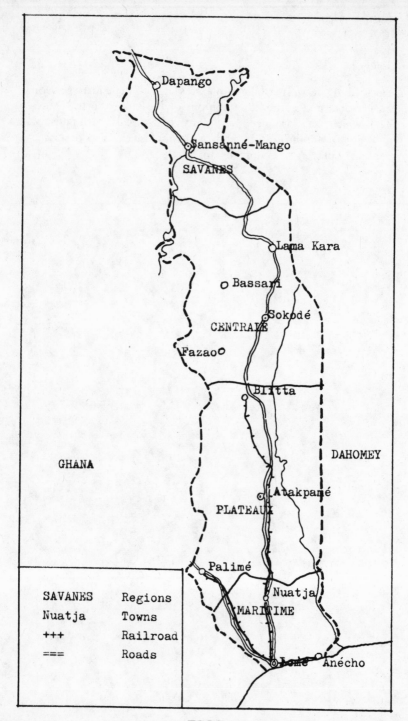

TOGO

3 The Benevolent General:
Military Rule in Togo

THE ETHNIC AND ECONOMIC INFRASTRUCTURE

In many respects Togo is a mirror image of Dahomey, with similar geographical and ethnic configurations, small size, a weak economy, external pressures, intense regional cleavages, and interelite strife. In Togo too, the army has played a dominant political role since 1963, though its record in office has been dramatically different from that of its counterpart in Dahomey. Nine years of direct military rule (since the 1967 takeover) under a remarkably cohesive army has brought Togo a measure of political stability, social tranquillity, and economic development. Though skimmed over in studies of African political systems, Togo's experience with military rule is unique and instructive, because it is a rare exception to the generally negative record of military regimes.

As in Dahomey, the most permanent and persistent feature of Togo's social, economic, and political life has been its ethnic cleavages. Within Togo's arbitrarily defined borders are to be found over forty ethnic groups (see table 3.1) that are traditionally broken down into three broad cultural and linguistic clusters.[1] Ewe and Ewe-speaking elements (Ouatchi, Mina) predominate in the south. Tracing their descent to the great migrations from Ketou (Dahomey) that also led to the establishment of the Dahomean kingdoms of Allada, Abomey, and Porto Novo, Togo's Ewe clans were linked by strong ties of cultural affinity. Constant pressures from their traditional enemies, the Fon in the east and the Ashanti in the west, coupled with individualistic values rooted in their psychology and religion, precluded the evolution of a centralized Ewe protostate. Instead, the 100 to 120 Ewe clans and subtribes maintained their separate identities without a common political

1. See Robert Cornevin, *Histoire du Togo*.

TABLE 3.1
Togo: Ethnic Breakdown, 1960

		Population	%
1.	Ewe cluster	753,000	44%
	(a) Ewe	(362,000)	(21%)
	(b) Ouatchi, Mina, Fon, Adja, etc.	(391,000)	(23%)
2.	Kabre cluster	399,000	23%
	(a) Kabre	(241,000)	(14%)
	(b) Losso, Lamba, Tamberma, Mossi, Logba	(158,000)	(9%)
3.	Moba cluster	122,000	7%
	Moba, Konkomba		
4.	Kotokoli cluster	122,000	7%
	Kotokoli, Bassari, Tchamba		
5.	Central Togo cluster	77,000	5%
	Akposso, Bassila		
6.	Gurma	76,000	5%
7.	Yoruba cluster	46,000	3%
	Nago, Ana		
8.	Hausa, Fulani	29,000	2%

Note: All figures estimated.

organization or throne, cooperating in times of external threats and reverting to traditional interclan rivalries and jealousies when the threat receded. Their inability to unite and the highly decentralized heritage of Ewe political life hampered not only the consolidation of a precolonial Ewe state but also the pan-Ewe unification and nationalist movements prominent in the two decades prior to independence.[2] Moreover, with the advent of popular suffrage many of these traditional village and clan rivalries became politicized on the national level, which lead to strains on the cohesion of the modern Ewe political elite.

The less densely populated central part of the country is very much an ethnic transition area in which reside segments of northern and southern tribes, a numerically important group of

2. Claude E. Welch, Jr., *Dream of Unity*, chapters 2 and 3. See also J. C. Pauvert, "L'Evolution politique des Ewe," pp. 161–92; D. E. K. Amenumey, "The Pre-1947 Background to the Ewe Unification Question"; James S. Coleman, *Togoland*.

Yorubas, as well as the Akposso. In the north population density once again increases (though with wide disparities) in areas inhabited by the Paragourma (Bassari, Gourma, Konkomba, Moba) and the Kabré (Kabré, Kotokoli, Lamba, Naoudemba) tribal groups. With two small exceptions, consolidated states did not emerge here either; intervillage raiding and clan wars flourished each dry season. Though patterns of social organization varied widely, traditional authority and chiefly powers were much more entrenched in the north than among the Ewe; contact between them was superficial and intermittent.[3]

As in Dahomey, Togo's regional cleavages do not reflect merely the historical isolation of disparate ethnic groups that have retained feelings of exclusiveness and mutual suspicion within the borders of one political system but also have cultural and economic dimensions. In the mainstream of new outside influences and with a value system that stressed individualism and was conducive to change and adaptation, Ewe society rapidly evolved and modernized under the impact of missionary activity and, later, German colonization. Avid pursuers of Western education, Christianity, modern avocations, and styles of life, and intensely upwardly mobile, the Ewe were soon designated as future administrators of the German colonial empire in Africa.[4] With the establishment of the French mandate southern Togo became an exporter of trained administrative personnel (fluent in French as well) to other parts of French Africa where, confused with the Fon, they were both collectively referred to as "Dahomeans."

Selected to be Germany's *Musterkolonie* (showcase colony), Togo was divided into two sections: Eweland, which was developed socially and economically, and the northern regions, largely ignored except as a source of cheap labor for development projects in the south. The administrative distinctions, springing as they did from strict differentiations between the potentials of tribal groups,

3. See J. C. Froelich, Alexandre Cornevin, Robert Cornevin, *Les Populations du Nord Togo*; J. C. Froelich, *Les Konkomba*; Robert Cornevin, *Les Bassari du Nord Togo*; H. Enjalbert, "Paysans noirs, les Kabrés du Nord Togo."
4. See D. E. K. Amenumey, "German Administration in Southern Togo."

resulted in a lopsided development of the country. Railways, roads, clinics, schools, and missions blanketed the south but stopped short of the north, from which European visitors and missionaries were barred. This bias was largely continued, though not as rigidly, when Togo became a French mandate in 1917, and it continued to be reflected in the discriminatory policies of Togo's first independent Ewe-dominated government.

By independence, ethnic and cultural cleavages had been widened and institutionalized with growing disparities between the two regions in practically every respect. Statistics on literacy rates, medical and social facilities, economic growth rates, and political representation all resembled data from two different countries. The disparities have only slowly diminished despite over a decade of northern-influenced regimes (1963–76). As recently as 1970 approximately 50 percent of children between ages six and fourteen attended school (44 percent of those in the six- to eighteen-year-old group); the regional spread ranged, however, from 99 percent in Lomé to 18.6 percent in Sansanné-Mango in the far north.[5] Attendance levels in the Maritime and Plateaux regions were practically identical but were 25 percent higher than in LaKara (the core of Kabré county and major recipient of development aid since Kabré elements gained ascendance in Lomé), 53 percent higher than in the Central region, and 280 percent higher than in the Savanna area.[6]

Togo's regional fissures have had a pervasive and detrimental effect on the development of political life. Ewe nationalism and northern resentments at southern domination spawned ethnically exclusive political parties that were unable to cooperate, let alone coalesce. The leadership that emerged, however, was radically different from that in Dahomey. Devoid of strong kingdoms or other large precolonial entities that might have provided natural foci for electoral support and allegiance, Togo's leadership has tended to be more diffuse, lacking in strong traditionalist credentials, and less in control of its political networks. This has allowed

5. *Togo-Presse*, August 7, 1970.

6. G. Sigisbert, "L'Enseignement vise à former les hommes qu'exige le développement du pays," p. 31.

the easier eclipse of regional leaders without the subsequent total alienation of their supporters as in Dahomey. The Ewe leadership mantle has, moreover, gravitated around "Brazilians" such as the Olympio cousins (Pedro and Sylvanus) and De Tovi and Anani Santos, while the northern leaders (Antoine Meatchi, Nicholas Grunitzky), though of chiefly lineage, have not possessed absolute control over their power bases in the hinterland. As elsewhere the multiplicity of reinforcing cleavages, personal antagonisms, and competition for supremacy in a political system with few alternate channels to patronage or power has only sharpened political strife, exacerbated regional tensions, and encouraged a zero-sum mentality among political aspirants.

The Togolese economy also exhibits vast regional disparities, with the cultivation of cash crops and hence higher per capita incomes concentrated in the south (especially in the cocoa- and coffee-producing Palimé region), where the important phosphate industry is also located. By contrast, income levels in the north, parts of which are overpopulated and suffering from soil erosion, have been extremely depressed due to the absence of industrial or cash crop activity and the nonexistence until recently of all-weather roads connecting the region with Upper Volta and the coastal areas. This regional disparity should be viewed, however, within the context of a generally erratic and, until recently, stagnant economy with very low internal growth rates. Thus, despite major development during the *Musterkolonie* phase and a further spurt during the early 1950s, Togo had the lowest economic growth rate of all twelve French excolonies during 1956–65.[7] Fluctuating agricultural output (constituting 65 percent of exports) whose potential growth is limited,[8] combined with strong phosphate exports (especially since 1966–67) still cover only an average of 75 percent of imports (see tables 3.2 and 3.3). It is the phosphate industry that has saved Togo from the economic plight of Dahomey.[9] Rapidly expanding phosphate exports have generated

7. *Togo-Presse*, December 2, 1967.

8. Amin, *L'Afrique de l'ouest bloquée*, pp. 125–34, 148–49. See also Banque Centrale des Etats d'Afrique de l'Ouest, *Commerce du Togo*, p. 2.

9. First discovered in 1952; the decision to exploit the resources was made in 1957, with the mining beginning in 1961.

TABLE 3.2
Togo: Imports/Exports, 1959–73
(in millions CFA francs)

	Imports	Exports	Balance of trade	Exports as % of imports
1959	3,747	4,348	+ 601	116.0
1960	6,452	3,588	− 2,864	55.6
1961	6,476	4,615	− 1,861	71.2
1962	6,724	4,239	− 2,485	63.0
1963	7,166	4,509	− 2,657	62.9
1964	10,286	7,448	− 2,838	72.4
1965	11,100	7,184	− 3,916	65.3
1966	11,668	8,872	− 2,796	76.0
1967	11,133	7,894	− 3,239	70.9
1968	11,623	9,549	− 2,074	82.1
1969	14,572	11,477	− 3,095	78.7
1970	17,928	15.176	− 2,752	84.6
1971	19,455	13,627	− 5,218	70.0
1972	21,381	12,659	− 8,722	59.2
1973	22,388	13,755	− 8,633	61.4

Sources: Banque Centrale des Etats d'Afrique de l'Ouest, *Le Commerce exterieur du Togo*, p. 3; and idem, *Indicateurs économiques togolais*, May 1972, p. 7, and February 1975, pp. 8–9.
Note: Percentages computed by author.

higher state revenues especially since the government acquired a growing share in the industry. (In 1975 the company was nationalized.) This, in turn, has resulted in balanced budgets since 1968 (see table 3.4), growing developmental allocations, the relatively satisfactory completion of the First Five-Year Plan (1966–70), and the adoption of the Second Five-Year Plan (1971–75).

Even prior to the recent budgetary stability (and notwithstanding a persistent urban unemployment rate of 25 percent), all governments have had to accommodate a swollen, top-heavy civil service that consumed more than 55 percent of the budget. In many respects the bureaucracy serves as a system of state compensation to skilled Ewes redundant in Togo's small private sector and swept out of their positions elsewhere in francophone Africa following the indigenization of civil services. Attempts to disencumber the budget of part of this wasteful expenditure have been largely unsuccessful. The trade unions, extremely docile when compared to their Dahomean counterparts, have drawn the line when governments have tried to reclassify or redeploy the civil service and lower the retirement age. Though salaries have remained frozen and fringe benefits have been nibbled at, the general insecurity of the Olympio and Grunitzky governments until 1967 and the recent economic upturn have made any serious pruning of the underemployed civil service impossible, especially since neighboring Dahomey provided clear examples of the potential negative repercussions.

With the advent of direct military rule in Togo, a new factor affected the economic picture: the 1968 liberalization of import-export tariffs. Within a matter of months Togo's free trade policies, in contrast to Ghana's austerity and high taxation system, brought about an unprecedented boom in smuggling along their common frontier. Windfall profits were reaped by Ewe middlemen in both Togo and Ghana, and Togo's customs revenues swelled as consumer goods moved from Togo to Ghana and primary goods

TABLE 3.3
Togo: Principal Commodity Exports, 1960–73
(in millions CFA francs)

	Phosphates	Cocoa	Coffee
1960	—	1,381	635
1961	154.8	1,287	1,246
1962	488.6	1,182	1,428
1963	1,068.4	1,177	802
1964	1,948.0	1,632	2,525
1965	2,197.5	1,687	1,365
1966	3,771.1	1,688	1,953
1967	3,032.0	2,349	838
1968	3,237.0	2,314	1,602
1969	3,356.0	4,063	1,748
1970	3,720.0	6,336	2,657
1971	4,787.0	4,246	2,435
1972	4,794.0	3,719	2,599
1973	6,267.0	3,556	1,801

TABLE 3.4

Togo: Budgets and Selected Breakdown of Expenditures 1961–74
(in millions CFA francs)

	1961	1962	1963	1964	1965	1966	1967	1968	1969	1970	1971	1972	1973	1974
Receipts	3,375	3,511	3,644	4,850	4,879	5,202	5,667	6,261	7,418	9,867	11,723	12,283	13,434	16,244
Expenditures	3,455	3,845	4,474	5,050	5,360	5,614	5,838	6,173	7,348	9,585	11,723	12,283	13,434	16,244
Education	573	594	643	741	814	889	936	1,003	1,138	1,356	1,527	1,921	2,247	2,708
Public Health	383	346	371	444	429	412	459	480	501	522	716	799	881	943
Social Services	33	35	38	17	28	27	65	90	117	167	118	147	161	148
Defense	66	144	228	682	678	583	629	670	734	829	948	1,104	1,261	1,604
Deficit	80	334	830	199	481	412	171	+88	+69	+281	—	—	—	—

Source: Banque Centrale des Etats de l'Afrique de l'Ouest, *Indicateurs économiques togolais*, January 1971, p. 10, and January 1974, p. 12.

(especially coffee and cocoa) moved in the reverse direction.[10] Thus the bleak economic picture of the early 1960s was transformed into the somewhat rosier one of the early 1970s because of two basic factors: increased government revenues from the new phosphate industry and customs duties on a larger volume of imports and exports, up to one-third of which is a result of smuggling. Since real internal economic growth has not yet begun,[11] these twin circumstances provide only a temporary though vital breathing space to an economy that is intrinsically not much more developed or diversified than that of Dahomey.

THE CIVILIAN ERA

Togo attained independence under the patriarchical leadership of Sylvanus Olympio, head of the Comité de l'Unité Togolaise (CUT), Africa's first nationalist movement. Originally established with French support as a convention of notables to combat pro-German Ewe sympathies during World War II, the CUT was taken over by Olympio elements in 1946 and transformed into a pan-Ewe pressure group. Its unification platform (with the Anlo Ewe of the Gold Coast) soon convinced the French administration that it was a "subversive" pro-British organization and led to attempts to eradicate it from the political scene. In order to prevent the CUT from capturing the Ewe constituency, Nicolas Grunitzky and Dr. Pedro Olympio (respectively, brother-in-law and cousin of Sylvanus Olympio) were aided in setting up a moderate pro-French southern party: the Parti Togolais du Progrès (PTP). In like manner northern chiefly elements (especially Bassari, Konkomba, and Tchokossi) were organized by Antoine Meatchi and Derman Ayeva (of the princely Sokodé family)[12] into a loose elite political body, the Union des Chefs et de Populations du Nord (UCPN).

Normal political ambitions and personality clashes favored the French when in 1951 the CUT's more radical youth wing

10. *Chronologie Politique Africaine*, March-April 1970, p. 71.

11. Amin, *L'Afrique de l'ouest bloquée*, pp. 125–34.

12. Robert Cornevin, *Le Togo: Nation-Pilote*, p. 114. It could also be noted that Grunitzky's mother came from the Atakpamé royal family. His father was a Polish officer in the German army in Togo. For further biographical data see Samuel Decalo, *Historical Dictionary of Togo*.

(JUVENTO) broke away from its parent organization under Anani Santos (francophone Africa's first indigenous barrister). The PTP also spawned a splinter party in 1952 headed by Pedro Olympio. The splintering of the Ewe vote and the dilution of its strength by the expansion of the franchise, which in 1946 had stood at 8,000, weakened the CUT. The French administration's heavy-handed intimidation, coupled with the manipulation of electoral registers, forced the CUT leadership to boycott all political contests from 1951 to 1958, clearing the way for successive PTP-UCPN coalitions and Grunitzky's 1956–58 Autonomous Republic administration.

The balance finally tipped in favor of Sylvanus Olympio when the United Nations supervised the 1958 preindependence election. The CUT gained 64 percent of the 317,669 votes cast and an absolute majority of the seats. A bloody settling of accounts followed the end of the CUT's seven years in the political wilderness. As soon as Togo became independent, harassment, intimidation, and imprisonment on trumped up charges rapidly eliminated sources of opposition to Olympio's regime. Under a presidential constitution that endowed Togo with "a President as powerful as that in the United States, and a Parliament as weak as that of [France's] Fifth Republic" [13] Theophile Mally, Olympio's Akposso minister of interior, jailed or exiled many of the preindependence political leaders, giving Togo the appearance of a harsh police state.

Olympio presided over his cabinet and the Togolese economy with authoritarian paternalism. Guided by orthodox accounting practices he had employed as general manager of the United Africa Company in Togo, Olympio introduced budget balancing, thrift, and conservative fiscal policies that attracted a lot of foreign praise even as they stifled possibilities of economic growth. To "achieve a balance between public expenses and our country's own resources" [14] was his goal; for with fiscal orthodoxy and drastic administrative belt-tightening Togo's dependence upon France would decrease, allowing Togo to become internationally non-aligned, possibly Olympio's highest goal.

13. Robert Cornevin, *Le Togo*, p. 94.
14. *Africa Digest*, June 1963, p. 203.

It was essentially Olympio's draconian economic policies that undermined his control of the country by alienating the very groups that had catapulted the CUT (renamed the Parti de l'Unité Togolaise, PUT) to power. Olympio's conservative trade policies and the closing of the Ghana-Togo border after a deterioration in relations between the two countries endangered the livelihood of Lomé's powerful market women. The modest levy on cocoa (five francs per kilo) enraged the traditionally pro-CUT Ewe planters of Palimé and Akposso. A freeze on salaries aggravated unionists, who saw their pay scales outstripped by their more aggressive compatriots in Dahomey, while the freeze on civil service appointments alienated others in the Ewe middle class condemned to remain among the skilled unemployed of Lomé and Anécho.

In a country where over 50 percent of the population is under eighteen years old, Olympio's frequent derision of youth and its academic training deeply antagonized the new generation, which was demanding a greater role in the decision-making process. He clashed bitterly with the Catholic hierarchy and especially with Lomé's archbishop (issues of *Présence Chrétienne* were banned several times), undercut chiefly authority throughout the country, and exacerbated regional resentments by his neglect of non-Ewe areas. Merchants, petty traders, clerks, and civil servants alike felt the oppressive nature of his rule. Long before the assault that was to topple him, the Olympio regime had become only an empty shell divorced from its sources of power. Olympio's political throne was increasingly maintained less by his network of Ewe power brokers than by Theophile Mally's police and informants, who ferreted out plots, intimidated opposition, packed jails with political prisoners,[15] and tried to keep track of the growing number of political exiles in Accra and Cotonou.

Ironically, it was not Togo's 250-man army that overthrew Olympio in 1963, though elements in it participated in the coup, but rather unemployed Kabré veterans of French colonial forces wishing to join the Togolese army. Over three hundred of them, recently demobilized, were dispatched to Lomé by the French government, which was dismantling most of its colonial forces.

15. *West Africa*, March 23, 1963.

Unskilled in other crafts, unemployable, ill-at-ease as Kabré in a southern city, and loath to return to their stagnant and neglected villages in the north, they petitioned for integration into the national army. Olympio did not hide his contempt for the "petits nordists," replying to their request that if Togo's army was to be enlarged he would rather staff it with Lomé's unemployed than with mercenaries who had helped France oppress their Algerian brothers.[16] Citing the wasteful nature of military expenditures, he also rejected counterproposals of the leaders of the veterans, Sergeants Emmanuel Bodjollé and Etienne Eyadema, for the integration of only sixty of the best-qualified men.

The complaints of the Togolese veterans coincided with anti-Olympio sentiments in the largely Kabré army where Olympio's pro-Ewe, antimilitarist biases and policies were resented. Moreover, several officers and NCOs (including the army's Kabré commander, Major Kleber Dadjo) and some French technical advisers favored the expansion of the Togolese army, because it would afford them greater scope for professional advancement and personal prestige. Thus, when the coup was mounted there was close cooperation between the leaders of the unemployed veterans and their supporters in the armed forces.

Though the conspirators aimed to avoid violence, Olympio, forewarned by Theophile Mally, was shot by Eyadema and some of his men at the gates of the American Embassy.[17] His death did not evoke visible emotions among the Ewe, though seven thousand Dahomeans flocked to the funeral in his native village of Agoué in Dahomey.

The coup had profound effects on Togo's internal power structure and external position. Olympio's early nationalist posture had cast a long shadow in African circles, especially since his

16. E. Milcent, "Tribalism et vie politique dans les états du Benin." See also Dennis Austin, "The Coup in Togo," pp. 56–60.

17. There was no speculation at the time as to why the group was not led by Bodjollé. Later, in 1965, when the coup leaders fell out, it was revealed that Bodjollé did not join the rebels at the last moment, while a mysterious call to the Presidential Office had been placed by someone with complete knowledge of the plans of the plotters. Bodjollé's secondary position within the military hierarchy that emerged from the coup can be linked with these events.

domestic authoritarian tendencies had not been well-known. His attempts to disengage Togo from the major powers had evoked the respect of other African leaders, as had his unyielding stand in face of threats from Nkrumah. Hence, the Lomé coup was greeted elsewhere in Africa with immense disapprobation, which even the electoral legitimation of the successor civilian regime did not dispel.[18] This was, after all, the first military coup in West Africa and only the third political assassination in black Africa. In contrast, the coup in Togo four years later hardly caused a ripple in a continent grown jaded by military interventions and bloody upheavals.

The 1963 coup also created a new elite in the armed forces, which dramatically expanded from 250 to 1,200 soldiers, 80 percent of whom were Kabré and from the north. The new military elite was drawn from the clique of privates and NCOs who struck at Olympio's regime and who are today majors and colonels in the army and police; at the core of the new military leadership emerged three ex-sergeants: Etienne Eyadema, Albert Alidou Djafalo (both Kabré), and James Assila (Ewe). While other civilian leaders (such as Grunitzky and Meatchi) and military officers (Bodjollé and Dadjo) played a role in Togolese politics after 1963, ultimate political power was all along held by the military trio who later, in 1967, emerged squarely in the center of the power hierarchy.

THE SECOND REPUBLIC

Politically the 1963 coup turned back the clock to the preindependence era and returned to power the politicians who had been roundly defeated by Olympio in 1958 or had been chased out of Togo or imprisoned during 1961–62.[19] The Military Insurrection Committee headed by newly promoted Captain Bodjollé chose Grunitzky as provisional president, with Meatchi as his deputy, despite the army's preference for the latter and pressure from

18. *West Africa*, January 19, 1963.

19. Howe argues in support of overt connivance of Ghana—or at least Meatchi—in the 1963 coup. See Russell Howe, "Togo: Four Years of Military Rule," pp. 6–12.

northern tribal leaders in support of him.[20] Grunitzky's categorical refusal to serve under Meatchi (his former minister and deputy from Lama Kara) and France's opposition to a Meatchi presidency carried the day, especially since Togo's new officer corps was anxious to consolidate and legitimate their status. Moreover, Grunitzky appeared to be a more pliable leader who would readily accede to demands for an enlarged army. As one observer pointed out, "Grunitzky is likely to remain a satisfactory front man for the junta only if he does what Mr. Olympio refused to do—create jobs with appropriate status for the unemployed soldiers." [21] The new government, in which each political faction was represented, was massively ratified in the May election, though some of the top UT leaders (Theophile Mally and Noë Kutuklui, UT secretary-general and Olympio's political heir) boycotted it, opted to stay out of the new power array, and worked to topple the new regime.[22]

Despite his success at the polls, Grunitzky was unable to impose his will or leadership on his coalition partners or to obtain the unequivocal support of any of the Togolese power formations. He spent considerable time touring the country and calling for unity, honoring religious (especially Moslem) groups, and rehabilitating northern chiefs deposed by Olympio, but to no avail. The Ewe masses refused to accept him as their leader after having rejected him in 1958. The militant JUVENTO was contemptuous of his conservative policies and regarded him as a front man for the army and for French interests; the northern UDPT (a merger of the PTP and the UCPN) preferred Meatchi to Grunitzky; the army could not forget that he was, after all, Olympio's brother-in-law.

The new coalition was a very unstable arrangement that forced together unnaturally a variety of ideological positions and political ambitions. If the Olympio regime had been harsh and authoritarian, Grunitzky's years in power were tarnished by his personal indecisiveness and frequent vacillation between the carrot and the stick. Without a significant power base, Grunitzky's role was

20. *West Africa*, April 27, 1963.
21. Helen Kitchen, "Filling the Togo Vacuum," p. 10.
22. Several plots masterminded by Mally and Kutuklui were reported in 1963 and 1964.

essentially one of balancing the various factions and personalities in his government. Unpretentious, devoid of personal charisma, and by nature not cut out to be authoritarian, he suffered continuous assaults on his authority from his ministers and from his vice-president. The ethnic-regional, ideological, and personal tugs-of-war in the factionalized cabinet often resulted in stalemates and inaction. Grunitzky's vacillations, the continuous challenges from his subordinates, the failure of the "reconciliation" effort, the government's southern bias, and fears that his collapse might lead to popular agitation for a PUT-led government, finally alienated his army sponsors and resulted in his eventual overthrow.

Grunitzky's efforts to balance the various factions in his government was complicated by the need to satisfy the demands of the civil service while keeping the new military elite happy as well. And all this had to be accomplished within the same fiscal constraints operating during Olympio's lifetime but without the harsh austerity policies that had irritated most segments of society.

The first pledge to be honored by Grunitzky's new government was the creation of a second battalion in the army. Togo's armed forces showed the largest numerical net increase (569 percent) in Africa between 1963 and 1967 and the second largest jump in budget allocations.[23] The 1964 budget showed a 300 percent increase in defense allocations even though France picked up much of the tab for equipment (see table 3.4). Similarly, important concessions had to be given to the burgeoning, preponderantly Ewe civil service and to the restless unionists who had suffered from low wages during the Olympio years. In exchange for wage increases the government obtained union support for a series of austerity programs. However, grievances rapidly built up during 1965, aggravated by the army's brutal dispersal of authorized services at Lomé's cathedral commemorating Olympio's death. A similar dispersal of the May Day processions, which were politicized by PUT elements plunged government-union relations to a low, leading to a confrontation in December 1965. Faced with the threat of a general strike, the government retreated from an attempt to restructure and reclassify the civil service.

23. Morrison et al., *Black Africa*, p. 116.

As in Olympio's days frustrations were also building up among the commercial groups in the coastal areas, in particular among Lomé's powerful market women who dominate much of the retail trade. The postcoup Ghana-Togo honeymoon was brief, and the border was again closed by Nkrumah, creating great hardships in Lomé's retail and transit trade. Grunitzky was never able to convince the traders that the closed border and consequent economic stagnation were not of his doing; nor was he able to convince cultivators in the Palimé region that his government had no control over the catastrophic 50 percent drop in the world price of cocoa in 1965. Major demonstrations also erupted when the regime tried to enforce the taxation of several commodities and the government had to beat a hasty retreat.

By 1966 the political situation had become critical and the Meatchi-Grunitzky tug-of-war was heading toward a showdown. The two differed on practically every issue to come before the cabinet, with Grunitzky getting his way largely owing to the support of his cronies, Apedo-Amah, the foreign minister, and Fousseni Mama, the northern UDPT interior minister. The cabinet was polarized behind the two contestants, with each group trying to embarrass and undermine the other. Then too, Meatchi's aspirations for supremacy were affecting the military as his friends tried to recruit the support of key officers.

The crisis broke out into the open in a November cabinet meeting presided over by Acting President Meatchi while Grunitzky was abroad. Fousseni Mama claimed that his security forces had discovered that Meatchi was the sponsor of anti-Grunitzky tracts distributed on Lomé's streets. Hotly denying this, Meatchi dismissed him, precipitating the resignation of two southern PUT members of the cabinet. Though Grunitzky tried to patch up his shaky coalition, the disillusionment and resignation of the moderate southern politicians unified the PUT and set the stage for the upheaval that was to erupt early the next day when demonstrators converged on the center of the capital after a radio appeal for an urban revolt. The swelling crowds (estimates ranged from 5,000 to 50,000) were addressed by Kutuklui and other PUT leaders and marched on the Presidency. There they were blocked by troops that had retaken the radio station and had assumed positions around the capital.

It was not until noon that the order came down from Eyadema to disperse the mobs and arrest their leaders. The drawn out discussions of the officer corps preceding this decision indicated that automatic support for Grunitzky was not forthcoming. Yet, to side with the PUT-led Ewe demonstration was equally inconceivable. (Indeed, in the 1965 confrontation with the civil service the army had supported Grunitzky even though its sympathies were with the unions.) Such an action would have enhanced Kutuklui's position, and a key plank of his wing of the PUT was the arrest and trial of Olympio's assassins. Even the establishment of a military regime at this juncture appeared hazardous. The army was not popular in the south and the PUT, aware that it had indirectly toppled Grunitzky, might press its gains and demand that the army itself step down. Thus there was really no choice but to support the embattled Grunitzky government even as plans were made to topple it later.[24]

There is no doubt that Grunitzky's fate was sealed by November 1966, if not earlier, though he was to remain in power for two more months. By now totally repudiated by even the moderate PUT leadership, he belatedly tried to consolidate his authority in the cabinet by progressively demoting Meatchi (November 26), abolishing the vice-presidency (December 14), and finally shunting his rival to the low-keyed Ministry of Public Works (December 23). This only caused unrest in Meatchi's northern areas of support and further isolated Grunitzky.

On January 13, 1967, the fourth anniversary of Olympio's assassination and a date of such personal significance to Eyadema that it was declared a national holiday, the army demanded Grunitzky's resignation. Eyadema justified the coup by noting Grunitzky's and Meatchi's "power struggle—one trying to eliminate the other—and disorder consequently being established in the

24. Agence France Presse reports that the army decided in advance to have Grunitzky's collapse coincide with the anniversary of its 1963 coup. *West Africa*, January 21, 1967. This was confirmed in interviews by the author in Lomé. See also *West Africa*, December 17, 1966.

country with the threat of civil war." [25] An eight-man National Committee of Reconciliation was set up headed by its sole military officer, Colonel Kleber Dadjo.[26] To further soothe tempers an amnesty was declared for the November 1966 plotters and the prisons were emptied of their inmates.

The fact that five of the NCR members were PUT supporters, including several just released from prison (though only three were Ewe or Mina), allayed southern suspicions and resulted in an influx of refugees from abroad, the most prominent of whom was Mally. Kutuklui, who had escaped to Cotonou in November 1966, was one of the few politicians not to return. A rumor spread rapidly in the coastal cities that the attempted takeover in November had succeeded, even if in a paradoxical manner, with the military about to usher in an Ewe government.[27] As tracts appeared in Lomé calling for speedy free elections, fears arose in the north at the prospect of another southern "takeover." At this stage, on April 14, Eyadema intervened again. Citing appeals from all segments of the population—a theme to be repeated numerous times over the next few years—he dissolved the NCR and at the age of 30 declared himself president (Africa's second youngest) and head of a twelve-man cabinet including four officers and five former NCR members.[28] Shortly afterward leaders of the four Togolese parties were summoned and their parties officially dissolved on the ground that "every time one of your groups comes to power . . . it concentrates on hunting out or locking up the leaders of the other parties, in order to be in sole command." [29] Togo's brief experiment with civilian rule was at an end.[30]

25. *West Africa*, January 27, 1967. An interesting account of the coup is given in *Civilisations* (Brussels), vol. 17 (1967), pp. 132–33.

26. It was obvious, however, that Dadjo was only a temporary front man for Eyadema. Official posters distributed soon after showed a hierarchy headed by Eyadema, Alidou Djafalo, and Assila, followed by Dadjo and his civilian committee. *West Africa*, February 25, 1967.

27. The fact that Meatchi was retired to his old nonpolitical position as director of agricultural services seemed to confirm this belief.

28. See *Africa Research Bulletin*, May 1967, for the composition of the government.

29. *Afrique Nouvelle*, May 11, 1967.

30. Howe, "Togo," argues with a certain amount of validity that the Grunitzky era should be regarded as *indirect* military rule.

THE ARMY IN POWER

Any analysis of the Eyadema regime must begin with a delineation of several unique characteristics of the Togolese army that sharply differentiate it from other African military hierarchies. The stability and relative success in office of the Togolese military regime and the absence of internal army factionalism or cleavages based on age, education, rank, or tribal origin (especially when compared to the military in neighboring Dahomey) stem from several factors, the most important of which was the colonial recruiting practices in French West Africa. The continuation of some of these practices by the group that rose to power in the military in 1963 assured the unity of the officer corps and the virtual absence of interethnic friction between it and the enlisted rank and file.

The mandate and trusteeship provisions under which Togo was governed by France prohibited active recruitment in the country. At the same time even the limited possibilities for upward mobility offered by a military career appealed to Kabré and other northern youth socially and educationally locked out by France's lopsided developmental policies. The fact that Kabré country had traditionally been poor and overpopulated provided another powerful impetus for the short trek from the Lama Kara region to Djougou and other recruitment centers in Dahomey and enlistment in the French colonial armies as "Dahomeans." French recruitment agents in Dahomey were sympathetic to such transfusions from Togo because they needed to fill West African quotas and preferred soldiers from the less developed "warlike" tribal groupings.

Few southerners from Togo joined the French colonial armies. Alternate channels to social and economic advancement existed in the coastal areas, notably education and the civil service. Those Ewe and Mina who did join much later on tended to end up in the technical services (engineering, logistics, medical corps) because of their superior training and educational background.

At independence, Togo's 250-man army was a recently created, docile, largely Kabré force with few indigenous Togolese officers and NCOs. When France started demobilizing its colonial armies in 1962 the Togolese "Dahomeans" were sent to Lomé to face not only functional unemployment because of Olympio's refusal to enlarge his standing army, but also the very same socioeconomic stagnation that had originally driven them from their northern villages. Their unwillingness to accept this fate led, as we have seen, to the 1963 confrontation, and their assassination of Olympio essentially assured that the enlarged army would always remain near the center of political power out of fear of possible future retribution if it lost power.

The complicity in the 1963 coup of the Kabré commander, Kleber Dadjo, assured the stability of the established hierarchy of command after the coup. The young NCO coup leaders such as Eyadema, Bodjollé, Kongo, Namadali, and Assila (the Ewe odd man out) immediately assumed intermediate officer rank. They set the tone in the army even though Dadjo (who was 15 years older) was retained as the nominal chief of staff. Etienne Eyadema, one of the youngest and brightest of the ex-sergeants, a soldier from the age of sixteen (enlisting in 1953) and veteran of the Indochina and Algerian wars, rose to the top when he seized the mantle of leadership in the 1963 coup.

The officer clique that gained control of the army in 1963 was therefore roughly of the same age, had shared similar experiences, including combat duties, had assimilated similar cultural values abroad, and were of the same ethnic grouping—also the dominant grouping of the rank and file.[31] With the exception of the purge of Bodjollé, who backed out at the critical moment in 1963 and then attempted to reassert his position through divisive tactics in the army,[32] and Dadjo, gently promoted to nonoperational duties since

31. See Cornevin, "Les Militaires," pp. 65–84.
32. Involved in a power struggle and personality differences with Eyadema, whose roots went back to the 1963 coup, Bodjollé was displaced from his command position in 1964 and sent back to Kumea, his home village, on January 7, 1965. When northern elements petitioned on his behalf, he bounced back to a largely honorary position as head of Grunitzky's military cabinet. His intrigues against Grunitzky and Eyadema, including his creation of a circle of Moba officers and NCOs personally loyal to him (and a subsequent small mutiny in the Tokoin barracks), led to his final replacement and imprisonment. Later one of his relatives attempted to kill Eyadema: the bullet, fired from 13 feet, was deflected by a

he was never an integral part of the inner clique and was a generation removed, there has been remarkable unity and continuity in the chain of command. After leapfrogging to officer rank in 1963, promotions became routinized without undue discrimination against the few non-Kabré officers. There has also been a conscious attempt to preserve the hierarchy of command, avoiding purges and demotions that might cause personal resentments and factionalism and split the army into competing groups. The emphasis on professionalism by the nonprofessional NCOs-turned-officers is best illustrated by the acceptance of Dadjo as chief of staff and by the retention (until mid-1972) in top government and army positions of Lieutenant Colonel Assila, an Ewe from Nuatja, despite a kidney ailment that kept him incapacitated in a Paris sanatorium for two years.

Possibly more than anything else, however, the internal unity of the officer class is cemented by mutual complicity in the Olympio assassination. Even if Eyadema were neither politically inclined nor ambitious, he could not afford to allow political events to get beyond his control. The establishment of a PUT- or Ewe-dominated regime not under his control would seal his fate. The fact that Noe Kutuklui and other PUT politicians have continuously stressed that the trial of Eyadema for murder would be their first order of business once in power has practically guaranteed that an independent Ewe government would not be allowed to come to power. Grunitzky was elevated from obscurity by the military because he was the one experienced, nationally known politician acceptable to France and willing to forget the 1963 events. Even when strains developed between Grunitzky and his sponsors, notably over reductions in defense allocations[33] and his continued pro-south developmental policies, the army had no choice but to support him. When he completely alienated northern chiefs by demoting Meatchi and when the last vestiges of his influence among the Ewe dissipated over the Fousseni Mama affair, his

notebook. Bodjollé was freed in November 1967, with his village chiefs pledging that he would not leave the village. For further details see J. C. Froelich, *L'Année Africaine* (1965); *West Africa*, February 13, 1965, and April 29, 1967; and *Afrique Nouvelle*, November 30, 1967.

33. *Le Monde*, January 14, 1967.

usefulness to the army ended and the military had to move in and rule directly without the legitimizing facade of a civilian government.

The relative success of army rule in Togo and the existence of other considerations that impelled the army to seize power in 1967 should not obscure this elemental and crucial fact. The success of army rule serves to legitimate a regime which, because of the personal and corporate considerations just discussed, can never afford to loosen its stranglehold over political life. The various anti-Eyadema plots and assassination attempts (masterminded by Kutuklui and his followers) that have punctuated the rhythm of military rule over the past nine years overlook the fact that Eyadema is not the only military figure standing between them and a civilian Ewe-led government. The entire ranking hierarchy of the army has, in differing degrees, a personal stake in maintaining and preserving army control. By the same token, no matter how much civilianization or liberalization the army may be willing to undertake, the key officers involved in the 1963 murder of Olympio are unlikely to allow the formation of a genuinely civilian regime except in the most dire possible circumstances.

Characteristics of Military Rule

The army has consolidated its rule in Togo through a variety of policies that have linked the economic satisfaction of group interests with continuation of military rule. In this Eyadema has been greatly aided by rising revenues from the expanding phosphate industry, which was eventually nationalized. Moreover, a major reduction (50–80 percent) in import duties on luxury items (alcohol, perfumes, tobacco) has led to a boom in the enormously profitable smuggling operations into Ghana to the intense satisfaction of Lomé's market women, the "principal socioeconomic force in the country." [34] The increased imports and exports caused by the illicit trade have generated even higher revenues for the government through customs duties. Progressively larger budgets (since 1968 nondeficit) have allowed Eyadema to use patronage to wean away potential Ewe opposition elements, satisfy army interests,[35]

---

34. "Togo: Une Remarquable Stabilité," pp. 67–72
35. One could note, for example, that the defense targets in the First Five-Year

and engage in the first serious efforts to develop the northern regions.

Though at the outset the austerity policies of the previous regime were not relaxed—indeed, in some areas they were pursued even more zealously—care was taken to blunt their effect upon the coastal populations. Thus, the freeze on civil service salaries was continued for the duration of the First Five-Year Plan (1966–70), but plans for mandatory retirement at fifty-five were quietly shelved and it was made optional. The freeze on new appointments was similarly relaxed somewhat, with the civil service growing by 7.8 percent during 1968–71 to just over 11,000 officials, or a per capita ratio of 1 : 200. Key labor leaders were co-opted into advisory committees, and in turn they persuaded their unions to support the government's austerity policies. By 1969 the economic vise was relaxed and the unionists obtained major fringe benefits, including paid four-week vacations and an unemployment compensation fund. In 1970 minimum salaries in the agricultural and professional areas were raised by 10 percent and in January 1971 (in part to avert discontent over the unexplained death of three political prisoners) there was a 10 percent across-the-board raise for all employees.

The moderate austerity policies, increased revenues from import duties, and royalties from Togo's 32 percent stake in the Kpémé phosphate industry resulted in the first balanced budget since 1961 (see table 3.4). Subsequent higher budgets have also been balanced without new taxes or levies, while expenditures on social services, education, defense, and health went up by 230, 57, 35, and 22 percent respectively between 1968 and 1971. And while not all the projections of the First Five-Year Plan were attained, the economy's growth rate was just over 5 percent. The more ambitious Second Five-Year Plan (1971–75) specified an annual growth rate of over 7 percent.[36]

Togo's improved economic position has also permitted supple-

Plan (1966–70) were overfulfilled while other projections were not reached and that these military allocations were granted priority over other allocations.

36. See the articles in the special "Togo" issue of *Europe-France-Outre-Mer*, November 1971.

mentary development budgets financing a major road improvement program that has paved the entire north-south axis, linking Upper Volta with the new German-built port of Lomé (currently being expanded) and weaning away some of Upper Volta's transit trade, previously divided between Abidjan and Accra.[37] Having started with a road network inferior to that in Dahomey, Togo has surged ahead of its neighbor and integrated its northern regions with the commercial mainstream of the nation. Facilities such as hospitals, schools, and other public buildings have also mushroomed in the north in what is essentially the first consistent effort to develop the region. Moreover, Lomé has also had a major face-lifting with the building of a modernistic Presidential Palace, sports stadium, Organisation Commune Africaine et Malgache (OCAM) village (for the 1972 conference), and a vast conference hall that also serves as headquarters for the Rassemblement du Peuple Togolais (RPT), the national party established in 1969.

Particular attention has been paid to Lomé's market women, who have become Eyadema's staunchest supporters. Continuation of Togo's liberal import code has been pledged on numerous occasions to their delegations. Promises have been made to exclude aliens (Lebanese, Asians, and Ibos) from the retail trade,[38] and new markets have been built across the country. Moreover, a woman— Marie Sivomey—was appointed mayor of Lomé, and in other localities efforts have been made to appoint women to administrative posts. Significantly, when Eyadema established the RPT, Lomé's market women joined en masse and made a collective contribution of 500,000 CFA francs.

The regime has also moved to consolidate its links with the traditional authorities throughout the country. Chiefs' salaries, greatly cut by Olympio, were raised 50 percent, and the government has initiated a series of conferences of traditional chiefs

---

37. Of the funds of the 1966–70 plan, 36 percent went into transportation and communications, rural development received 20 percent, and urban development and housing 16 percent. Fifty-two percent of the total allocations went to the south and 48 percent to the north. See Banque Centrale des Etats de l'Afrique de l'Ouest, *L'Economie togolaise*, pp. 2–5. See also the bank's *L'Exécution du premier plan du developpement économique et sociale du Togo.*

38. *West Africa*, June 20, 1970.

following which recommendations are delivered to Eyadema. This recognition of the continued importance of the chiefs and their new contacts with the government have alleviated some of the inherent tensions between modern and traditional authority. The annual conferences have also opened up an important avenue of communication between the masses and the regime while at the same time providing a supplemental means of social control in the countryside.

Politically, Eyadema's nine years in office fall into two periods. The first two years were spent largely in the assertion and consolidation of military rule while continuous allusions were made to an eventual return to civilian rule and party politics. Committees were set up, with members as disparate as Meatchi and Mally, to draft a new constitution, suggest means to achieve national unification, sponsor civic education, and recommend guidelines for the return to civilian government; these, in typical Togolese style, were either rarely heard of again or extremely slow in their work. Eyadema periodically announced that neither the army nor he himself were interested in political power; carefully orchestrated demonstrations were then staged across the country urging him not to relinquish power to the politicians. So transparent was the stage-managing that *West Africa* quipped on one occasion that Eyadema was "perhaps a Bokassa pretending to be a Lamizana," [39] alluding to the different political styles and personal ambitions of the heads of the military regimes in the Central African Republic and Upper Volta.

Eyadema's 1967 cabinet was composed of twelve members, four of whom were officers: Lieutenant Colonels Eyadema, Dadjo, Alidou Djafalo (head of the *gendarmerie*), and Assila, the only non-Kabré of the group. The eight civilian ministers were individuals who were personally loyal to Eyadema and were equally representative of north and south. (For the ethnic composition of cabinets under Olympio, Grunitzky, and Eyadema see table 3.5.) As in the officer hierarchy, the degree of stability of Eyadema's civil-military cabinet is striking; most of the civilians brought into the government in 1967 were still there in 1973. Among them can

39. *West Africa*, October 18, 1969.

TABLE 3.5

Togo: Ethnic Representation in Cabinets
(in percentages)

Ethnic group	As % of population	Represented at Independence	Represented in Grunitzky's last cabinet	In Eyadema's cabinet
Ewe	44	67	70	25
Kabré	23	22	20	42
Moba	7	0	0	8
Central Togo	5	11	0	0
Gurma	5	0	0	0
Kotokoli	7	0	10	17
Others	9	0	0	8

Source: Donald Morrison et al., *Black Africa*, p. 363.

be noted in particular Joachim Hunlédé, foreign minister (Mina), Benoit Mallou, minister of education (Kabré), and Barthelemy Lambony, minister of labor and social affairs (Moba). The first reshuffle did not occur until August 1969 when the retiring Colonel Dadjo was replaced by Lieutenant Colonel Janvier Chango (Kabré) and two young technocrats were brought in. A second reshuffle in 1972 maintained the civilian ethnic balance, promoted Lambony to the Ministry of Interior (he had actually been performing these duties during the absence of Assila in a Paris sanatorium) and replaced two civilian ministers with younger, highly respected technocrats. A more recent cabinet reshuffle again preserved the ethnic balance while retaining some of Eyadema's 1967 appointments.

Through these policies, many of which were possible only because of the improved economy, Eyadema and the army have been able to consolidate and legitimize their rule. Through patronage, popular economic policies, and astute cabinet appointments, attention to the demands of all segments of the population, and, in the final analysis the omnipresent but largely invisible police and army, Eyadema has been able to nibble at Ewe opposition to his rule, which has become progressively less vocal and less united through massive defections. Whether this is regarded as "opportunism" by Ewe leaders—as is the view in some expatriate Togolese circles in neighboring countries—or merely a cogent example of the government's ability both to satisfy and intimidate potential opposition is somewhat beside the point. More telling is the fact that Noë Kutuklui's 1970 attempt to displace the regime did not evoke much support among elements in Lomé that were unwilling to see Eyadema toppled.

The Institutionalization of Military Rule

On January 13, 1969, Eyadema officially announced that the army had completed its self-imposed task of bringing about national reconciliation "and no longer has any reason for ruling"; political activities could be resumed, though the army would "judge the ability and determination of . . . politicians to transcend vain political quarrels." [40] Promptly, "carefully staged demonstrations demanding that [Eyadema] stay on developed all over the country," with the government paying for telegrams of support and village delegations that flooded into Lomé.[41] "Bowing" to public pressure, the cabinet annulled its authorization of political activities on January 17. One could view the original decree and its annulment as yet another example of the stage management of politics in Lomé; yet it actually marked the beginning of efforts to institutionalize (and eventually constitutionalize) military rule along the lines developed by Eyadema's idol, General Mobutu, in Zaire. Both the institutions set up since 1969 (especially the RPT political movement) and Eyadema's new posture and policies attest to an effort to reach out beyond the traditional bases of his support (the army and the north) and to acquire wider credibility as a popular national leader, albeit a Kabré in military garb.[42]

In order to give the regime at least the facade of popular legitimacy some tangible form of popular approval was necessary, beyond the periodically organized demonstrations in its favor. Moreover, new political institutions were required to lend credibility and provide a structural base for the political reality of a

---

40. *Africa Research Bulletin*, February 1969.
41. *New York Times*, May 25, 1969. See also *West Africa*, January 18, 1969.
42. See also Theophile de Chardon, "Togo's Liberal General."

permanent "civilianized" military regime. While moving to legitimize itself and willing to share a measure of its absolute political
control, however, the army could not compromise its dominant
position in the political arena. The problem was a complicated one
and carried with it significant risks. With liberalization a myriad of
factors might lead to a situation in which the army might be swept
from power by a determined southern popular upheaval or
compelled to use force to maintain itself, thus losing the support it
had assiduously amassed in the south over three years.[43] The
decision to move toward a normalization in the political sphere was
not easy to make, but by 1969 Eyadema and the officer corps felt
confident enough to move in this direction.

In March 1969 the semiofficial daily *Togo-Presse* put out the first
feelers when it published a series of articles proposing a new
political party that would not stand, as the former ones did, "for
hatred, division, strife and personal interest." [44] In September
Eyadema officially "endorsed" the idea when he proposed the
creation of a national political movement to encompass all
Togolese. As expressions of support came in from traders, market
women, and northern groups, he convened a meeting of all
Togolese traditional chiefs in Anécho where he further expounded
on his proposal. Having obtained their pledge of support, he
proclaimed the establishment of a "national" Rassemblement du
Peuples Togolais (RPT); a party not of "hate . . . , settlement of
accounts, divisions, hegemony struggles, personal interests" but
one that would be "the high location of honest, democratic
struggles, assuming the real participation of every citizen in the
task of political peace and fundamental restructuring of our
economy." [45] A Constitutive Congress that met late in November
promptly declared that the RPT's function would be "to direct and
control the life of the nation in its political, economic, social and
cultural aspects" and that in light of the army's immense contribu-
tions to national unification "the participation of the military in

43. *Afrique Nouvelle*, January 23, 1969.
44. *Togo-Presse*, September 22, 1969.
45. Cited in Simon Kiba, "Le Régime militaire au Togo II." See also *Togo-Presse*,
September 22, 1969, and *West Africa*, September 27, 1969.

public affairs is expressly recognized." [46] Eyadema was specifically invited to stay on at the helm of the nation. Edouard Kodjo, a highly competent Ewe official, was elected secretary-general of the RPT in a calculated move to gain support for the party in the south.

The next few months saw renewed efforts on the part of the regime to project itself as not overly tied to military interests. A variety of complaints had piled up relating to petty corruption in the army, the sudden enrichment of a few officers, and the entry of some officers into commercial (and smuggling) activities in direct competition with civilian economic groups. Charges of petty corruption in the Togolese army (as in other African armies) were not new,[47] but in a small country like Togo, with limited economic activity, it stood out prominently, which was especially embarrassing to a military regime seeking popular endorsement. (Eyadema himself has always been acknowledged as relatively honest; he has maintained a modest style of life, preferring to live in a small house in the Tokoin camp.)

Several internal and highly confidential directives were disseminated within the army command and on February 10, 1970, Eyadema publicly declared that engaging in commercial activities or transactions of any kind was incompatible with military service. Offending officers were given until the end of the month to dispose of any lucrative enterprises they might be engaged in or face dismissal from the armed forces.[48] Major Robert Adewui, commander of the Second Motorized Battalion and key participant in the 1963 coup,[49] was then relieved of his command (though retained in the army) because of his trucking enterprises. There

46. *Afrique Nouvelle*, December 11, 1968.

47. *West Africa*, August 12, 1967, and June 8, 1968. In 1968 an issue of a Dahomean newsletter was banned by the military regime in that country because it alleged that there was close cooperation between Togolese and Dahomean officers in smuggling activities.

48. *Chronologie Politique Africaine*, January-February 1970.

49. Adewui held the keys to the army's arms depot in 1963 and was hence instrumental to the success of that coup. Since the Togolese army takes care of its own and rarely dismisses officers who might consequently constitute a threat, Adewui was actually promoted to major in March 1970.

were reports of other personnel being ordered to refrain from commercial activities. The purge of officers with economic interests was accompanied by an efficiency and antimoonlighting drive in the civilian sphere. In a series of early morning visits to government buildings Eyadema surprised civil servants accustomed to arriving late and division directors and other employees conducting their personal affairs during office hours, all part of the relaxed style of Togolese bureaucracy. As in the military shakeup, dismissals were announced in the civil service for dereliction of duty.[50]

The decision not to revert to the pre-1967 style of party politics, Eyadema's efforts to broaden and further legitimize his government's authority, and the creation of the RPT led to another attempt to remove him from power. A double plot, allegedly planned by Kutuklui from Cotonou, was discovered on the night of August 8, 1970. Seventeen people, mostly non-Togolese, were surrounded and arrested when they convened prior to arming themselves for an assault on the Tokoin barracks and Eyadema's home.[51] Accounts of the plot are still murky and contradictory. The open trial included testimony by an obvious *agent provocateur,* and this further confused what had actually transpired. One popular interpretation of what was at best incredibly naive and sloppy planning suggests that the affair was a government-engineered attempt to locate and flush out residual sources of opposition.[52] Several lawyers and judges who walked out of the trial in disgust were later themselves put on trial, lending further credibility to this interpretation. The revelation of the plot did, however, spark Lomé's first truly spontaneous demonstration of support for Eyadema as a massive crowd marched in solidarity to the Presidency; however, even here militants interfered, "organizing" and swelling the ranks of the crowds. There could be little doubt, however, that though many southerners still could not ally themselves with the military regime, they were paradoxically also unwilling to see it collapse.

50. *Afrique Nouvelle*, March 26, 1970
51. *Africa Research Bulletin*, January 1971; *Le Monde*, August 12, 1970; "Behind the Togo Coup."
52. "Togo Coup?", pp. 8–10.

In November 1971 the RPT's first congress was held in Palimé, the southern center of the cocoa-growing district, with the participation of 2,000 carefully screened delegates. The decision to convene the meeting in the south was another calculated attempt to obtain active support from the Ewe and Mina, who had by and large remained uninvolved in the RPT. Palimé was specifically chosen because of the recent prosperity of the region and its cultivators, who had seen cocoa prices go up from 80 to 93 CFA francs per kilo between 1969 and 1971.[53] The congress, after promoting Eyadema to general for "exceptional services," turned to the major issues on its agenda. It "rejected" the recommendation of its own Central Committee that power be returned to a civilian regime, declaring that "the people consider the idea of constitutionalizing the regime as inopportune and premature." On the other hand, a popular referendum was approved on the question, "Do you wish General Etienne Gnansigbé Eyadema to continue the mission given to him by the Army and the people as President of the Republic?" Finally, turning to its own organizational structure, the RPT abolished the positions of the secretary-general and his two assistants (Kodjo had become too zealous and ambitious) and created instead a fifteen-man Political Bureau. The latter was packed with loyal Eyadema supporters, civilian and military, a majority of whom were northerners.[54] The convention closed with the announcement that the next congress would be held in 1972 in Lama Kara, the capital of Kabré country.

The referendum that was to legitimize the military regime was held in January 1972. Significantly, voting in the hinterland was in the form of "village units," though it is doubtful whether individual balloting in the north would have affected the results. The highest turnout ever was reported by *Togo-Presse*. Of 880,930 registered voters there were only 10,941 abstentions, 170 spoiled ballots, and 878 negative votes, while 99.09 percent of the voters confirmed Eyadema's rule.[55] The vote was interpreted by the government as approval of the transformation of the military regime into a unique

53. "Letter from Kluoto."
54. *Afrique Nouvelle*, November 26, 1971.
55. *Afrique Nouvelle*, January 17, 1972; *Togo-Presse*, January 14, 1972.

kind of civilian government in which army elements form an integral part.[56] From this point of view, the circle that started with the January 13, 1967, coup was completed exactly five years later in 1972.

There can be no quarrel with the contention that new civil-military arrangements may be needed to accommodate the special circumstances in developing countries. This does not erase, however, the distinction between such new composites and a civilian government in which the military is subservient to civilian hierarchies. Whatever nomenclature is adopted to classify the Togolese governmental hybrid the fact remains that its military component is the most prominent one and is in ultimate control of the country. Though the regime has turned out to be quite liberal, flexible, and tolerant of civilian transfusions of new blood, the limits of social and political freedom are specific. Again, though the government has been lenient in granting amnesties and pardons for political intrigues, it is an army clique that is the wielder, arbitrator, and guarantor of political power. Hence Togo's regime, official rhetoric aside, cannot be regarded as anything but a civilianized military autocracy quite unlike the pre-1974 Voltaic civil-military coalition with which it superficially invites comparison.

In evaluating the regime's potential to further popularize itself and achieve future stability one is struck by several disquieting factors which, though they may not be destabilizing in the immediate future, suggest possible areas of stress. As has been noted, much of the support of the regime in the advanced coastal areas has been attained through the satisfaction and furthering of various economic interests. But many of these achievements depend upon external factors—world market prices of cocoa, coffee, and phosphates, Ghana's restrictive import-export code, foreign (especially French and German) aid, and continued good harvests. In 1975 Togo's fiscal situation was remarkably good, allowing for an 80 percent increase in the budget and across-the-board 10–15 percent increases in salaries—all thanks to a dramatic increase in world commodity prices for phosphates and phosphate products. But world prices drop as well as rise. Any change for the

56. From interviews in Lomé in July and August 1972.

worse in the external factors that so affect Togo's economy may severely contract the government's revenues, which in turn may lead to social friction in conditions of acute economic scarcity. This is especially true in light of Eyadema's stress on the socioeconomic uplifting of the north and the eradication of gross disparities between the various regions of the country.[57] This major commitment of capital outlays for the development of the socioeconomic infrastructure of the north has had to be undertaken without significant cutbacks in developmental programs in the very wary and jealous south. The magnitude of the fiscal juggling task required to satisfy demands from competing regions for scarce developmental funds may have been a major factor leading to the surprise nationalization of the Kpémé phosphate mines in January 1974, though Eyadema has cited other reasons.[58]

Equally significant for Togo's drive toward national unification and stability is the fact that the RPT is still very much a hollow structure—essentially a decentralized organization of Eyadema loyalists, with low levels of Ewe participation. Establishing and sustaining a mass party is no mean task in Africa, so conceivably the RPT may still blossom in the future. Eyadema's peculiar penchant for the formal trappings of legitimacy does raise a question, however, as to the degree of enthusiasm with which the government will further the expansion of the RPT and encourage its development into a more assertive and/or quasi-legislative body. To date there has been no sign that the RPT, and especially its Political Bureau, is anything but a tightly controlled ancillary

57. Actually between the coastal and the Kabré areas, since the other minority regions have been relatively neglected under all administrations including Eyadema's.

58. The nationalization was announced shortly after Eyadema's escape from an air crash on January 24, 1974. Claiming that this accident had in reality been an assassination attempt sponsored by the foreign interests controlling the phosphate industry, the nationalization was decreed in retaliation. (His plane was involved in yet another crash less than a year later—which he also claimed was a retaliatory attempt on his life.) See *West Africa*, February 4 and 11, 1974, and January 6, 1975. Whatever the validity of the charges against the international consortium, the nationalization of Togo's most profitable industry began pumping new funds into the state treasury, which were greatly augmented by the startling rise in world prices for phosphates in 1974–75.

organization that clears its most minute "decisions" and "recommendations" with Eyadema before pronouncing them to the public. The patronage and outlet for political careers that it provides may not be substantial enough to keep its galaxy of powerful personalities satisfied. On the other hand, Eyadema has been open to the suggestions and recommendations of technocrats, so that a sharing of responsibilities between the government and the RPT may yet develop along tension-free lines.

As to Ewe participation in the RPT, Eyadema has been very astute in deciding that pressure or intimidation should not be used in order to gain adherents in the south;[59] his stated preference has been for a party of true "believers" and supporters of his cause, even if this means a numerically small membership. Low-keyed membership drives have been conducted in the south, but despite some success in some areas the results have been largely disappointing. The Ewe, who had originally withdrawn into their private affairs with the 1967 coup, have only recently started to emerge from isolation. Their jump onto the Eyadema bandwagon has been spotty.[60] and optimistic forecasts about growing support for the regime in the south are still somewhat premature. Partially to acquire a national image and wider popularity as a statesman in the more militant south, Eyadema has opted since the 1972 plebescite for certain nationalistic, symbolic policies. These have included a low-keyed "cultural revolution" that has required public figures to drop Christian names for ethnic ones,[61] changes in the names of towns (for example, Anécho became the precolonial Aného), and a somewhat more assertive position vis-à-vis France (though manifestations of the latter were only visible when it became diplomatically safe to be assertive, namely, after *other* leaders had broken the ground and France had yielded). Undoubtedly these policies appeal to more militant elements in the south (and according to some accounts a nationalistic posture was forced upon Eyadema by them), though it is equally true that some disillusion followed

59. *Togo-Presse*, September 11, 1971.

60. *West Africa*, November 15, 1969; *L'Année Politique Africaine* (1970), pp. 67–72.

61. For example, Foreign Minister Joachim Hunlédé became Ayi Houenou Hunlédé and Secretary of State Michael Eklo adopted the first names Yao Kunalé.

when the largely symbolic nature of these postures became evident.

Paradoxically, the Ewe, who have spawned so many intellectuals and politicians in the past, have failed to produce (admittedly, with the cooperation of Eyadema's security forces) alternative political leadership. Certainly Noë Kutuklui, who has been behind practically every attempted coup in Togo, is not the undisputed leader of the Ewe; indeed, it is doubtful whether as an individual, rather than as a symbol of anti-Eyadema opposition, he has any significant support in the south. Nor have the "Brazilian" families, who figured so prominently in the colonial and immediate postindependence years, produced any popular leaders who might draw together Ewe sentiments and aspirations.

The political picture of the future is therefore clouded by uncertainty about the continuity of Togo's economic development, low levels of political institutionalization, and the equivocal position of the most developed third of Togo's population, who still cannot enthusiastically bring themselves to support the regime but are unwilling to see it collapse. In light of Togo's sharp socioeconomic cleavages this is possibly all that could have been expected within the short time that has elapsed since the army took over. Certainly, however, despite its faults and its unwillingness to relax control over the political arena, the Eyadema regime is exceptional among African military governments.

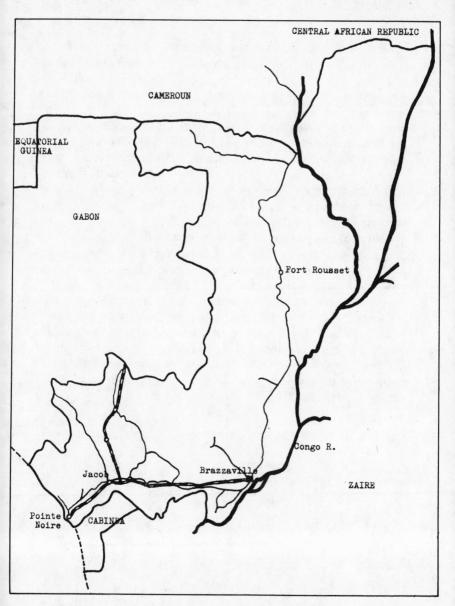

PEOPLE'S REPUBLIC OF CONGO (CONGO/BRAZZAVILLE)

4 Revolutionary Rhetoric and Army Cliques in Congo/Brazzaville

Congo/Brazzaville is Africa's first people's republic and one of the continent's most enigmatic and fascinating polities. Seemingly thriving on internal contradictions and inconsistencies and one of Africa's most ideologically politicized countries, it frequently appears to outside observers to present an undecipherable, kaleidoscopic procession of events. Yet beneath the ideological rhetoric are some of the same factors that have led to decay and instability in other countries such as Dahomey. Indeed, while the uniqueness of the Congolese case study is impressive, it is the systemic similarities between Congo and other unstable polities that are most striking and significant to the comparative analyst.

Congolese sociopolitical evolution has traditionally been tumultuous and punctuated by periodic upheavals. The country's rural-urban balance was drastically affected by major demographic dislocations caused by unusually brutal colonial exploitation. The construction of the Congo-Ocean railway and the establishment of Brazzaville as capital of the French Equatorial Africa Federation were two events that contributed to making Congo one of the continent's most urbanized and proletarianized countries. With over 35 percent of the population in four urban centers in the south and with postindependence Brazzaville transformed overnight from a federal administrative center to an oversized capital of a small country, Congolese politics have become progressively radicalized under the pressure of large masses of rootless, unemployed youth and union militants. The process of radicalization spilled into the armed forces, which rapidly lost all semblance of organizational unity. Just as revivalist symbols captured the allegiance of significant elements in this region in the past (for example, the Bakongo reunification aspirations and syncretic quasi-religious movements such as Matsouanism) so the quest for "Scientific Socialism" has caught the attention of contemporary

Congolese bureaucrats and officers. Yet underlying all of the anachronisms and the peculiar interaction between cultural values and heritage, on the one hand, and modern institutional and/or ideological concepts, on the oher, are the unique features of Congo's classic, fully developed praetorian system, within which the military faction is trying to consolidate its power through a variety of institutionalization experiments.

THE PULVERIZED SOCIOCULTURAL AND ECONOMIC INFRASTRUCTURE

Patterns of socioeconomic organization and political evolution in Equatorial Africa have been deeply conditioned by ecological factors unique to the region and the different impact of colonial rule in this less favored part of Africa. The Congo—richest of the four states in quality of manpower, though still relatively poor in terms of material resources—is no exception. Most of the population of less than one million reside in the central and southern parts of the country's 132,000 square miles. The major ethnic groups in the south are the Batéké and the Bakongo, who comprise 20 percent and 47 percent of the total population, respectively. The Bakongo grouping encompasses several clans: the largest and most dynamic is the Lari (45 percent of the Bakongo), and the second largest is the coastal Vili.[1] In the geographic center of the Congo are found the Mbochi (11 percent) many of whom have been drifting to the south. The northern regions are very sparsely populated, totally isolated in the Congo's *cuvette* of ill-drained, little explored swamps and heavy tropical forests. Land communication along the country's north-south axis is nonexistent beyond Fort Rousset, except by small dugout canoes, and extremely poor between Fort Rousset and Brazzaville. The country's 200 miles of poorly maintained paved roads run southward from the capital and are supplemented by the Congo-Ocean railroad, built to carry river traffic beyond the Congo River's cataracts to Pointe Noire on the coast.[2]

1. Morrison et al., *Black Africa*, p. 211.
2. On the other side of the river in Zaire runs the parallel Leopoldville-Matadi railroad built by the Belgians for the use of their colony.

The French penetration of what was to become the colony of Congo occurred at a time when all three major ethnic groups were either engaged in aggressive expansion or had recently arrived at a new territorial equilibrium following conflict over strategic trade routes and land. The Mbochi, expanding southward, had broken Batéké control over the riverine trade, and the latter were also retreating under pressure from Bakongo clans expanding northward from the Brazzaville littoral to the fertile Niari region. The slave traffic, which according to one estimate had drained over thirteen million people from this region alone,[3] had evoked deep antagonisms among the victimized interior populations against middleman interior tribes in Gabon and Congo and coastal elements there that traded with European companies. Interethnic animosity, hostility, and violence have always been close to the surface in contemporary Congo, since ethnic grievances have been deep and relatively recent. Indeed, the country was neither fully pacified nor totally occupied by the French until around 1918.

The contemporary Bakongo-Mbochi antagonism reflects not only a continuation of precolonial strife in modern guise but also tensions visible elsewhere in Africa between more socioculturally advanced and upwardly mobile coastal populations and less advantaged interior groups. Unequal patterns of socioeconomic evolution have sharpened and entrenched interethnic cleavages. In the Congo, however, the picture has been further complicated by different patterns of acculturation and social stratification within the major ethnic groups (especially among the various Bakongo clans) and by varying reactions to the harsh colonial rule imposed on the area. Moreover, the manpower requirements for the construction of the Congo-Ocean railroad in the 1920s and 1930s resulted in the rapid pulverization of traditional life and norms and the urbanization and proletarianization of large segments of society. (Around 25 percent of the adult population of Congo was involved in the construction of the railroad.) The composite result, at independence, was an extremely badly integrated, transitional society permeated with complex cleavages: a society marked by

3. See Georges Balandier, *The Sociology of Black Africa*, p. 60. See also J. M. Wagret, *Histoire et sociologie politiques de la Republique du Congo/Brazzaville*.

deep interethnic hostilities, syncretic religious protest movements (social frustrations channeled by indigenous anticolonial churches), urban-rural imbalances, and radicalized incipient class consciousness in the cities.

Of the various ethnic groups at the time of the French occupation, the Bakongo sought most eagerly to adjust to and exploit the new socioeconomic and political order. Since they were proud of their heritage—the medieval Kongo empire—and considered themselves the unvanquished coequals of the colonial intruder, they found adjustment difficult. For French policy in Equatorial Africa—especially as interpreted and practiced by both private companies and French administrators—was quite different from that in Togo, Dahomey, or for that matter much of French West Africa. The cultural "arrogance" of the Bakongo—who clung tenaciously to their values and life-styles—was viewed by France as overt resistance to its "civilisatrice" effort and potentially dangerous to French rule. The Bakongo were not granted the same privileges or role in the development of the colony as were, for example, the Ewe and Fon of Togo and Dahomey. As a result, the Bakongo (especially the Lari), alternated between rejection of the new order and rapid assimilation of new values or life-styles when the perceived advantages appeared overwhelming.

Nowhere is this more strikingly illustrated than in the history of French efforts to reorganize patterns of rural settlement to conform better to the economic needs of the colony. For two generations Bakongo groups strenuously resisted French efforts to relocate them in other regions, though there was a quasi-spontaneous relocation along the new railway line once its economic potential was realized.[4] On the other hand, so many Bakongo perceived the advantages of a modern education that the French administration became worried in the 1940s about the educational imbalances that had developed between ethnic groups and initiated discriminatory policies in an attempt to correct them. (These policies together with increasing urbanization and the general postindependence spurt in education resulted in a 70 percent school attendance rate in 1971,[5]

4. Virginia Thompson and Richard Adloff, *The Emerging States of French Equatorial Africa*, p. 479.
5. *Afrique Nouvelle*, March 25, 1971.

with the Congo leading Africa in a number of educational indices.)[6]

Bakongo efforts to secure economic and political benefits through the acquisition of Western life-styles were often thwarted by a callous and harsh colonial administration and a sluggish economy thoroughly monopolized by French concessions. In assessing the complex interaction between Bakongo aspirations and French rule in the Congo and the intense frustrations unleashed by the clash between them, one must recollect that to the French Colonial Service a posting in Equatorial Africa was regarded as a major demotion and the lowest rung in the profession.[7] More often than not the Congo was the dumping ground for the dregs of the service, for "no matter how inefficient or brutal, most administrators were considered good enough for service in the Congo."[8] Functionaries transferred from other colonies for alcoholism, drug addiction, mental breakdown, "bizarre" actions, and outright brutality inevitably found their way into Moyen Congo. While abuses of power, maladministration, and cruelty were not infrequent in other parts of Africa, distance from France and the unglamorous nature of a Congo posting, together with pressures to fill unrealistically high district tax quotas in a poor colony, led to numerous atrocities and a brutalization of the peasantry by promotion-seeking, incompetent, or frustrated administrators.[9]

Much of the Bakongo ambivalence toward colonial authority and values stemmed from the clash of their aspirations with the inconsistent behavior and periodic anti-Bakongo policies of the French.[10] The development of a Prospero-Caliban relationship[11]

6. See the Education tables in Morrison et al., *Black Africa*, pp. 62–73.

7. For an excellent study of the French Colonial Service see William B. Cohen, *Rulers of Empire.*

8. Ibid., p. 81.

9. Ibid., pp. 30–31, 80–82. For one popular report on the situation in France's equatorial colonies see André Gide, *Voyage au Congo*, p. 27 passim. See also Jules Saintoyant, *L'Affair du Congo, 1905.*

10. Balandier, *Sociology of Black Africa*, p. 9.

11. O. Mannoni, *Prospero and Caliban.* See also the critique of Mannoni in chapter 4 of Franz Fanon, *Black Skin, White Masks*, and Albert Memmi, *The Colonized and Colonizer.*

was especially visible in the field of education (avidly sought as the prime means of entry into the civil service), where the religious message and French values transmitted by missionary teachers were often rejected or drastically modified. The ambivalence is seen in the relative success of non-French Protestant sects[12] (including Swedish Evangelists, Jehovah's Witnesses, and the Salvation Army), which were more flexible in allowing Western religion to be mixed with indigenous forms of self-expression and worship. It is also evident in the eruption of pent-up frustrations through syncretist religious protest movements, so common in the Congo basin and in Equatorial Africa in general.

Many of these syncretic movements swept into the Congo from the Bakongo "diaspora" across Stanley Pool in the Belgian Congo (now Zaire) or from Angola and originally appeared as sociopolitical reformist or protest movements. Their rapid spread on both sides of the Congo River underscored the discontent that had been generated by the heavy-handed administrations of both France and Belgium's King Leopold I. Their transformation into remarkably resilient evangelical *religious* movements was the result of colonial intolerance of any form of political opposition (religious freedom was guaranteed in the Congo Basin Treaty), the rich role of symbolism and fetishism in traditional Bakongo culture, and the needs of a proud but oppressed people to unite around an indigenous symbol of cultural independence and equality. But the quite explicit rejection of French cultural domination in the various doctrines of these movements demands that they also be viewed as manifestations of Bakongo protonationalism emerging through social, cultural, and religious conduits.[13]

Of all the syncretic movements, Matsouanism had the most profound effect upon the evolution of political life in the Congo. Developing into a monumental social protest and xenophobic religious movement only after the arrest and banishment of André Matsou Grenard, who merely intended to set up a modest Amicale

12. In 1959 there were an estimated 187,000 Catholics, 48,194 Protestants, and 27,000 members of the Salvation Army. At the same time, however, there were 27,000 followers of Lassyism (one of Congo's syncretic movements) in Pointe Noire alone.

13. See Balandier's analysis in *Sociology of Black Africa*, especially pp. 389–472.

fund-raising organization, Matsouanism rapidly united large segments of the Lari behind a policy of passive (though at times violent) resistance and total rejection of French colonial authority.[14] The ultimate effect of Matsouanism was to completely remove from the social and political life of the country one of the most resourceful, vital, and Westernized ethnic groups precisely when the Congo's political pace started to quicken. This withdrawal of large segments of the Lari, their rejection of involvement with the colonial power, and their immersion in the Matsouanist ethos and ritual directly contributed to the more rapid evolution of other ethnic groups during the immediate pre- and post-World War II period. The educated coastal Vili, in particular, gained an early political ascendance. The Mbochi—hitherto slow to grasp modern opportunities—made rapid social and economic strides, aided by a French policy of curbing the Bakongo stranglehold over the indigenous civil service. Paradoxically, though withdrawn from the modern social and political spheres by their own volition, the Lari observed the advances of their traditional rivals as further proof of the anti-Lari and anti-Bakongo bias of the French administration.

General Features of the Economy

Congo's internal social tensions have traditionally been exacerbated by the inability of the economy to match the needs or expectations of the growing urban masses and the neglected rural population. The country, it is true, prouces a remarkable variety of commodities, has immense reserves of exploitable ores and minerals, and is one of francophone Africa's most industrialized countries—all of which place it in the same category as the Ivory Coast, Gabon, and Cameroun.[15] Yet poor communications, the small scale of most industries, the competitive edge of Zaire (the industrial giant to the south), the continuing stranglehold of foreign companies, and inept development plans that pay little attention to

14. See especially Martial Sinda, *Le Messianisme congolaise*. See also E. Andersson, *Messianic Popular Movements in the Lower Congo*, and idem, *Churches at the Grass-Roots. A Study in Congo-Brazzaville*; Etienne Bazola, "Le Kimbanguisme" H. W. Feheran, "Kimbanguism Prophetic Christianity in the Congo"; John M. Janzen, "Kongo Religious Renewal: Iconoclastic and Iconorthostic."

15. *Marches tropicaux et mediterranéens*, April 19, 1969.

the economic priorities of neighboring countries have all helped stunt Congo's economic growth. Moreover, despite the fact that Congo has attracted significant aid from a variety of donors (including China, Italy, Russia, Cuba, North Korea, Belgium, and France), total administrative anarchy and crass mismanagement and corruption in the public sector ("organized bungling," according to Colonel Ngouabi)[16] have resulted in a waste of scarce resources.

Though foreign capital still operates under conditions more liberal than those in the Ivory Coast,[17] most foreign consortiums have not been anxious to invest funds to open up new areas of exploitation in the Congo, especially since the declaration in 1969 of a people's republic. Indeed, since 1969 little fresh capital has filtered into the country despite France's continued guarantees of private investment. The drying up of investment capital and the persistence of a monopolistic and exploitative approach by existing foreign enterprises has resulted for example, in poor conservation policies and little, if any, reseeding in Congo's important timber industry. This has led to the rapid depletion of the most accessible forests (along the Congo-Ocean railroad) and resistance to fresh investments in new areas. Since until recently timber has been Congo's most valuable export (with diamonds, smuggled from Zaire, a poor second), the net effect has been a worsening trade balance and reduced state revenues from taxes and fees. Nor have prospects been improved by the radical rhetoric of Congo's political elites (suggesting to nervous entrepreneurs eventual nationalization) or by the fact that Congo has no capability to either control or supervise the big foreign combines.[18]

Congo's chronic trade imbalance (see table 4.1) has been further aggravated by heavy imports, an estimated 40 percent of which are consumed by the country's resident foreigners, and by the continuing inability of the agrarian sector to either feed or support itself and the burgeoning city populations. Congo's stagnant agriculture

16. *West Africa*, April 9, 1973. See also *West Africa*, February 13, 1971.

17. *Le Monde*, March 26, 1970.

18. Congo has only two forestry engineers and only four Water and Forest Service agents. See *Le Monde*, April 27, 1971, for some of the controversy regarding the role of French timber companies in the country.

TABLE 4.1
Congo/Brazzaville: Imports/Exports, 1963–72
(in millions CFA francs)

	Imports	Exports	Balance of trade	Exports as % of imports
1963	15,269	10,295	− 4,974	67.4
1964	16,006	11,702	− 4,304	73.1
1965	15,974	11,518	− 4,456	72.1
1966	17,188	10,659	− 6,529	62.0
1967	20,239	11,730	− 8,509	57.9
1968	20,614	12,189	− 8,425	59.1
1969	20,292	11,383	− 8,909	56.1
1970	15,910	8,564	− 7,346	53.8
1971	21,910	10,960	− 10,950	50.0
1972	22,608	13,211	− 9,397	58.4

Sources: United States, *Area Handbook for People's Republic of the Congo,* pp. 159–60; United Nations, *Statistical Yearbook* (New York: United Nations, 1965, 1970); and *Africa Research Bulletin*, Economic, Financial and Technical Series, September 1974, p. 3243.

(in part a continued peasant reaction to the brutal crop promotion practices of the colonial era) manifested its immunity to revitalization efforts when only 60 percent of the targets of the 1964–68 plan were fulfilled even after the targets were revised downward in midstream. At the same time state revenues from porterage, transit, and railroad fees from the upriver traffic have declined as Chad, Gabon, and the Central African Republic have diversified their trade routes. On the other hand, significant new resources have recently been opened to exploitation, altering the lopsided trade imbalance. Currently there are high hopes for the immense potash deposits at Hollé (among the richest in the world), conveniently located near the port of Pointe Noire. Recent offshore petroleum strikes refined locally in Pointe Noire at a time of boom prices, other discoveries of mineral resources, and a potentially important cane sugar industry all place Congo in a completely different economic category from either Dahomey or Togo.[19]

19. Yet Congo ranked last among thirty-two states in terms of balance of trade as percentage of GNP. See Morrison et al., *Black Africa*, p. 131.

Yet, it is difficult to conceive of a true transformation of the basic features of the Congolese economy. Government policies have for some time been based on a *mise en valeur* approach that relies on revenues from extraction of primary resources. The ecological and developmental parameters are particularly harsh: a very small population increasingly concentrated in economically nonproductive urban centers; a poor infrastructure to which the French only belatedly and halfheartedly turned their attention;[20] an extremely high percentage of youth under the age of sixteen (estimated at around 60 percent of the population), many of whom became unemployed after moving into the urban centers; and a dormant and decaying agricultural sector that has difficulty feeding the essentially parasitic urban sector.[21] Superimposed upon these severe restraints on economic development is the heavy-handed exploitative monopoly exercised by French private capital in the extractive sector—a monopoly that no Congolese regime to date has either dared antagonize or been able to harness for the creation of the infrastructure the country needs.[22]

Despite diversification and industrialization efforts, the Congolese economy has remained essentially extractive and heavily monopolized by foreign interests. Dependence upon French aid deters any Congolese regime from seriously pressuring or threatening the foreign monopolies, and Congo's other limitations (size and population distribution in particular) do not auger well for any such policy if it were attempted. In the meantime fiscal bottlenecks, heavy debts, and current outlays prevent a more rapid and extensive development of the economy (though some important strides in this direction were made in 1974), just as the drying up of risk capital further slows down exploration and exploitation of

20. Until 1913 Congo's exports to France exceeded imports from the metropolitan country, as the colony was one of the last in Africa to receive any infrastructure aid. Henri Brunschwig, *French Colonialism 1871–1914*; p. 91. As late as 1930 the Congolese colonial budget allocated only 2 percent of its expenditures on public works and other infrastructure building to rural areas.

21. The poor topsoil in this tropical rain forest area of Africa (except for the fertile Niari region) is still another reason why the agrarian sector is stagnant.

22. See, for example, Pierre Philippe Rey, *Colonialisme, neo-Colonialisme et transition au capitalisme*.

known reserves. Whether or not one adopts a neo-Marxist interpretation of Congo's economic dilemma,[23] it is clear that radical rhetoric, import substitution drives, neoautarchy, and diversification of developmental aid donors—all adroitly attempted by the current leadership—may be but poor palliatives that only nibble at the basic economic problems.

While Congo's regular budgets have not usually shown a deficit (see table 4.2), French aid figures prominently in the supplemental (capital goods) budgets. The dramatic fivefold increase in expenditures between 1960 and 1973 and the country's respectable (for Africa) $200 per capita income reflect the success of pressures by urban elites for administrative positions and social services. All governments to date have been forced to acquiesce in the expansion of the already bloated civil service. At the same time

TABLE 4.2
Congo: Budgets, 1960–75
(in billions CFA francs)

	Revenues	Expenditures	Deficits
1960	4.9	4.9	—
1961	5.9	6.4	0.5
1962	7.3	8.0	0.7
1963	8.7	8.7	—
1964	9.3	9.2	+0.1
1965	9.6	10.5	0.9
1966	12.2	12.1	+0.1
1967	13.3	13.2	+0.1
1968	13.2	13.2	—
1969	15.9	15.9	—
1970	18.1	18.1	—
1971	19.5	19.5	—
1972	21.8	21.8	—
1973	24.7	24.7	—
1974	43.8	43.8	—
1975	70.0	70.0	—

23. Samir Amin and Catherine Coquery-Vidrovitch, *Histoire économique du Congo 1880–1968.* See also Catherine Coquery-Vidrovitch, *Le Congo au temps du grandes compagnies concessionaires.*

there has been an additional influx into the administration of
thousands of Congolese expatriates who like their Togolese and
Dahomean counterparts were squeezed out by nationalistic drives
throughout Africa. This continuous pressure for an ever-expanding
civil service is a dominant feature of Congolese politics, and its
importance is difficult to exaggerate. If the root of contemporary
political strife in Africa is conceptualized as competition for jobs in
a context of acute economic scarcity—as has recently been
argued—then the intensity and violence of Congolese politics may
emerge in proper perspective.[24] With Congo's basic human and
economic parameters and with a massive unemployed proletariat,
governments may ignore demands for material benefits only at
their peril. Fulbert Youlou, Congo's first president, whose economic policy (if he had any) was laissez-faire, discovered the
suicidal consequences of neglecting the urban masses. No regime
since then has made this error.

The net effect has been the development of a bloated, under-
worked, inefficient, corrupt, urban-based bureaucracy. It can be
functionally viewed as composed of highly autonomous mutual
advancement pyramids that are cemented by regional, ethnic, clan,
or personal patron-clientelist bonds and are relatively immune to
purges (even those based on ideology). Its personnel is currently
estimated at over 30,000 (around 8 percent of all adults or 3 percent
of the entire population), who consume up to 75 percent of the
regular budget[25] (or over 20 percent of the GNP); its annual rate of
increase shows few signs of slowing down. Indeed, with the shift in
the ethnic balance of power that accompanied the rise of the
Ngouabi regime and the fuller integration of Congo's youth in the
state's central and administrative apparatus, new pressures have
built up for government largesse, causing the state payroll to
skyrocket further.

24. As Lee has correctly noted, *Le Monde* may well have been banned from
Brazzaville in 1969 because an article hit too close to home by referring to the
preservation of existing methods of controlling public sector jobs as possibly being
the main consideration in Congolese politics. See *Le Monde*, November 11, 1969,
and J. M. Lee, "Clan Loyalties and Socialist Doctrine in the People's Republic of
the Congo," p. 46.

25. *Le Moniteur du Commerce et de l'Industrie*, August 10, 1972.

The intense pressure for positions in the public sector—virtually a question of physical survival to Congo's urban unemployed—is greatly aggravated by the state educational system, which even as it disburses 5 percent of the national budget in the form of scholarships churns out increasing numbers of youth who choke the southern cities, especially Brazzaville. They attempt to eke out a miserable existence working at temporary casual jobs, urban agriculture, and petty commerce or by calling for doles from their better-placed kin (contributing to the latter's proneness to illicit or corrupt practices). One recent estimate projected an urban unemployment figure of 450,000 by the year 1985.[26] Even if this estimate turns out to be unnecessarily pessimistic, the awesome dimensions of Congo's urban and employment crises and their potentially destabilizing effects are transparently clear.[27]

Congo's youth has exerted a dominant influence in politics since independence. This floating pool of unmobilized rootless manpower is searching restlessly for a political role as well as for economic security. Prior to Youlou's demise, Congo's youth was internally divided on many planes and used as a stepping-stone to power by a variety of political aspirants. It came politically of age with the trade union-youth demonstrations that toppled Youlou. Since then both Massemba-Debat and Ngouabi have tried to harness this "political age class" [28] through the co-optation of its leaders into the ruling hierarchy or the civil service and by the creation of unified youth structures with specific developmental or security responsibilities, such as the JMNR (the youth wing—Jeunesse—of the post-Youlou single party, the *Mouvement National de la Revolution*) and the Civic Defense Units (the armed wing of the JMNR). The zeal with which youth fulfilled its often self-defined duties, the harsh manner in which it exercised its newly gained powers (especially in areas of intergenerational tension), and its rapid radicalization and politicization underscore the importance of this new amorphous force in Congolese politics. Indeed, for a

26. *West Africa*, January 8, 1972. See also Roland Devauges, *Le Chômage à Brazzaville: Etude Sociologique*.

27. For a theoretical discussion see Huntington's seminal article, "Political Development and Political Decay." See also J. P. Nettle, *Political Mobilization*.

28. See Pierre Bonnafé, "Une Classe d'age politique."

few years after it was formed, the JMNR for all practical purposes set the political tone of the country and assumed symbolic leadership—so much so that some observers regard Ngouabi's rhetorical shifts as attempts to keep in ideological tune with this constituency, to which he and his regime are ultimately accountable.[29]

However that may be, the social mobilization and politicization of the youth, the unionists, and the military, and the high permeability and eventual destruction of civil-military boundaries —in the context of regionalism, ethnic strife, and economic scarcity—have created a highly volatile and atomized praetorian system marked by endless jostling for power and influence by personalist and factionalist cliques.

POLITICAL RADICALIZATION UNDER YOULOU AND MASSEMBA-DEBAT

As in Togo and Dahomey political activity in Congo after World War II was characterized by the coalescence of ethnic blocs behind modern regional-ethnic elites. Unlike Dahomey, however, traditional leaders have wielded less power on the national level and have also had a restricted role as rural power brokers. Social uprooting and the pulverization of traditional norms prevented the emergence of powerful regional power wielders from among the traditional chiefs in spite of the idealization of the concept of kingship in Bakongo folklore. Moreover, Bakongo and Batéké tribal chiefs traditionally possessed greater magico-religious than political functions,[30] and the spread of fetishist cults and quasi-modern religions (including messianic movements) eroded even the traditional sacramental functions of the increasingly secularized office of chief. Hence with the extension of the franchise Congo's rural village chiefs assumed the function of delivering the local vote to the ethnic regional leaders with few exerting any other meaningful influence on the national level. Indeed, following Youlou's collapse in 1963 and the general radicalization of society, tradi-

29. United States, *Area Handbook for People's Republic of the Congo*, p. 107. See also, Michel Croce-Spinelli, *Les Enfants de Poto-Poto*.
30. Balandier, *Sociology of Black Africa*, p. 383.

tional chiefly authority was directly challenged, and many of its functions were taken over by party militants and organized youth groups that began to terrorize the countryside.

Until 1956 Congo's regional "bosses" were André Matsoua (who had died in exile in 1942), Felix Tchicaya, and Jacques Opangault. With 90 percent of the Bakongo sympathetic to the Matsouanist movement, those who participated in Congo's first elections (and many remained aloof) overwhelmingly voted the dead Matsoua as Congo's first deputy to Paris. This occurred both in 1945 and 1951 with many voters returning to Brazzaville from domiciles in Zaire in order to cast a vote for Matsoua;[31] by default the French administration declared Tchicaya, the runner-up, as elected. Tchicaya, an ex-sergeant, had risen to prominence by uniting the Pointe Noire Vili, the Batéké, and some of the uncommitted Bakongo behind his Rassemblément Democratique Africaine-affiliated Parti Progressiste Congolais (PPC). But he was totally unable to present himself as Matsoua's heir in Lari areas. Meanwhile the Mbochi had been organized behind their ethnic leader, Opangault, who headed the French Socialist Party (SFIO) branch in Congo, later to become the Mouvement Socialiste Africain (MSA). The power balance was tilted strongly in favor of Tchicaya, however, if only because of the numerically larger Bakongo electorate.

The electoral picture dramatically changed with the January 2, 1956, elections and the meteoric rise of Abbé Fulbert Youlou as spiritual heir of Matsoua and supreme "chief" of the Lari and other Bakongo clans. Youlou's rise was assisted by Tchicaya's prolonged absences in Paris, which he preferred to his hometown, during which Youlou was able to lure to his cabinet several key Vili politicians such as Stephane Tchichéllé, who later became his foreign minister. While weakening Tchicaya's hold over Pointe Noire, Youlou also presented himself as a symbol of Lari renascence and opposition to the French establishment. And the more

31. Sinda, *Le Messianisme congolaise*, p. 256. Since Matsoua was not ritually buried (and complex death rites and cults are rife in Equatorial Africa) he could not be considered dead—one reason for the contemporary resistance of Matsouanists to the idea of his death.

the French tried to discredit the flamboyant and ambitious defrocked priest the more the Lari flocked to his banner. A demand by Brazzaville's archbishop that the faithful reject Youlou's electoral candidacy (read in all churches) boomeranged in Bakongo areas in particular as Youlou was then cast in the role of another Matsoua whom the colonial power was trying to eliminate. Adroitly exploiting his religious background[32] in cultivating Matsouanist support, Youlou affected a massive transfer of Lari sentiments to his candidacy and party, the Union Democratique pour la défense des Intérèts Africaines (UDDIA). By 1957 Youlou, overwhelmingly voted in as mayor of Brazzaville, and Opangault, with whose MSA the foundering PPC had merged in desperation, held near parity in the Territorial Assembly; shortly afterward Youlou wrested control of the government from Opangault (having been minister of agriculture in his coalition cabinet), transferred the capital to Brazzaville, and emerged as independent Congo's first president.

Youlou's administration was notable for its increasing corruption and autocracy[33] and its reactionary political and economic orientation.[34] Ethnic tensions were greatly exacerbated when Youlou moved to institutionalize a uniparty state after Opangault and other non-Bakongo leaders had been co-opted into the government. Even before independence Youlou's rapid consolidation of power triggered several sharp and bloody riots as Mbochi-Bakongo and Lari-Vili animosities flared and as Youlou's youth gangs turned against hard-core Matsouanists who persisted in their passive opposition to the Youlou government by refusing to carry identification cards, pay taxes, or participate in censuses.

Youlou's reactionary foreign policy—paranoid fear of communism, support for Tshombé and opposition to Lumumba, overtures

32. Boganda, Central African Republic's first nationalist leader, was also a priest, as were several other political leaders in Equatorial Africa.

33. The National Assembly had "granted" Youlou the power to rule by decree.

34. For a deeper analysis of the civilian era see John A. Ballard, "Four Equatorial States"; Ronald Matthews, *African Powder Keg*, chapter 4; F. Constantin, "Fulbert Youlou 1917–1972"; J. L. Lacroix, "Evolution de l'économie et transformation des structures au Congo depuis 1960"; and Samuel Decalo, "The Development of a Praetorian System in Congo/Brazzaville."

to Portugal, plots to resurrect a pan-Bakongo empire encompassing parts of Congo/Kinshasa and Angola while offering northern Congo to the Central African Republic, and so on—was combined with laissez faire economics. He was extremely docile vis-à-vis French expatriate interests in Brazzaville, which supported him openly, and his administration totally lacked clear economic priorities or developmental plans beyond the Kouilou dam project. The conspicuous consumption, sensuous venality, and scandalous affairs of Youlou and most of his ministers (who tended to invest their "profits" in bars and nightclubs in Brazzaville or in diamond smuggling ventures) contrasted starkly with the poverty of Brazzaville's unemployed. Profligate expenditures on prestige projects such as a television station for less than 300 sets and free-flowing patronage dispensed from the state's permanently semiempty coffers contrasted with the scant attention given to the inflation-ridden salaries and growing social needs of the urban masses. At the same time Youlou's overt contempt for Congo's youth and the minimal role he assigned to it in his administration created a dangerous and volatile backdrop to his increasingly unpopular rule. The degree to which the regime had lost contact with social realities was manifested during Sekou Touré's state visit in June 1963 when Congo's unionists and youth wildly applauded the Guinean leader while greeting his host with jeers of "Down with Abbé Youlou."

All the simmering grievances and disenchantment with Congo's first independent government came to an explosive boil in August 1963 as Youlou clashed with the unions, which he had been unable to subdue or control, in announcing his establishment of a highly centralized one-party state. The three days of demonstrations and strikes that finally dislodged Youlou ("les trois glorieuses" of August 13–15, 1963) were neither a revolution—as they are viewed in Brazzaville—nor a classical coup by Congo's then minute, largely French-officered army. They bore a striking resemblance to the 1963 unionist-student upheaval that toppled Maga in Dahomey.[35] The intensity of the demonstrations in Brazzaville, France's

35. For one comparative analysis see Terray, "Les Révolutions congolaise et dahoméenne." See also W. H. Friedland, "Paradoxes of African Trade Unionism."

unwillingness to come to the rescue of Youlou, and the volatile
government-union stalemate that ensued nudged the largely Mbochi army to withdraw its support from the beleaguered regime, thus
assuring its downfall. The army then rapidly presided over a
transfer of power to the choice of the unionists, Alphonse
Massemba-Debat.

Massemba-Debat, schoolteacher by profession and a moderate
Socialist, had served in various capacities in Youlou's government
including president of the National Assembly. He had been forced
to resign a few months before the coup because of his opposition to
Youlou's increasingly autocratic policies. It was largely Massemba-
Debat's political integrity, experience, and leftist credentials that
made him the acceptable choice of the factions that had helped
topple Youlou; and it was these characteristics and his known lack
of consuming ambition that enabled him to retain power for nearly
five years despite the rapid radicalization and politicization of the
Congolese scene after 1963 and the resultant intense jostling for
power and influence by competing groups.

Massemba-Debat achieved in months what his predecessor had
failed to achieve—a uniparty system and unified ancillary organizations (such as a single union movement)—[36] but he was never
fully in control in the party, government, or country. The
government's announcement that Congo was henceforth a socialist
state based on Marxist-Leninist principles was not accompanied by
social and economic policy shifts. The extreme caution with which
the new "socialist" regime acted on concrete issues rapidly
polarized the militant left into ideological factions while Brazzaville's radical rhetoric alienated conservative Youlouists, Matsouanists (who rejected Massemba-Debat's Lari credentials), and
Catholics, all still powerful in Congo. Indeed, in the 1964 municipal
elections over 48 percent of eligible voters shunned the polls.
Clandestine plotting and tract warfare by elements purged after the
coup indicated that sources of opposition to the new regime were

36. The single union was created over the opposition of the Catholic unionists
who had been instrumental in bringing Massemba-Debat to power. The unions had
not been against Youlou's projected single union but demanded prior restructuring
of the government and major ideological and political shifts in policies.

deeply entrenched. The nationalization of education and youth movements, which primarily affected Catholic schools and youth groups, and the progressive purge of Catholic union leaders and other political moderates in the new party, the Mouvement National de la Revolution (MNR) and the National Assembly only enlarged the pool of disenchanted elements, providing a solid base for the various power grabs that were to be attempted periodically.

The interpenetration of civil-military boundaries following the 1966 decision to create a "people's army" and the politicization of youth and unionists—who assumed important governmental and party positions—greatly expanded the range of ideological views, corporate needs, and personal ambitions requiring accommodation. This in turn reduced the efficacy of the decision-making organs in which conflicting pressures were manifested, thus further complicating Massemba-Debat's juggling and balancing role within a system without a solid core of authority and legitimacy increasingly challenged by semiautonomous groups. Attempts to restructure a French expatriate-dominated economy, satisfy the demands of the civil service and the unemployed, and keep the unruly and role-expansionist youth movement and armed forces in line, while balancing ideological cliques and warding off personalist challenges in the MNR Politburo and National Assembly progressively taxed Massemba-Debat's abilities.

The regime, for example, was never truly able to impose its authority upon the country's youth. For some six months after the 1963 upheaval in response to the government's request for help in ferreting out sources of opposition, "committees of vigilance" and other roving youth cliques terrorized the countryside in the name of the revolution, "stamping out" Youlouist opposition and bourgeois and fetishist practices. In mid-1964 these highly autonomous formations were organized as the youth wing of the MNR, but though they were theoretically subservient to the MNR leadership, neither Massemba-Debat nor the Politburo were able to fully control a JMNR that undertook to "purify" the revolution and protect it from its enemies. Perpetual JMNR harassment of "capitalist" U.S. embassy staff and armed roadblocks and car searches in Brazzaville and in the countryside were reasons for the U.S. withdrawal of its embassy from Congo. (In retaliation Congo broke diplomatic relations with the United States.) JMNR elements also crossed the river to Kinshasa in an attempt to assassinate Youlou, who had escaped house arrest on March 25, 1965, and were involved in several political liquidations in Brazzaville itself.[37]

Throughout Massemba-Debat's tenure in office the JMNR was very much a barbed and vocal thorn in his side, and late in 1967 there was evidence that certain of its factions were preparing to attempt a coup. The JMNR also continuously antagonized and clashed with both the *gendarmerie* and the armed forces over some of its self-assumed paramilitary responsibilities. The 1966 military mutiny, for example, was directly sparked by the corporate threat to the army from the growing paramilitary capabilities of the JMNR. Falling under the control of ambitious political aspirants such as André Hombessa, the powerful minister of youth and later of interior, the JMNR became a stepping-stone to power for radical militants.

Paradoxically, however, while impatient with Massemba-Debat's cautious policies, the ultraleft JMNR was also the government's bulwark against the increasingly autonomous and mutinous army. Dwarfing the regular armed forces by sheer numbers, tapping independent sources of weapons, and possessing a Cuban-trained armed wing (the Civil Defense Corps), the JMNR's power was curbed only in 1968 after a bloody battle with Ngouabi's troops. Following this confrontation the JMNR's armed units were absorbed into the army and the new Ngouabi regime drastically curtailed their autonomy and responsibilities. As will be noted, however, the merger of JMNR units with the armed forces simply multiplied the army's internal cleavages without significantly reducing the new regime's need to watch carefully the mood of its youthful constituency.

From both within and outside the party Massemba-Debat was under continuous pressure to radicalize Congo's posture especially vis-à-vis French expatriate interests. Congo's dramatic post-Youlou

37. Such as the February 1965 kidnapping and murders of Congo's Supreme Court president, attorney general, and director of information, all considered moderate. *Afrique Nouvelle*, February 25, 1965; *Le Monde*, February 19, 1965.

volte face toward the East and the new militant rhetoric from Brazzaville did little to appease the growing radicalism among segments of the urban masses. The erection of a commerce and industry state sector and the influx of Chinese, Russian, Cuban, and other Communist assistance missions did little to camouflage the fact that the core of Congo's economy remained virtually untouched by the new "Marxist-Leninist" regime.[38] Private French capital continued to be courted as the only means to develop and diversify the economy, few new limitations were placed upon foreign entrepreneurs old or new, and nationalization remained in the province of rhetoric. As Massemba-Debat once retorted in exasperation with JMNR criticisms, "there is nothing to nationalize in this country!" [39]

Congo's dependence upon French government financial and technical assistance continued unabated and, indeed, increased despite a sharp proliferation of aid from other countries.[40] Consequently, the regime's radical rhetoric tended to be greatly muted when France's interests were at stake, which further aggravated militants.[41] Despite this, private foreign capital shunned the country, relations with France became increasingly strained, and the economy suffered a decline at a time when the administrative costs of the new state sector (corruption-ridden and inefficient), the expanded bureaucracy, and the newly combined armed forces were exerting intense pressures.

Lack of progress in disengaging the economy from foreign control set the stage for many of the ideological clashes within the MNR Politburo—the center of power in Congo[42]—with Massemba-Debat striving to keep himself from being overpowered by the strong undercurrents while he resisted pressures from all

38. Amin and Coquery-Vidrovitch, *Histoire économique*, p. 145.

39. *Afrique Nouvelle*, April 26, 1967.

40. France's aid to Congo elevated it to third rank in Africa in terms of per capita assistance received from former colonial powers. Morrison et al., *Black Africa*, p. 137.

41. House, "Brazzaville." See also *Le Monde*, March 26, 1970.

42. The MNR was officially the initiator of policies which the government executed. See *Afrique Nouvelle*, January 1, 1966, and *Africa Research Bulletin*, February 1966.

factions to make his government fully accountable to the Politburo. The violent tug-of-war between the various cliques in the Politburo and National Assembly (whose intransigent "Maoist" president, Leon Angor, mounted a powerful drive to shackle the cabinet to the party) set the tone for much of Massemba-Debat's presidency. And the factional cleavages spilled over into ancillary organizations with the JMNR forming a semipermanent, ultraleft opposition.

Viewing this cauldron of ambitious personalities and ill-defined ideological factions, Africanists have often contradicted each other in their attempts to identify and separate the "ultra-revolutionary" from the "revolutionary" and "radical" elements or the pro-Chinese from pro-Russian from pro-Cuban cliques. Each embassy in Brazzaville (including the French) maintained links with and subsidized its supporters in the political hierarchy; yet the ideological coloration of these mutual advancement alliances has more often than not been fluid and opportunistic, with most cliques maintaining a foot and an outstretched palm in several camps. Sudden metamorphoses from moderate to radical and the reverse have not been unusual; growing pressure from the ultraleft JMNR made one day's radicals appear as the next day's moderates. Within such a context the "true" moderates were very rapidly either purged or forced underground, which made assessments of "revolutionary" credentials highly relative and contingent upon the specific ideological power balance of the moment. More importantly, however, any attempt rigorously to separate the various ideological camps is somewhat irrelevant for a real understanding of the jostling for power in Brazzaville and the policy outcomes of power shifts among the top contenders and cliques.[43]

Thus the distinction between Massemba-Debat's first (1964–66) government under Dr. Pascal Lissouba (who began as a radical and was forced out by Angor for being a moderate) and his second (1966–68) under Ambroise Noumazalay (who though pro-Chinese replaced Lissouba in order to placate France)[44] pales in compari-

43. See *Le Monde*, September 24–25, 1972.
44. For an example of complete disagreement among observers of the Congolese scene as to the radical credentials of Lissouba and Noumazalay, compare *Le*

son to the policy similarities of the two administrations. This is not to imply that there were no meaningful differences between Lissouba's premiership, during which the basic patterns of a mobilizational polity[45] were laid, and Noumazalay's, when heightened revolutionary rhetoric was tempered by increasing efforts to mollify France and attract foreign investment capital. Nor is it to imply that the sharp ideological cleavages within the MNR or Massemba-Debat's political gyrations as he shuffled, promoted, and demoted radical or moderate cliques in his cabinet were meaningless. Rather, that much of the revolutionary zeal in Congo camouflaged personalist ambitions, while the factional "ideological" clashes and purges often covered up interethnic competitions and the settling of old accounts; and that militant rhetoric became functionally institutionalized as the lingua franca of elites rebelling against a frustrating neocolonialist reality while groping for a more self-satisfying revolutionary posture and a unique "role" in Africa.[46] It was against this backdrop that Massemba-Debat began to founder in 1967. When opposition to his leadership suddenly merged with corporate gripes in the army and Captain Marien Ngouabi's ambitions, the highly politicized army moved squarely into the middle of the political arena.

Praetorianism, Corporate Grievances, and Congo's Armed Forces

Congo's armed forces originated early in 1962 when a small *gendarmerie* and a minuscule army of 700 men were set up with indigenous troops detached from France's colonial armies. Total

---

scene as to the radical credentials of Lissouba and Noumazalay, compare *Le Monde*, May 9, 1966, with *Africa Contemporary Record* (1968), p. 455. For biographical data on Congo's political personalities see Virginia Thompson and Richard Adloff, *Historical Dictionary of the Republic of the Congo (Congo-Brazzaville).*

45. See Introduction in James S. Coleman and Carl G. Rosberg, Jr., eds., *Political Parties and National Integration in Tropical Africa.*

46. According to one observer, Congolese youth may have developed "a culture of the word, in which spoken words seemed all powerful. . . . The management of words . . . were regarded as the key to the social drama in which they were all involved." See P. Erny, "Parole et travail chez les jeunes d'Afrique Centrale" (also cited in Lee, *African Armies and Civil Order*, p. 54). See also P. Erny, "The White Man as seen through the eyes of Congolese (Brazzaville) children."

personnel in both forces barely numbered 1,500 and they were under direct French officer and NCO command. Franco-Congolese military accords signed at independence provided for the slow indigenization of the command hierarchy, the supply of materiel and technical advisers at favorable terms, and direct French military assistance in case of internal or external threats. Small detachments of the armed forces (frequently company size) were designated as the country's "Navy" and "Air Force"; others became the Signal Corps, Supply Corps, and so forth, but Congo's dire financial straits and inadequate technical infrastructure and communications clearly ruled out any significant expansion of the armed forces. Indeed, the one-battalion army was essentially conceived of as a symbol of the country's national sovereignty and a glorified superpolice that could come to the aid of the *gendarmerie* in case of domestic turbulence.

From their inception the armed forces reflected the wider societal cleavages in Congo. Ethnic tensions were intense, with the rank and file largely northern (Mbochi, Kouyou), while southern (Bakongo) elements held key positions in the officer corps. The involvement of several officers in commerce and smuggling across the Congo River tended to sharpen ethnic animosities as did the general smugness and self-assurance of the southerners.[47] Rumors of attempts by Youlou to induce more Lari to join the army or to create extraordinary officer slots as sinecures for his supporters (which failed because of relatively low pay scales and opposition by the French officers)[48] further fostered discontent in the largely northern army.

As in Togo and Dahomey resentments and frustrations developed among upwardly mobile and ambitious elements over the

47. Major David Moutsaka, the chief of staff in 1966 and Massemba-Debat's cousin, was especially unpopular among the troops, while Major Felix Mouzaba-kani, the former chief of staff, was one of those whose commercial activities deeply annoyed the junior ranks. Also, the level of corruption in the Congolese armed forces has always been high. For example, Captain Norbert Tsika, head of the *gendarmerie* from 1963 to 1966, was arrested for embezzlement only to be freed in the 1968 Ngouabi takeover and reinstated in his old command. A year later he was demoted to private for cowardice at the time of the attempted putsch.

48. From interviews in Kinshasa in July 1972.

extremely limited prospects for promotion in a battalion-sized army with few NCO or officer positions and a top rank of major.[49] Petty jealousies were also rife between officers promoted from the ranks (for example, Lieutenant Poignet) and those who had attended academies in France (Captains Ngouabi and Raoul). Tensions and antagonisms deepened between garrisons in the smaller urban centers (especially among the Pointe Noire personnel) and the elite paracommando Brazzaville unit. Discipline was generally badly maintained, and the military was permeated with competing loyalty pyramids. Indeed, several months before the upheaval that was to topple Youlou, the army was rocked by a short, unreported mutiny, and a similar eruption occurred in November 1963. Thus despite its small size Congo's army manifested many of the tensions and cleavages present in other, larger African armed forces.

Garrisoned in the southern cities the army could hardly be kept immune from the mushrooming mood of dissatisfaction with Youlou's regime. This was especially true of the troops in Brazzaville, who were in daily contact with unemployed northerners in the Poto Poto quarter. Thus when the anti-Youlou demonstrations broke out in 1963 the army was instantly polarized, with most of the rank and file sympathetic to the grievances of the unemployed and unionists; the Lari-Bakongo officers, on the other hand, were somewhat equivocal, because they feared they might unwittingly help to bring about a Mbochi political ascendance and/or a new radical regime.

France's decision not to heed Youlou's appeal to it to honor the Franco-Congolese military accord, and especially De Gaulle's rejection of Youlou's telephone request for the dispatch of French troops to crush the demonstrations, sealed the fate of the Abbé's regime. The French officers in nominal command of the Congolese army were ordered to remain neutral in the conflict, and the indigenous officer hierarchy, under pressure from the crowds and aware of anti-Youlou sentiment among their troops, decided to

49. With the expansion of the armed forces after 1963 colonel became the highest rank.

withhold the army's support from the beleaguered regime. On August 15, in the presence of trade union leaders, the army's senior officers, Captains David Moutsaka and Felix Mouzabakani, requested and obtained Youlou's written resignation.[50] According to accounts Youlou then fainted and upon recovering tearfully telephoned De Gaulle to announce "J'ai signé, mon general." [51] In appreciation of the army's "constructive" role, the Massemba-Debat government speeded the Congolization of the officer corps, appointed Moutsaka chief of staff, and promoted many of the key officers by one rank.

Since the "revolution" that toppled Youlou was very much a limited urban upheaval (estimates of the demonstrating crowds vary between 7,000 and 10,000), the postcoup political elite was quite conscious of its narrow base of support. This was evident when pro-Youlouist tracts surfaced in the south and plots to return him to power were discovered. The extent of the resistance to the upheaval is also attested by the low turnout for the 1964 municipal elections, when only 50 percent of the electorate voted in a race dominated by leftist candidates. To assure the survival of the socialist regime the MNR and Massemba-Debat deliberately embarked upon a policy of politicizing the army that had helped them come to power and utilizing the unemployed youth as a clout against opposition. In retrospect it is clear that the absence of intraelite cohesion and strong control mechanisms encouraged the proliferation of factional assaults on the weak institutional center of authority, which directly worked toward the creation of a highly unstable praetorian system.[52]

It is hard to exaggerate the role of the JMNR in this process. It continuously threatened Massemba-Debat from the Left (where, as a moderate, he was most exposed), becoming the power base of ambitious competitors such as André Hombessa, "the wild man of

50. See "Brazzaville: Ten Years of Revolution," part 1.

51. Over a year later when Youlou escaped from house arrest with the assistance of supporters in the *gendarmerie*, his requests for landing rights and asylum in France were denied and his plane was diverted to Madrid where he was to die in exile in 1973.

52. See the comments on Congo in Valerie P. Bennett, "The Intransferability of Patterns of Civil-Military Relations," pp. 76–82.

the Congolese revolution," Claude Ndalla, and Michel Bindi[53] in the left wing of the MNR. More importantly, the JMNR's "revolutionary" unruliness ("a mixture of revolutionary idealism and juvenile delinquency"),[54] antiarmy bias, and pretensions to power constituted a direct corporate challenge to the military. Rhetoric about the "unity of workers and party" aside, the army was the regime's only prop. By the 1968 JMNR-army showdown the JMNR had become 35,000 strong and had acquired independent sources of finance, supplies, and arms, with a variety of donors ranging from Cuba to North Vietnam. Quite apart from the JMNR's significant paramilitary capability, an elite, well-armed, 1,000-man Civil Defense Corps (frequently referred to as "the people's militia") had been recruited from its most militant and dedicated members. The militia acted as a praetorian guard against enemies of the revolution and the regime and as a buffer against any armed assaults including those emanating from the regime's own support organizations—the army and the *gendarmerie*.

Ideologically and militarily trained by Cuban instructors, the militia (whose size was later doubled to 2,000 to give it parity with the expanded army) rapidly began to conceive of itself as the only true guardian of the socialist revolution in Congo. Headed by the ambitious and radical Ange Diawara, it viewed the army as a decadent bourgeois leftover from the colonial era (which was somewhat true) and the *gendarmerie* as a hotbed of reactionary Youlouist sentiments (also true). Its relations with both were bitter, antagonistic, and competitive. The militia's self-assurance was greatly enhanced by the fact that the MNR frequently supported it

53. For detailed biographies see Thompson, *Historical Dictionary*: Both Hombessa and Bindi were ministers of interior under Massemba-Debat. Hombessa moved to that post in April 1965 after organizing the JMNR as his fiefdom and climbing on its shoulders into the cabinet as minister of youth, a position he relinquished to Ndalla. Hombessa's demotion in January 1968 precipitated a government crisis. His replacement was Michel Bindi, the general director of security, who was sentenced in 1969 to ten years for the 1965 murders (see footnote 37). Both men encouraged the JMNR Biafra camp shootout with Ngouabi troops in 1968.

54. According to a 1965 observation in *Jeune Afrique*. Cited in United States, *Area Handbook*, p. 103.

in its clashes with the *gendarmerie*, over which it rapidly gained ascendance. Thus, for all practical purposes, by 1968 the Civil Defense Corps and the JMNR had usurped many of the *gendarmerie's* responsibilities and had developed the notion that they were the government's main security prop, if not the power behind the throne.[55] This view greatly exasperated many in the army's officer corps who regarded themselves as the true buttress of the revolution and who rankled at the privileges and powers granted to what they considered undisciplined hooligans. At the same time more conservative and/or Youlouist elements in the army feared that further aggrandizement and arming of the JMNR would completely foreclose the option of a return to the nonsocialist political hierarchy of the past.

Moreover, while both the JMNR and the militia had started as unpaid ancillary organizations, by 1966 most of their officials and many of their members were receiving state salaries, free lodgings, and donations—overt or covert—from sympathetic Eastern embassies in Brazzaville. This, too, threatened the corporate integrity and prestige of the regular armed forces by restricting the amount of funds and foreign subsidies available to them. Thus, for example, after 1966 some of the army's private financial pipelines to East European embassies began to dry up, though key officers were still able to obtain lucrative subsidies.[56]

In June 1966 the MNR decreed that the Congolese army would be transformed into a "People's Army" under its direct control, with a collegiate command structure and a Political Directorate to supervise ideological indoctrination. The move, which had been decided upon as early as January 1965, was an attempt to impose tighter political control over the faction-ridden army and to curb the growing ideological friction between the regular and paramilitary forces. The past few years had cogently indicated the degree to which sources of opposition to the regime were entrenched in the

55. See *Le Monde*, July 31, 1965. On a number of occasions Premier Lissouba reminded JMNR formations that they were *not* the government and even Hombessa admitted once to the National Assembly that his "shock troops" were simply uncontrollable.

56. House, "Brazzaville," p. 20.

army and *gendarmerie;* in August 1964, for example, Chief of Staff Major Mouzabakani and several other soldiers had been purged for an alleged Youlouist plot that included gunrunning from Leopoldville. In March 1965 Youlou escaped to Zaire with the aid of elements in the army and *gendarmerie;* later the same year two other plots were discovered in which army and *gendarmerie* officers were involved.

The decision to demolish civil-military boundaries and to completely politicize the army further opened up the armed forces to a wide variety of political crosscurrents and influences. Even before the French training mission's activities were wound up in 1966 the army had received materiel and advisers from Russia, China, and Cuba, and military factions had become attached to one or another of these ideological camps. MNR cliques and aspiring politicians such as André Hombessa, Claude Ndalla, Michel Bindi, and Ambroise Noumazalay worked at establishing alliance pyramids with officers and troops.[57] More importantly, however, the decision to begin full-scale indoctrination of the army caused intense resentments among the northern troops and officers, who viewed this as yet another Bakongo plot to keep them in a subordinate position.

The degree to which antigovernment grievances had built up in the army and highly autonomous personalist power formations had been forged by individual officers came to light in June 1966 with the Mbochi-Kouyou mutiny in the Brazzaville garrison. The rebellion was sparked by the demotion and reposting from Brazzaville of the popular Kouyou Captain Marien Ngouabi for insubordination over the political indoctrination of the army and its future linkage with the JMNR. His loyal Kouyou troops promptly went on a rampage, arresting Chief of Staff Moutsaka and other senior officers. They then ransacked the MNR party headquarters and chased its Politburo, Noumazalay, and the cabinet to the municipal sports stadium around which the Cuban-led Civil Defense Corps loyal to the government set up a protective

57. For the logical conclusion of this process, the development of "private armies" (in Zaire), see Jean Claude Willame, *Patrimonialism and Political Change in the Congo*, chapter 4.

cordon until tempers cooled. Peace was restored only after Ngouabi's demotion was rescinded and a junior officer appointed chief of staff to replace the unpopular Moutsaka. Soon after, Ngouabi was appointed commander of Brazzaville's paracommando battalion, an ideal base for any praetorian assault in the future. However, the Cuban instructors of the militia were not disposed of as demanded by Ngouabi and indeed the militia was further strengthened.[58]

Though the immediate conflict between Ngouabi and Massemba-Debat was resolved, relations between them never really improved. The two were mismatched in terms of personalities and the young self-made northerner chafed at the manner in which he was continuously being pushed around by the paternal school-teacher-turned-politician. As the government increased its efforts to impose ideological control over the army, friction between Ngouabi and Massemba-Debat multiplied and Ngouabi started to search for allies among the president's powerful left-wing enemies.

Ngouabi also did not get along with many of the southern officers in the army though he did cultivate the friendship of several, including Cabinda-raised Captain Alfred Raoul of the Signal Corps, who emerged as his principal lieutenant after the 1968 coup. The fact that the easygoing and bon vivant Raoul has always been a pro-French political moderate may appear paradoxical in light of the reputation Ngouabi acquired of being a pro-Chinese "Maoist." Yet the apparent inconsistency is resolved if one remembers that in spite of rhetoric or appearances ideological considerations have usually been of secondary importance in Congo, especially in the army where ethnic cleavages and personal competitions polarized the officer corps much more strongly and meaningfully. Another example of this is Ngouabi's link with the conservative Lari (though born in Fort Rousset) Major Joachim Opango Yhomby, to whom he entrusted the Brazzaville battalion in 1968 the *gendarmerie* in 1969 and promoted to chief of staff in

58. See *Africa Research Bulletin*, July 1966. Aware of the explosive nature of this particular grievance, Massemba-Debat slowly phased out the Cubans or posted them into the interior where their presence was less visible. Interestingly, the Cubans were popular with the population and youth while Russian and Chinese assistance teams were viewed as too aloof.

1970.[59] Ngouabi's leftist "credentials"—which became "visible" to the outside world around 1967—were largely a result of his tactical alliance with the Noumazalay clique in the MNR in the months prior to Massemba-Debat's political collapse.

During 1967 and early 1968 the government's moderate posture vis-à-vis France came under increasing criticism from the MNR left wing, the JMNR, and politicians shut out by Massemba-Debat's recent cabinet shuffles. André Hombessa, demoted early in 1968 from the Ministry of Interior to the Ministry of Information, was in the process of rebuilding his anti-Massemba-Debat youth power base—referred to in Brazzaville as the "Hombessa-JMNR." Similarly, Noumazalay, dropped from the premiership in January 1968 because of personality and policy differences, was mounting a challenge against Massemba-Debat, utilizing his support in the party, of which he had been secretary-general. The army was once again seething with grievances. Tracts were surfacing daily in Brazzaville attacking the servility, moderation, and immobility of the regime, which was allegedly selling out the country to the "imperialists." Increasingly, Massemba-Debat found himself isolated and in need of moderate supporters, the kind he helped purge during his administration's leftist phase. Yet the discovery of two rightist plots seemed to discredit the logic of a pro-France appeasement policy, which had not previously paid off significantly in terms of increased private or public investments.

The long-simmering governmental crisis, exacerbated by the January cabinet reshuffle, came to a head on July 22, 1968. Aware that leftist intransigents in the MNR and the JMNR were plotting his overthrow with the support of the militants in the army and weary of continuously fighting for his government's autonomy vis-à-vis the Politburo, Massemba-Debat met the crisis head-on. On July 22 he publicly challenged his opposition (for the second time that year) to produce a leader with better solutions to Congo's problems, asserting that he would gladly step down from power in favor of such a person. When the challenge went unanswered (and scattered demonstrations erupted in his favor) Massemba-Debat moved to neutralize the power base of his opponents: the National

59. Yhomby's prompt support in 1972 saved Ngouabi from the Diawara putsch.

Assembly and MNR Politburo were declared dissolved, and the *gendarmerie* (mostly Lari and still loyal to him) began arresting a large number of youth and party leaders (including Ngouabi) suspected of plotting against the regime.[60]

While Massemba-Debat's purge of his opposition might have succeeded, since it was but another phase in his perennial tug-of-war with the party Politburo, the arrest of Ngouabi was a tactical mistake. He was undoubtedly guilty of plotting Massemba-Debat's demise (few in Brazzaville were totally innocent of this), but he was not yet strong enough to resist the purge and might have bided his time. His arrest, however, brought the armed forces into the fray, caused Massemba-Debat to make a humiliating about-face, and pushed Ngouabi to further solidify his commitment to Massemba-Debat's enemies. Thus the ultimate outcome of the crisis was the coalescence of a stronger anti-Massemba-Debat clique and the decision by Ngouabi to assume a more vigorous political role. The attempts to purge him presaged not only Massemba-Debat's eclipse but also that of the Bakongo political hegemony over the country.

Ngouabi's arrest, as in 1966, brought into the city Kouyou troops, which promptly freed their commander as well as other arrested military personnel. Among these was Felix Mouzabakani, in prison for his 1964 plot, who was temporarily appointed minister of interior. A chaotic situation then ensued as political factions scrambled to join the new power structure that appeared to be developing. Aware that he did not control the entire army and that his alliance with the MNR left wing was not yet powerful enough, Ngouabi called upon Massemba-Debat, who had left for his home village, to "pluck up his courage" and resume his office—though with greatly circumscribed powers—since "the Army was not thirsting for power." [61]

When Massemba-Debat returned to Brazzaville he was confronted by a new chief of staff, Ngouabi, and a National Council of the Revolution (CNR) to whom his cabinet was directly subordi-

---

60. *Le Monde*, August 5, 1968. See also *Marches Tropicaux et Mediterranéens*, October 26, 1968, and *Afrique Nouvelle*, August 15, 1968.

61. *Le Monde*, August 6, 1968.

nated. His attempt to disencumber himself from the control of MNR militants therefore resulted only in his becoming thoroughly shackled to a much more powerful civil-military coalition. The CNR and its central directorate were chaired by Ngouabi. Packed with many of Massemba-Debat's opponents (for example, Noumazalay and Diawara) within a short time they forced him to drop his provisional premier, Pascal Lissouba, and accept Captain Raoul in his stead. For all practical purposes, the Massemba-Debat government had become the administrative organ of the CNR central committee.

The final stage in Ngouabi's consolidation of power occurred on August 29 when diehard segments of the paramilitary forces (in particular the Hombessa-JMNR) refused to surrender their arms and submit to the army's authority as Ngouabi demanded. A brief but bloody battle ensued when the army converged on their headquarters (the meteorological camp that they renamed "Biafra") and over 100 of the 300 youthful defenders of the "revolution" were killed.[62] The fighting gave an excuse for a major settling of personal scores both in Brazzaville and across the country that was only quelled with some difficulty. On the same evening Massemba-Debat resigned and retired from the political scene.

MILITARY RULE IN A PEOPLE'S REPUBLIC

One of the most important factors that triggered off the 1968 coup was the encouragement given to Ngouabi by left-wing MNR elements striving to rid themselves of Massemba-Debat's leadership. The early composition and rhetoric of the CNR, as well as the declaration of a people's republic and a People's National Army (APN) at the end of 1969 certainly projected the image of a major reassertion of Congo's radical left. Yet rhetoric and the new structural trappings of a Communist state aside, and viewed over its seven years in power, Ngouabi's regime has been remarkably nonrevolutionary and devoid of striking socialist policies or

62. Reports that Hombessa and Bindi joined the insurgents were probably untrue, though the camp was definitely supplied with arms and ammunition just before the army attack.

changes.[63] Structurally the new government introduced innovations in the state administration, promulgated a new (1973) constitution, and reorganized the armed forces; it nationalized several flagging French enterprises, established a "new" Marxist-Leninist party, the Parti Congolais du Travail (PCT), and left OCAM. Greater stress on Marxist-Leninist jargon and accoutrements, heightened radical rhetoric, and grand international gestures have not been matched until recently by serious economic militancy.

The regime's sensitivity to French expatriate economic interests did not at the outset differ markedly from that of all previous administrations. Significantly, the huge, newly discovered phosphate deposits were handed over for exploitation to a company in which the Congolese government held only a 15 percent interest—a strikingly lower share than many conservative African states enjoy in similar concessions.[64] As one observer pointed out, "Socialism has made little difference to either the vast mass of the people, living on subsistence agriculture in the country and largely unaware of the political leaders in the towns; or to the country's economy, which remains largely under the control of French interests."[65] And *Le Monde* jadedly concluded that Ngouabi's regime has been "less concerned with ideological options than with remaining in control of the state."[66]

The ideological zigzag course charted by Ngouabi as he tried to balance the various civil and military factions and the intermittent assaults on his position from both conservative and leftist elements can also be viewed as a direct continuation of Massemba-Debat's juggling act while in office. Indeed, Congo's political experience since 1963 is dramatic proof that in Africa "Plus ça change, plus c'est la même chose"; it illustrates also the difficulty of disengaging a developing economy from a neocolonialist relationship and mobilizing a fragmented population for the tasks of national reconstruction.

63. *New York Times*, October 25, 1969. Indeed, at the outset Youlou and Opangault supporters were invited to join the new government.

64. *Africa Contemporary Record*, 1969–70, p. B419.

65. Ibid., 1970–71, p. B305.

66. *Le Monde*, November 11, 1969. See also Gilbert Comte's "Le Socialisme de la parole," p. 3, and "Les Européens inquiets mais prosperes," p. 4.

Two features that do set off Ngouabi's regime from those of his predecessors are the eclipse of the political predominance of the Lari and the more acute polarization and splinterization of the armed forces. These two processes are directly interlinked. Growing Mbochi influence deeply threatened the Bakongo political and social establishment and set off strong ripples of discontent in Bakongo-dominated structures such as the civil service, the police, and the *gendarmerie*. The latter in particular felt threatened by the ascendance of the army, especially in light of the various plans to either totally restructure it or directly subordinate it to the regular armed forces. Elements of the *gendarmerie* and police have directly or indirectly been involved in all the plots and attempted coups against Ngouabi's regime. Not even the reorganization and subordination of the *gendarmerie* to new regional military commanders rid the force of its "counterrevolutionary" tendencies. And its eventual dismantlement only drove sources of opposition underground.

TABLE 4.3
Congo: Ethnic Representation in Cabinets, 1960–67
(in percentages)

Ethnic group	As % of population	Independence cabinet	Prior to 1963 coup	Massemba-Debat 1967 cabinet
Bakongo	47	43	57	50
Batéké	20	7	7	10
Mbochi	11	21	21	10
Mbété	7	—	—	10
Sanga	5	7	7	—
Others	10	23	7	20
N =		14	15	11

Source: Donald Morrison et al., *Black Africa*, p. 213.

Under both Youlou and Massemba-Debat an effort had been made to keep the representation of Congo's ethnic groups in the cabinet approximately at par with their actual strength throughout the country (see table 4.3). Indeed, neither of Massemba-Debat's two premiers, Lissouba and Noumazalay, were Bakongo. Though the Lari overrepresentation in the civil service could not be compensated for by the promotion of unskilled Mbochi, efforts were made to regularly hire northern candidates with the necessary educational qualifications. But the reality of a Lari-controlled patronage system often prevented the execution of such an ideal policy, and neither Youlou nor Massemba-Debat really cared about northern Congo. Moreover, during the period 1960–68 Congo's meager or nonexistent development budgets simply did not allow for any serious improvements of the infrastructure in Mbochi areas even had the regime been so disposed. Given the grievances and economic pressures in the southern cities, an antinorthern fiscal and economic bias continued until the 1968 coup.

The rise of Fort Rousset-born Ngouabi ended the neglect of Congo's undeveloped central and northern regions and the political and administrative superiority and dominance of the Bakongo. Both to consolidate his popularity with northern elements (especially those in Brazzaville's Poto Poto quarter) and to intimidate and dislodge potential southern and "reactionary" sources of opposition to his regime, Ngouabi began to divert development funds to the north,[67] while selective purges of high-level Bakongo politicians and civil servants commenced. The latter were camouflaged under the guise of a general attack on "counterrevolutionary" and "bourgeois" elements in the country. Their purpose was to dislodge high- and middle-level Bakongo power wielders and sources of patronage in the administration and civil service and replace them with Ngouabi's Mbochi appointees. Yet, again, the pragmatic limitations of power in Congo prevented a complete purge or intimidation of the urban Bakongo upon whose tacit acquiescence the stability of the regime depended. Even as many high-level Bakongo politicians and civil servants were removed from lucrative sinecures, important new positions had to be created or found for them, to the detriment of the "austerity" financial policy periodically declared by Ngouabi. In this respect, too, Ngouabi's regime strikingly resembled previous administrations, which found themselves totally incapable of any resoluteness when

67. In reality only the Fort Rousset region benefited from this new largesse, which took the form of basic infrastructure building (roads, clinics, schools).

wedged between the anvil of fiscal responsibility and the hammer of explosively escalating pressures for civil service positions.

The Bakongo shakeup of 1969 rapidly spun off a series of demotions and trials of individuals connected with Massemba-Debat's government, including non-Bakongo politicians such as Noumazalay, who had helped pave the way for the military takeover. Though political purges had occurred under Massemba-Debat, they now become an integral part of the new order. Real and/or imagined enemies of the "revolution" or of the clique in power were periodically "uncovered" and placed on trial as Congo's political tensions heightened with the steady entrenchment of Mbochi influence. Moreover, stepping uncertainly into the political arena without any clear set of priorities or policies, Ngouabi was immediately engulfed and buffeted by the same pressures that had wrenched his predecessor's grasp from the reins of power. It was not until 1972, after severe challenges to his authority and leadership, that Ngouabi clearly emerged as the victor in his protracted struggle with Congo's personalist and ideological cliques—a struggle that sucked in the country's civil and military elites, ravaging and reducing both to shambles. The best indicator of the intensity of the strife is the decimation of the PCT's membership to less than 160 by 1972. At that date there remained only 3 members in the Politburo (out of 9) and 5 (of 18) in the party Central Committee.[68]

The Politics of the "Permanent Plot"

The first plot against the Ngouabi regime was the allegedly Youlouist February 1969 scheme of Major Mouzabakani (who at the time was minister of interior) and his aide Lieutenant Pierre Kikanga, the Lari paratroop instructor. Their trial merged with hearings before the Revolutionary Court of Justice of charges against the Vili "M'Pita group," who were exonerated,[69] and the

68. *New York Times*, July 17, 1972.

69. The M'Pita group trial clearly revealed that the regime had an ethnic bias and that it was using its judicial powers to intimidate potential Bakongo opposition. The group was allegedly aiming at the "restoration of the American capitalist system." See *West Africa*, March 8, 1969.

May 1968 Debreton conspirators.[70] In October it was Massemba-Debat's turn to be arrested, together with his two former premiers, André Hombessa, and twenty other top government officials. The group was accused of a variety of "crimes" committed between 1963 and 1968, including complicity in the 1965 political kidnap-murders of three Lari moderates.[71] Though the courts exonerated most of the defendants of serious wrongdoing (especially Massemba-Debat, Lissouba, and Noumazalay) their arrest, incarceration, and highly publicized trial were clear attempts to intimidate their supporters and political allies.

On November 8 another plot was discovered, allegedly planned by Youlouist elements led by Bernard Kolela, a Foreign Ministry official.[72] (Kolela had been sentenced to death in 1965 for an anti-Massemba-Debat plot, only to be reprieved and reintegrated into the civil service in 1968.) The intrigue had its repercussions in the armed forces, and several top military officers were purged in its aftermath: Major Norbert Tsika, head of the *gendarmerie*, was demoted to private and Major Alphonse Maballo, assistant chief of staff, was reduced to the rank of captain for "lack of courage." [73] Other personnel were summarily purged.

The wave of political intrigues and heightened turbulence in the country was considerably encouraged by the easy infiltration across the Congo River of opposition groups residing in Zaire. The long, porous borders were difficult to patrol because of manpower limitations and the unreliability of large segments of the *gendarmerie*. Security measures were nevertheless tightened, special CNR Vigilance Brigades (headed by militant officers) were set up, and an Emergency Tribunal and Emergency Court were created to deal with assaults against the regime. The tribunal and court churned out a large number of death sentences against the multitude of "counterrevolutionaries" and "adventurists" brought to trial, a fact that did not prevent the regime from commuting most of the sentences and periodically announcing wholesale amnesties.

70. In that affair several French citizens and Congolese officers were involved. *Le Monde*, May 31, 1969.

71. See footnote 37.

72. See the cynical analysis in *Le Monde*, November 11, 1969.

73. Ibid., November 15, 1969.

Growing dissidence, lack of discipline, and unrest in the armed forces led to an acceleration of the integration of all paramilitary units into the army, originally announced in 1968. Though the policy had always been justified in terms of the danger to the regime from the reactionary tendencies of the *gendarmerie* (which was more credible after the Mouzabakani-Kikanga plots), the reorganization of the armed forces also served to curb leftist and other irregular forces regarded by Ngouabi as a personal threat to his army power base. Hence, while assiduously paying homage to the revolutionary role of Congo's youth and promoting some of its leaders and ideologues to important posts—Claude Ndalla (former ambassador to Peking), Ange Diawara, Justin Lekoundzou, and Ange Poungui all ended up in the Politburo—Ngouabi at the same time eliminated the JMNR threat by integrating its armed wings into the newly restructured Congolese National Army. However, though he shackled one corporate threat that had plagued both Massemba-Debat and himself in the past, Ngouabi was in reality allowing the militant left direct and unfettered ideological access to the army. Under only nominal party control a Political Directorate headed by First and Second Commissars Lieutenant Diawara and Captain Kiboula-Kaya weeded out "reactionary" elements and conducted ideological indoctrination in accord with the PCT decree for the total politicization of the armed forces.[74]

The indoctrination process sparked off resentments on the part of persons who felt they were marked for a purge or had been bypassed in promotions for ideological reasons. It also deeply antagonized army professionals, who chafed at the way "outsiders" (such as Diawara) had moved into important military positions and were building up powerful personal power bases. These feelings were not unjustified, because the creation of Diawara's Political Directorate did give the radical left a military base from which to mount ideological or personal challenges against their commander-in-chief. Indeed, both Diawara and Kiboula-Kaya eventually led sections of the army against Ngouabi's regime, and the subsequent purge of the "contaminated" army was costly both in terms of

74. *Africa Research Bulletin*, February 1969. "Severe sanctions" were decreed against any civilian or soldier who claimed to be apolitical.

personnel and of the total erosion of the army's sense of corporate integrity.

The *gendarmerie* and the police were also structurally subordinated to Ngouabi's loyalist army. In November 1969 the *gendarmerie* was drastically reorganized. Its former three geographical divisions (north, central, south) were eliminated, the communal hierarchy fused with the army's, and individual units operationally linked to the army commanders of the seven new military zones into which Congo was carved. Later the national police was similarly reorganized and made operationally subservient to army commanders. As subsequent events were to illustrate, however, mere structural rearrangements were insufficient to erase group and ethnic resentments and personal ambitions deeply entrenched in these Lari-dominated forces. The subordination of Lari *gendarmes* to non-Bakongo military officers only tended to create new tensions and resentments, which became translated into greater Lari support for assaults against the northern-dominated regime.

Tension between the army and the *gendarmerie* was greatly aggravated by the second pro-Youlou putsch attempted by Kikanga on March 23, 1970. Leading his small force of thirty men across the river from Zaire, Kikanga fully expected to split the loyalties of the Congolese armed forces and to swing to his side the armed support of the *gendarmerie*.[75] The fact that this did not occur and that the assaulting force was promptly liquidated can be attributed less to a miscalculation on Kikanga's part about the extent of anti-Mbochi sentiment in Brazzaville and more to the swiftness with which Ngouabi's loyal paratroop battalion moved in to prevent the spread of the revolt. Many *gendarmerie* officers and NCOs were aware in advance of Kikanga's imminent assault,[76] and widespread sympathy for the attempted coup resulted in the refusal of certain units to move against Kikanga's force. The defeat of the uprising was therefore followed by a major purge of officers who had not rallied quickly behind the government, the disbanding of

75. *Le Monde*, March 24 and 26, 1970.
76. The chief adjutant of the *gendarmerie* and several other officers were sentenced to prison or death for their complicity.

the *gendarmerie*, and the creation of a people's militia from its more militant and loyal elements.[77]

The dissolution of the *gendarmerie* and the creation of a militia were a clearcut victory for the radical left faction in the PCT and a defeat for Ngouabi, who had always distrusted paramilitary forces outside his direct control. The addition of two more leftists to the Politburo (one of them Noumazalay) and the slow eclipse of Raoul (upon whose control of the Second Infantry Battalion Ngouabi had always relied) was further evidence of Ngouabi's eroding position. Increasingly, he appeared to be losing control of events and giving ground to the many militant and ambitious civilian factions.[78] His public posture, actions, and frenzied rhetoric were strikingly reminiscent of the desperate style and impotence of Massemba-Debat in the months prior to his collapse. By August 1970, under pressure to put order in his own bailiwick, Ngouabi began lashing out against the "embourgeoisement" of officers in high administrative posts and the "sink of corruption" in the army itself.[79]

The mounting pressure on Ngouabi's position finally developed into a major test of power in December 1971. It is doubtful whether Ngouabi—who had always been much more popular in the army than in the party—could have survived much longer as a puppet for the much stronger personalities in the Politburo and the Central Committee. As a moderate and pragmatic centrist, he struck a false note with his ideological rhetoric in comparison with the fiery invective of the country's "Maoist" clique, which appealed to wide sectors of the restless youth and urban unemployed.[80] Though Ngouabi attempted to project the image of the "revolutionary

77. The fact that antigovernment demonstrations had erupted in the south on the eve of the attempted putsch pushed the Politburo to decree the immediate dismissal of all traditional chiefs and their replacement by cells of PCT militants.

78. Ironically, in September 1970 the former minister of public works, Stephane Nouarra, was sentenced to two years in prison for building up a personal network in the government in anticipation of a Ndalla-Diawara-Kiboula Kaya anti-Ngouabi revolt, which indeed occurred. See *Le Monde*, September 26, 1970. See also Simon Kiba's interesting analysis of the various plots in *Afrique Nouvelle*, March 25, 1971.

79. *West Africa*, August 15, 1970, and April 2, 1973.

80. Claude Ndalla, for example, pushed strongly for the immediate expulsion of all French nationals and the nationalization of their assets and the entire private economic sector, as well as the closing of all churches and their transformation into party meeting halls.

intellectual, in a state of constant debate with his party militants, always ready to deliver long harangues to rally the faithful," [81] this was very much a learned response to the political temper of the country. As one observer cogently put it, "to survive at such a time you had to know the revolutionary jargon, at the very least." [82] Ngouabi not only mastered the jargon but also the Byzantine intricacies of developing a radical dialectic while holding centrist positions and purging the true militants in the political system.

The showdown with his Politburo opposition was triggered off in November 1971 by a series of violent student strikes in Pointe Noire. Student complaints of shortages of teachers, supplies, and facilities rapidly spread to other sectors and became politicized by Ngouabi's enemies into a broadside attack against the "hypocrisy" and "false revolutionary attitude" of the regime and some of its key figures. Both pro-French Raoul and Yhomby-Opango ("who lives like a capitalist in his luxurious villa")[83] were severely denounced, and the dangerous coalition between students, workers, and Ngouabi's Politburo opposition (and especially Ndalla) appeared to be on the verge of completely isolating Ngouabi and his few supporters. Since Ngouabi could not tolerate such a dual challenge to his civil and military authority the long-postponed showdown erupted. The army was ordered in to occupy the schools and disperse the strikers. In the process over twenty students were killed. Using the unrest as a pretext, a purge of allegedly "degenerate" and "fetishist" elements—catchwords for personnel not solidly pro-Ngouabi—commenced in the party. The purge toppled eight members of the PCT Central Committee (for "ideological deficiency") including the mayor of Brazzaville, the chairman of the youth movement (accused of witchcraft), four Politburo members (including Ndalla and Raoul), and a wide assortment of state officials such as the president of the Supreme Court, the mayor of Pointe Noire, and four of the government's nine regional commissioners.[84] Once again the dividing lines were

81. "Brazzaville: Ten Years of Revolution," part 2.

82. Ibid.

83. *Jeune Afrique*, March 11, 1972, and *Afrique Nouvelle*, December 8, 1971. See also *Africa Research Bulletin*, December 1971.

84. *Le Monde*, December 18, 1971.

not really on a left-right axis; rather, this was Ngouabi's settling of accounts with his opposition, the result being the strengthening those who were primarily loyal to Ngouabi, whether moderate or radical. The few remaining "independent" figures that survived the purge, such as Noumazalay, Poungui, and Diawara, suffered an eclipse in power and were removed from office in the second phase of the showdown.

However, the tenuous nature of Ngouabi's "victory" was strikingly demonstrated on February 22, 1972 when his regime survived its most serious challenge. Seizing the radio station with the aid of members of the infantry battalion under his command, Lieutenant Diawara caused temporary confusion in the security forces with the (false) announcement that he was moving to protect Ngouabi against a right-wing coup by Yhomby-Opango. The ruse nearly succeeded, for Ngouabi—then in Pointe Noire—hastily ordered the arrest of his loyal chief of staff. The latter, however, evaded arrest, marshaled his loyal troops, and crushed the short-lived rebellion.[85] For his prompt and loyal action Yhomby-Opango was later promoted to full colonel, the highest rank in the Congolese armed forces.

The ease with which Diawara could have achieved his goal, the hesitation, fence-straddling, and even support for the attempted putsch by elements in the army (including the undigested segments of the *gendarmerie*), and the rapid spread of the rebellion to other parts of the armed forces (such as the People's Militia under Lieutenant Ngolo) impressed upon Ngouabi the fragile nature of his hold over even his own military apparatus. The fact that Diawara and his principal aides were able to evade capture and continue residing in Brazzaville itself, while using public phones to solicit support for a renewed assault, in spite of a massive cordon, manhunt, and dragnet of informers severely shook Ngouabi, as it underscored the persistence of widespread opposition to his rule fully four years after he had assumed power.[86] It also rankled that

85. *West Africa*, March 10, 1972.

86. A wave of murders later in 1972 in Lari villages south of Brazzaville was attributed by the government to either Diawara supporters or to deserters from the Zaire-based Angolan National Liberation Front, though reliable sources maintain

several French Marxist teachers, especially recruited by Congo under France's technical cooperation program, were directly involved in the Diawara plot. For months prior to Diawara's death foreign observers commented on Ngouabi's "paranoid obsession" with his rival's whereabouts. As the usually reliable *Africa Confidential* pointed out, "it has been clear from the increasingly hysterical tone of some of Ngouabi's declarations that something had to happen about Diawara soon, or the regime would fall apart." [87] Only after Diawara was finally located and killed fourteen months later (and his corpse publicly displayed in Brazzaville to prevent the growth of a Matsouanist myth) did some of Ngouabi's public self-assurance begin to return.

Though Diawara's challenge to the regime was rationalized as an ideological dispute over socialist rectitude[88] it was primarily a continuation of the December 1971 personal power struggle.[89] The new political purge that followed Diawara's attempted coup badly truncated all state and party political organs and resulted in the arrest of Noumazalay, Ndalla, Raoul, and scores of others, many of whom could not have been ideologically connected with Diawara in any conceivable manner. In the subsequent trials 23 death sentences were passed (including one on Noumazalay); in typical Congolese style these were later commuted to life imprisonment, and by 1974 several of those convicted had been amnestied and two were back on the Politburo. Among the remaining 153 convictions Ndalla was sentenced to life imprisonment and Raoul to ten years.[90]

---

they were intended as intimidation by Mbochi agents of the government. The regime did its utmost to discredit Diawara by first calling him an admirer of Hitler who confused fascism with socialism and then accusing him of being a CIA agent. *West Africa*, March 17, 1972. See also Jean de la Gueriviere, "Republique populaire du Congo," pp. 22–23.

87. *Africa Confidential*, April 27, 1973.

88. The regime compared events in Brazzaville with events in China and Russia: "Who would have thought that Lin Piao would disappear from circulation? Or that Trotsky would betray Lenin's ideas? The socialist path is long, tortuous and full of pitfalls." See *Africa Contemporary Record*, 1972–73, p. B534.

89. *Le Monde*, March 11, 1972, notes that Ngouabi's opposition felt that he had *pushed* Diawara and his followers to mount their assault against the regime.

90. The trials aroused strong protests by Parisian leftists led by Sartre (*West Africa*, March 24, 1972). In the pardons announced in 1973 the regime stated it was

The power struggles of December 1971-February 1972 consolidated Ngouabi's position in the Congo but also exposed his reliance upon his control of the army (via Yhomby-Opango's iron loyalty) and the unswerving support of politicians such as Nze (promoted to the vice-presidency of the PCT) and literary prize winner Henri Lopes (soon to become premier). The army command was particularly demoralized by the attempted coup from its midst, the subsequent purges, and the continuing factional strife and plotting in the officer corps. Despite the shakeup in the security forces, army support for Diawara persisted and contributed to Ngouabi's acute unease until his rival was caught and killed. On a number of occasions in February 1973 Ngouabi—appearing in full combat uniform—sharply castigated the armed forces for their penchant for plotting and joining in coup attempts to gain personal and professional advancement. Boasting that he was "temporarily closing his eyes to what was going on" Ngouabi lashed out against the overpoliticization of the army: "Woe betide those who have not understood. . . . If people engage in coups d'état to become generals and colonels, well, we will arrange so that the highest rank in the Congolese army remains that of major." [91] On the latter occasion he announced the complete dismantling of the police force and the assumption of its duties by the army because of the discovery of yet another plot involving police personnel.[92] Officers from the paratroop battalion were also assigned to key state industries in conjunction with a major auditing and antiembezzlement drive aimed at reducing the enormous deficits of the state industries. (A year later Ngouabi was to complain about the fiscal irregularities of army personnel co-opted into the state industries.)

Congo's political institutions were also ravaged by the purges attending the December 1971–February 1972 power struggle. Indeed, the internal PCT housecleaning was on such a scale that it seriously depleted the party of both top officials and rank and

---

establishing a distinction between "incorrigible anti-Marxists," "tribal reactionaries led by Bernard Kolela," and the "deviationist gang led by Ange Diawara." See *Le Monde*, October 30, 1973.

91. *Africa Research Bulletin*, March 1973.

92. *West Africa*, February 26, 1973.

file.[93] Massive arrests throughout the country of "deviationist" party officials (that is, militants suspected of being Diawara followers) practically closed down a large number of PCT branches and brought party activities to a standstill elsewhere. The decimation of the party organization destroyed Ngouabi's facade of civil-military legitimacy and required massive infusions of new blood into the various hierarchies. Toward this end, the PCT Congress scheduled for 1974 was urgently convened late in 1972. The handpicked delegates promptly produced a new constitution (Congo's fourth).[94] new state structures such as a People's Assembly, and a slate of new appointees to staff the party administration.

The popular referendum that ratified the new constitution and the resolutions of the PCT Congress once again revealed the intensity and multiplicity of Congo's ethnic cleavages. Though 73.4 percent of the voters (in an 83.1 percent turnout) approved the constitution, voting followed ethnic lines. Abstentions and negative votes outnumbered positive votes in the Bakongo concentrations in the south. In Brazzaville's Bakongo districts 60 percent of the voters rejected the proposals, while in the Poto Poto quarter (Mbochi) 90 percent of the voters approved them.[95] No clear majority emerged either for or against the constitution in Congo's other main urban centers, Dolisie, Jacob, and Pointe Noire. Thus, despite the "constitutionalization" of the regime and the emergence of a new Politburo, Central Committee, and party administration, the tensions and contradictions inherent in the political system were hardly affected.

In sum, Ngouabi has been unable to establish either political peace or a new political order in Congo, just as these twin tasks evaded his predecessors. Indeed, under military rule the pace and intensity of disorder has been heightened because of the total—and possibly irrevocable—politicization of the armed forces. It is difficult today even to state that Ngouabi fully controls the army, let alone the armed forces, as he once did when he was the direct

93. For a partial list of those purged in the first phase see *Le Monde*, December 18, 1971.

94. Congo's previous constitutions dated from 1961, 1963, and 1970.

95. *West Africa*, July 9, 1973.

commander of the paratroop battalion. Though nominally loyal, the army is thoroughly riddled with highly autonomous factional cliques and mutual advancement alliances that can neither be checked nor controlled. Their support for the Ngouabi regime is essentially conditional upon the noninterference of the regime in their lucrative economic enterprises and/or personal power empires. An indication of the prevalence of these "private armies" are the increasingly frequent speeches in which Ngouabi has lashed out at the bourgeois and mercantilist tendencies of the armed forces; these diatribes are unaccompanied, however, by either demotions or disciplinary action against offenders.

Moreover, the rapid shifts in political loyalty in the country have necessitated continuous rotation of command personnel in the armed forces to avert the creation of alliances inimical to Ngouabi's position. Not even Yhomby-Opango was immune to this periodic reshuffling. Elevated to the highest rank in the army for his role in crushing the Diawara uprising, Yhomby was abruptly dismissed from his post in September 1973, being replaced by his deputy, Captain Victor Tsika Kabala. After being placed temporarily under house arrest (due to rumors that he was becoming "politically interested")[96] Yhomby was first appointed inspector general of the Army (a nonoperational command position) and then integrated into the Council of State as secretary-general with ministerial rank.

On September 26, 1974, it was announced that once again the armed forces command hierarchy would be reorganized to assure the fealty of the force to civilian and party control. (The armed forces had already been "reorganized" in October 1973 when Yhomby was appointed inspector general.)[97] Among the new structures set up for this purpose and headed by Ngouabi were a Defense Council dealing with general policies and a Defense Committee—a military high command—dealing with the specific details of training, promotion, ideological indoctrination, and so forth. The Defense Committee included Colonel Yhomby (as

96. From interviews in Washington (December 1974).
97. See *West Africa*, October 29, 1973.

Council of State delegate for defence and security, a newly created post), by now back in the good graces of the regime. At the same time the command of the General Staff was given to Major Louis Sylvain Goma (previously minister of public works and transport and a former chief of staff and defence minister), assisted by five deputies in charge of public security, Peoples' Militia, armed forces, political affairs, and economic affairs.[98] It is an open question whether this structural reorganization will fulfill its function of quelling revolts from within the armed forces. Certainly, however, the sources of such upheavals are neither structural nor amenable to simplistic solutions such as command reorganizations, and this helps explain Ngouabi's sensitivity to the vested economic interests of large segments of the armed forces.

The regime cannot afford to alienate the urban working and middle classes nor, for that matter, the increasing number of school graduates.[99] Despite an official policy of austerity, the size of the civil service slowly increased through 1974, and the national budget was squeezed to provide larger allocations for "sovereignty, security, and foreign commitments" [100]—that is, the armed forces. The pressure in Brazzaville for civil service jobs, compensation for spiraling inflation, and satisfaction of the demands of the armed forces were so intense that clampdowns on such expenditures could well have sparked a general upheaval. Early in 1975, flush with major new oil revenues, the regime announced important concessions to the urban masses when minimum wages were boosted by 80 percent and price freezes were declared on many staples. Clashes between the government and youth continued, however, and climaxed with Ngouabi's decision early in 1974 that scholarship disbursements would be made monthly (instead of by semester) and would be granted only to ideologically "good"

98. *Africa Research Bulletin,* October 1974.

99. Up to 90 percent are unemployed. The situation was so bad in 1971 that secondary school graduates were asked to attend school for another year since there were no job openings for them anywhere.

100. The 1972 budget, for example, included a 30 percent increase in such allocations. See *Africa Research Bulletin,* Economic, Financial and Technical Series, January 1972. See also *West Africa,* December 3, 1973, for new increases in defense allocations in the 1974 budget.

elements from the poorer strata of society. This decision came in the wake of a little-reported but major student upheaval at Brazzaville's university in which twenty-four student leaders were expelled (for "reactionary" attitudes) and drafted into the army for two years.[101] Simultaneously the General Union of Students and High School Pupils was banned (for its "shameful, anarchist, antinational, and dogmatic attitude"),[102] and a "structural reorganization"—the creation of a twenty-two person governing council with Ngouabi as chairman—was decreed as the solution to university unrest.

The regime has also been sensitive to complaints by domestic traders of foreign African competition, and in mid-1972 various restrictions were placed on non-Congolese merchants. But it was only after the 1973 war in the Middle East, which brought in its wake the united cartel of oil-producing nations and a quadrupling of oil prices, that Brazzaville's regime began to assert itself vis-à-vis companies owned by French expatriates in Congo. The first major decrees came in January 1974. After complaining publicly several times about the paradox of increased Congolese oil exports from the Pointe Noire region accompanied by declines in available supplies of refined oil in the country, Ngouabi announced the nationalization of all oil companies. Though the nationalization decree was not as straightforward as it sounded, it did result in a sixfold increase in government income from Elf-Erap, the oil company.[103] These new funds constituted some 75 percent of Congo's greatly expanded 1974 and 1975 budgets and were channeled into the ailing and quasi-bankrupt state enterprises,[104]

101. *West Africa*, February 4 and 11, 1974. Later it was revealed that the students were allowed to continue studying in army barracks and were to be demobilized at the end of the semester.

102. *West Africa*, April 8, 1974.

103. Ibid., February 4, 1974.

104. One example of the gross mismanagement and plundering of the state sector is provided by S.I.A.-Congo, the country's sugar company and largest industrial unit. The company has been having an annual deficit of 1,000 million CFA francs (four million dollars) when original projections and, later, expert evaluations posited a net annual profit of 2,000 million CFA—see *Le Monde*, April 30, 1975. In 1974 some 4,000 million CFA were spent to sustain the state enterprises, most of which had been set up with expectations of profitability.

and into an ambitious three-year development plan. The oil bonanza also allowed the regime to reduce the national debt and to capitulate to unionist strikes for across-the-board salary increases that had previously been opposed.[105] Other measures were announced in March, nationalizing all private insurance companies and giving the state a majority holding in all foreign banks.[106] At the same time the regime declared that it would not allow any new private investment projects unless state funds were also involved in the form of joint companies.

Thus Ngouabi's regime has only recently begun to adopt economic nationalism, less under the instigation of local elements or the dictates of its own ideology than as a result of external events and forces. The regime has adroitly appealed for, and received, development assistance from a wide array of international donors. However, much of this aid has been used for the creation of sinecures for the hard-pressed middle class and army command. The impotence with which both party and army chief of staff face the blatant dissipation of scarce resources and the myriad challenges to authority in Brazzaville is a striking testament to Congo's full-blown praetorian system.

105. *West Africa*, August 11, 1975.
106. Ibid., February 4, 1974.

5 The Politics of the Personalist Coup: Uganda

Few African states have received such a flood of scholarly attention as Uganda since it was catapulted into world prominence by the rise of General Idi Amin in January 1971. Possibly more than in any other military regime in Africa the demise of civilian rule has resulted in dramatic shifts in national priorities and international linkages. These reorientations, however, have been largely a consequence of Amin's peculiar political style and less the result of a planned program of action by the military as a whole. Uganda's experience with civil-military relations and military rule is invaluable for comparative purposes not only because it provides an East African and ex-British tutelary example, but also because it illustrates a relatively rare case of personalist dictatorship and "imperial style" [1] in black Africa.

ETHNIC CLEAVAGES AND CULTURAL SUBNATIONALISM

As elsewhere, at the core of some of Uganda's most intractable political problems is a historic power imbalance, which has resulted in an unequal socioeconomic development of the country's ethnic components. Uganda's estimated population of 9.5 million is divided among twenty-one major ethnic groups, or thirty-odd tribes, eighteen of which number over 100,000 (see table 5.1). The country is also the geographical juncture of Bantu, Nilotic, Nilo-Hamitic, and Sudanic language families, segments of the latter three having been brought under effective central control only in the 1920s. The different forms of internal social organization of the various ethnic components of these linguistic groups (and in particular, the cleavage between "decentralized" and "centralized" forms of social control), assured wide disparities in their reactions to Western influences and modernization.[2] More-

---

1. See Samuel Decalo, "The Imperial Style in Africa."
2. See Meyer Fortes and E. E. Evans-Pritchard, *African Political Systems*, p. 5.

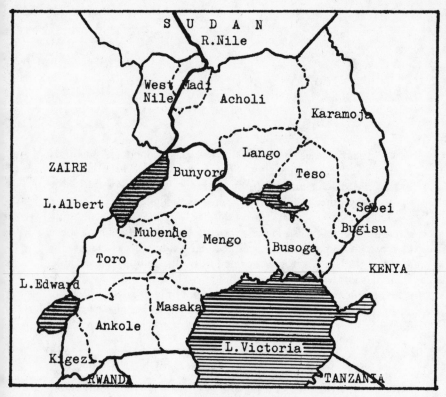

UGANDA

over, the region has been the arena for persistent ethnic conflict between southern Bantu tribes and Nilotic and Nilo-Hamitic groups. The latter two have traditionally feared and resisted Bantu expansion and domination and have carried their mistrust and resistance into the modern era.

TABLE 5.1
Uganda Major Tribes, 1959

Tribe	Population
Baganda	1,044,878
Iteso	524,716
Banyankole	519,283
Basoga	501,921
Bakiga	459,616
Banyaruanda	378,656
Lango	363,807
Bagisu	329,257
Acholi	284,929
Lugbara	236,270
Batoro	208,300
Banyoro	188,374

Source: East African Statistical Department, *Uganda General African Census.*
Note: Recent estimates put the entire population at 9.5 million with figures for the Baganda 50 percent higher than those of the 1959 census and similar increases for other ethnic groups.

When colonial rule was imposed over the territory that became Uganda there were several kingdoms in the country vying for military primacy. The British intrusion in the area overlapped with a renewed tug-of-war between Buganda and Bunyoro, the two most developed and centralized kingdoms, with the smaller Toro, Ankole, and Busoga essentially tributary states to one or another of the two protagonists.[3] This latest phase of intertribal warfare in the

3. For some representative literature on the various ethnic groups and kingdoms in Uganda see in particular: J. H. M. Beattie, "Bunyoro"; idem, *Bunyoro*; Lloyd A. Fallers, *Bantu Bureaucracy*; idem, *Inequality*; idem, *The King's Men*; idem, *Law*

region's history of intense strife saw the erosion of Bunyoro's former supremacy and the militant reassertion of Buganda. Still, the latter might have remained but one of several powerful states had it not been for British aspirations in East Africa. Anglo-Bugandan mutual interests led to a de facto military alliance between them that brought about the total eclipse of Bunyoro power, the large-scale northward expansion of British authority (into Langi, Acholi, and Madi areas), and the establishment of the undisputed primacy of Buganda within the new British colony.[4] Buganda's rise to preeminence as a surrogate conqueror and, later, administrator sharpened existing interethnic resentments and complicated national integration in the modern era. At the same time the British practice of indirect rule via traditional authority froze and institutionalized the country's ethnic cleavages, encouraged the emergence of subnationalisms, and helped powerful traditional elites survive at the expense of modern political authority.

Buganda's historic special relationship with the colonial power was confirmed by the protectorate status granted it and by the 1900 Uganda Agreement that spelled out several mutual obligations.[5] The primary long-run outcome of the agreement was that it appeared to reaffirm the contention of Buganda elites as to their kingdom's uniqueness and preeminence in the colony. The fact that Buganda had accepted colonial rule as a result not of military defeat or conquest but of negotiations (based upon a multitude of opportunistic considerations on the part of the palace nobility and clan chiefs) had immense consequences for the future of all Uganda. For, though neither a binding treaty nor a constitution and soon losing whatever value it ever had in a fast-changing

---

Without Precedent; J. Middleton, *The Lugbara of Uganda*; K. Oberk, "The Kingdom of Ankole in Uganda"; C. Kottak, "Ecological Variables in the Origin and Evolution of African States"; M. S. M. Kiwanuku, *A History of Buganda to 1900*; A. R. Dunbar, *A History of Bunyoro-Kitara*. Kenneth Ingham, *The Kingdom of Toro in Uganda*.

4. See K. Ingham, *The Making of Modern Uganda*; M. S. M. Kiwanuku, "Bunyoro and the British."

5. In this connection see also A. Low, "The British and the Baganda"; Donald A. Low and R. Cranford Pratt, *Buganda and British Over-rule 1900–1955*; Donald A. Low, *The Mind of Buganda*; idem, *Buganda in Modern History*.

world, the 1900 Agreement was regarded by Buganda's kabaka (king) as attesting to the kingdom's coequal status with the colonial power. From this stemmed the concept that Buganda possessed the right to abrogate the protectorate relationship—as it indeed tried to in 1960[6]—whenever the kingdom's basic interests appeared threatened. This view strongly gained ground in the kabaka's palace with the advent of modern politics. The prospect of universal franchise and socioeconomic promotion of the less developed regimes directly threatened the kabaka's supreme political status within Buganda and the latter's preeminence in Uganda. For the ultimate result of any such policies would have been the electoral subjugation of Buganda to the dictates of the entire colony and the rise of a political leader above the social status of the kabaka himself, a sacrilege to the hallowed, quasi-divine status of the Buganda throne. Thus tensions and contradictions between concepts of Bugandan and Ugandan nationalism or, put differently, Ugandan unity and Ganda[7] separatism, are at the root of much of the unrest since the early 1950s.

Moreover, with British assistance Buganda had made large territorial gains in the precolonial phase of the elimination of Bunyoro power and had been poised for far more ambitious ones when reined in. These gains became the festering Bunyoro "Lost Counties" irredentist issue that poisoned Buganda's relations with neighboring kingdoms for over seventy years. The resolution of the issue against Buganda by the non-Ganda President Obote (in the 1964 referendum) underscored the kingdom's rapid loss of autonomy and control over events within independent Uganda, giving extra drive and urgency to Ganda separatist feelings.

The location of the colony's capital (and hence the government and commerce) in Buganda territory automatically assured a much more thorough, widespread, and deeper Western impact upon Ganda than non-Ganda society. Led by traditional elites—as was not the case elsewhere in Africa—the Ganda enthusiastically

---

6. See *Buganda's Independence*.

7. The word *ganda* is one of two adjectival forms for Buganda, the second being *kiganda*. With other prefixes *ganda* refers to the country (Buganda), the people (Baganda), an individual (Muganda), and the language of Buganda (Luganda).

embraced modern concepts of Western religion, cultivation, and education, becoming the most modern, well-educated, and prosperous group in the country. Indeed both the government and the missionary societies were hardpressed to satisfy the burgeoning demand for education and services. Yet at the same time the Baganda retained their traditional cultural and political values and their sense of cultural superiority.[8] This latter outlook and Buganda's frequently expressed arrogance as modernizing pacesetter for the colony further alienated traditional enemies as well as newly integrated peripheral groups, especially in the north.

The cleavages internal to Ganda society were thus not between conservative chiefs and a growing Westernized youth. Rather, as Fallers notes, "Ganda society has acculturated, as it were, from the top down, and hence the new culture tends to have universal legitimacy. . . . keeping a sense of cultural integrity and wholeness through a period of radical change."[9] Or, as Renwick has commented with respect to university students, "the younger elite has acquired neither a class consciousness nor a class culture. In fact the student is still linked to his tribal heritage in thought and speech, with a restricted and parochial outlook."[10] In particular, the strong personal loyalties of the Ganda to their kabaka have not been significantly eroded. These loyalties were tested on several occasions in the past (for example, when the kabaka was exiled by the British governor in 1953, when the Democratic party tried to garner support in Buganda, and when the monarchy was abolished in 1966) and have proved durable despite the challenges. The somewhat paradoxical situation thus arose where the most developed and sophisticated part of Uganda, which gave the country a powerful impulse toward modernization, was also the stronghold of ethnic chauvinism, restrictive cultural exclusiveness, and political traditionalism, with the contemporary impetus and pressure for national unification and political modernization increasingly coming from non-Baganda areas and elites.[11]

8. Fallers, *The King's Men*, p. 3. See also H. F. Morris, "Buganda and Tribalism."

9. Fallers, *Inequality*, p. 159.

10. Allan Renwick, "Makerere and Uganda's Elite," p. 11.

11. Fallers, *Inequality*, p. 159. See also Nelson Kasfir, "Cultural Subnationalism

The British encouraged the development of Buganda as the nucleus of the colony and a source of trained personnel for their administrative hierarchy. (At the same time the British followed a policy of recruiting into the police and armed forces elements from the less developed allegedly "warlike" northern populations.) Ganda administrators percolated into a wide variety of posts throughout the country, frequently introducing their forms of social organization or administration. This form of internal "colonialism,"[12] the often forcible introduction of Luganda language, and the condescending mannerisms of the Ganda bureaucracy evoked deep resentments that were not easily forgotten. Though with the spread of education to the hinterlands the early pro-Buganda bias was slowly corrected, the early Ganda advantage in most spheres of endeavor (except commerce, which they shunned) widened the gaps between the Ganda and many other ethnic groups. As late as 1960 statistics reflected the disparities among Uganda's different ethnic groups, as tables 5.2 and 5.3 illustrate.

A third major source of conflict in Uganda emerged with the spread of Christianity. In 1875 Stanley had sent his appeal to the *Daily Telegraph* for a greater missionary effort in the area. Two years later the influx of Catholic and Protestant workers began, greeted cordially by Kabaka Mutesa I—the thirtieth kabaka of Buganda—as a counterbalance to the Moslem threat from the coast and the expanding Egyptian empire to the north (parts of Acholi had been integrated into the latter's Equatoria province).[13] The fierce competition between Catholic and Protestant evangelists resulted in a major spurt in the building of schools and the spread of education, but it also polarized Buganda elites. Intense religious strife, massacres, and religious wars (in 1886 some 200 Christians were killed) characterized the early history of Christianity in Uganda as local political factions and ambitious aspirants became linked with one or another of the competing denominations, which

---

in Uganda"; David Apter, "The Role of Traditionalism in the Political Modernization of Ghana and Uganda"; May Edel, "African Tribalism: Some Reflections on Uganda."

12. A. D. Roberts, "The Sub-Imperialism of the Buganda."
13. J. Taylor, *The Growth of the Church in Buganda.*

TABLE 5.2
Uganda: Ethnic Representation in Education,
Police, and Higher Civil Service

Ethnic group	% of population, 1959	% of students in secondary schools, 1960	% of Makerere University African students, 1959	% of police force, 1961	% of higher civil service, 1961
Baganda	16.3	29.0	46.6	3.8	46.9
Iteso	8.1	10.6	6.1	15.2	2.0
Banyankole	8.1	6.5	6.1	2.6	4.1
Basoga	7.8	6.1	6.1	4.2	4.1
Banyaruanda	5.9	2.6	1.8	1.2	4.1
Langi	5.6	6.5	1.8	7.5	2.0
Acholi	4.4	7.1	4.3	15.5	4.1
Lugbara	3.7	2.6	0.4	4.5	2.0
Batoro	3.2	3.7	1.8	0.7	6.1
Banyoro	2.9	3.5	3.6	2.6	6.1
Karamajong	2.0	0.0	0.4	0.0	0.0
Alur	1.9	1.2	0.4	3.5	0.0
Madi	1.2	1.1	0.7	3.8	2.0
Samia	0.7	1.8	0.7	3.1	0.0
Kakwa	0.6	0.5	0.0	1.6	0.0
Jaluo	0.6	0.0	0.0	3.4	0.0

Source: Selected data from tables 2 and 4 in Kasfir, "Cultural Subnationalism," pp. 82–83, 127.

acted functionally as political parties. Ultimately, the British helped the Protestant factions to emerge victorious, and they established a political hegemony over Buganda. Yet statistical surveys indicate that fully 49 percent of the population profess to be Catholic as opposed to 28.2 percent Protestant and 5.6 percent Moslem though the latter have been consistently underestimated. This religious cleavage, reinforcing other social and political lines of division, remains a paramount polarizing force in Ugandan politics. A proper appreciation of the religious situation in Uganda is indispensable to the analysis of the political evolution of the

TABLE 5.3

Uganda: Language Group Representation in Education,
Police, and Higher Civil Service

Language group	% of population, 1959	% of students in secondary schools, 1960	% of Makerere University African students, 1959	% of police force, 1961	% of higher civil service, 1961
Bantu	65.7	66.3	81.5	29.8	85.7
Nilotic	14.5	16.6	9.3	34.8	8.2
Nilo-Hamitic	12.7	12.3	7.8	21.4	2.0
Sudanic	5.0	3.7	1.4	8.8	4.1
Other	2.1	1.1	0.0	5.3	0.0

Source: Part of tables 2 and 4 in Kasfir, "Cultural Subnationalism," pp. 83, 127.

country and underscores the magnitude of the societal upheaval
occasioned by General Amin's rise to power.

Until the elimination of the kabakaship in 1966 religious
affiliation was a primary criterion for upward mobility in the courts
and administration of Buganda, with patronage allocated on
denominational lines strongly biased in favor of Protestants. Thus,
for example, the allocation of the twenty *saza* (county) chieftain-
ships was strictly regulated along religious lines and the katikiro
(prime minister), treasurer, and other top administrators have
always been Protestant.[14] The situation—highly institutionalized
until the Christian denominations lost virtually all influence with
the advent of Amin's pro-Moslem policies and biases—assured the
proliferation of religious grievances. These were then transferred to
the political arena, with religious affiliation becoming the major
aggregative focus for political parties, which were popularly
identified as Protestant or Catholic.[15] In the preindependence

14. The denominational division of the kabaka's cabinet was traditionally four
Protestants, one Catholic, and one Moslem. Of the 20 *saza* chiefs, ten have
traditionally been Protestant and eight Catholic. In like manner this was the bias in
Ankole, Toro, and Bunyoro.

15. George W. Shepherd, Jr., "Modernization in Uganda," p. 324. See also F. B.
Welbourn, *Religion and Politics in Uganda 1952–1962*, and A. J. Hughes, *East Africa*,
p. 148.

elections the (Catholic) Democratic Party scored some significant victories in non-Ganda regions, because a vote for the DP became the political equivalent of venting one's frustrations at (Protestant) Buganda domination, though paradoxically most of the DP leaders were Catholic Ganda commoners. Within Buganda,[16] however, the predominance of Catholic adults in the voting population did not assure the rise to power of a Catholic party (such as the Democratic party), for by definition the latter was opposed to the Protestant kabaka and his court; any such victory would also have signified the totally unacceptable ascendance of a Ganda commoner over the quasi-divine kabaka.[17]

THE ECONOMIC BACKGROUND

When the British arrived, Buganda and the other major kingdoms had relatively well-established patterns of trade and commerce.[18] The transformation of the subsistence economy to one based on cash crops and catering to Europe's needs met with only moderate initial resistance. Both traditional leaders and peasants were quick to shift cultivation patterns and learn modern agricultural techniques. Cotton, and then coffee and tea, were introduced and were successful in Uganda's rich soil and high humidity.[19] From the outset these three commodities have constituted over three-fourths of Uganda's exports (see table 5.4).

Prospects for the expansion and development of Uganda's agriculture have always been considered bright.[20] The economy was regarded as basically buoyant, attracting the highest rates of investment and producing the largest per capita income growth in East Africa in the period 1960–65.[21] On the other hand, the

16. The Catholic-Protestant division in the rest of the country is much more equal.

17. See also K. G. Lockard, "Church-State Relations in Uganda 1962–1971."

18. Richard Gray and David Birmingham, eds., *Pre-Colonial African Trade: Essays in Central and Eastern Africa Before 1900*; C. C. Wrigley, *Buganda.*

19. For the shift in African outlooks on the cultivation of cotton see for example Uganda, *Report of the Uganda Cotton Commission*, pp. 29–30 inter alia.

20. See David H. Davis, *The Economic Development of Uganda.* Also, P. Clark, "Development Strategy in Early Stage Economy"; "Uganda 1972 Economic Survey."

21. *Uganda Argus*, December 20, 1966.

TABLE 5.4
Uganda: Principal Exports, 1964–71
(in thousands Ugandan £)

	Coffee	Cotton	Copper & alloys	Tea
1964	35,378	15,857	6,192	2,212
1965	30,421	16,762	7,994	2,388
1966	34,783	15,345	5,753	3,151
1967	34,600	15,160	5,470	3,480
1968	35,750	14,790	5,570	3,710
1969	38,996	12,548	6,014	4,653
1970	50,700	17,500	7,300	4,700
1971	49,117	17,595	6,887	4,772

Source: *Africa Contemporary Record.*

TABLE 5.5
Uganda: Imports/Exports 1962–71
(in millions Ugandan £)

	Imports	Exports	Balance of trade	Exports as % of imports
1962	14.0	40.6	+ 26.6	290.0
1963	18.2	54.8	+ 36.6	301.0
1964	32.8	66.4	+ 33.6	202.4
1965	40.8	63.9	+ 23.1	156.6
1966	42.9	67.0	+ 24.1	156.1
1967	41.3	65.5	+ 24.2	158.5
1968	43.8	66.3	+ 22.5	151.3
1969	45.5	69.9	+ 24.4	153.6
1970	43.3	87.0	+ 43.7	200.9
1971	68.1	84.0	+ 15.9	123.3

Source: Adapted from *Africa Contemporary Record*, vol. 1 (1968–69), vol. 2 (1969–70), and vol. 5 (1972–73).
Note: Postcoup figures are highly unreliable.

economy exhibited resistance to efforts at crop diversification, and the development of secondary industries has been slow. Perennial heavy dependence upon a few primary commodities subject to major vicissitudes in world market prices, coupled with the vagaries of private capital transfers (acute in light of the presence until

Amin's rise of Uganda's sensitive Asian minority), have all played havoc with attempts at orderly economic planning and budget balancing.

Thus, despite a positive trade balance (see table 5.5), which camouflaged, however, periods of stagnant commodity prices paid to farmers and fluctuations in crop production, services, invisibles, and transfer payments (which shot up sharply with Obote's leftward veer in 1969) contributed to the creation of balance of payments deficits and shrinkages in hard currency reserves. Such a situation developed in particular in 1970 and 1971, when a drop in coffee production (to 175,400 metric tons from a record high of 247,243 tons in 1969), combined with low world market prices, contributed to a major balance of payments crisis.

Poor budgetary controls, lack of adequate fiscal responsibility, corruption, and periodic massive overspending (especially by the military)[22] have also been recurrent problems. Deficit spending has cut into approved developmental budgets, slowing down programs of public investment in the country's growth.[23] (For Uganda's budgets see table 5.6.)

Neither the First (1962–66), Second (1966–70), nor Third (1971–

TABLE 5.6
Uganda: Budgets, 1968–73
(in millions Ugandan shillings)

	Recurrent expenditures	Development expenditures
1968–69	981	443
1969–70	1,025	412
1970–71	1,201	832
1971–72	1,364	837
1972–73	1,430	640

Note: Compiled from a variety of governmental sources. Figures are not highly reliable in light of major fluctuations in reported sums.

22. See, for example, *Uganda Argus*, June 18 and 20, 1969.
23. See Michael Tribe, "Uganda 1971."

76) Five-Year Development Plans attained their projected targets, and the GDP growth rate steadily declined from an annual pre-1966 average of 5.2 percent (and a 7.2 percent projection) to 4.8 percent during 1966–69, 3.2 percent in 1970, and 2.1 percent in 1971.[24] Since the military takeover, recurrent regular and development budget deficit expenditures have become the undisguised norm, with massive unbudgeted spending grossly inflating aggregate deficits at the end of fiscal years. Thus the planned deficits of 1970–71, 1971–72, and 1972–73 budgeted at, respectively, U£4.875 million, U£6.5 million, and U£14.95 million were exceeded by 245 percent, 267 percent, and 290 percent,[25] due largely to expenditures for (and fiscal irregularities by) the armed forces. These uncontrolled expenditures rapidly exhausted the central bank's capital reserves at a time when all foreign sources of financial assistance dried up as a result of Amin's increasingly erratic foreign and domestic policies. The quasi bankruptcy of the treasury and the country's isolation from the major money markets provided the backdrop against which Uganda's foreign policy was realigned toward the oil-rich states of the Arab Middle East.

THE ASIAN MINORITY

The rapid expansion of the Ugandan economy during the early years of colonial rule further entrenched the already dominant position of Buganda, whose farmers were among the first to extensively plant cotton and other cash crops. (The center of the cotton industry later shifted eastward.) The spurt in agricultural exports constituted a rationale for the extension of the railroad from the coast to Kampala, a virtual sine qua non for the export of Uganda's crops. And this in turn brought about a major influx of Asians (Indians and Pakistanis) from abroad.

The speed with which Asian traders and entrepreneurs moved in to monopolize large sectors of trade, commerce, and small industry, despite a host of restrictive and discriminatory British (and

24. "Uganda," *Africa 1973* (London: Africa Journal Ltd, 1973), p. 182.
25. Ibid., p. 183.

later Ugandan) legislation designed to contain their activities, is a cogent testimonial to the middleman role vacuum in the country as its economy developed. Capitalizing on Ugandans' lack of training, opportunity, capital, and inclinations, Asian entrepreneurs played a vital role in modernizing and building the country's economy, both prospering and becoming an indispensable class in the process.[26] By 1910 a three-tiered functional division of labor appeared to have emerged in Uganda as elsewhere in East Africa: "Administration and agricultural development were thought to be European occupations; trade and craftsmanship were relegated to Indians; and Africans were encouraged to work in the European agricultural system and to supply cheap labour in the towns. . . . The picture did not substantially change in the next forty years." [27]

The 1966 Ugandan census revealed the magnitude of the Asians' role in the economy in reporting that they controlled fully 73.6 percent of the wholesale trade as compared to Europeans' 21.5 percent and Africans' 4.6 percent. Indeed, as early as 1925 100 of the 145 cotton gins in the country were owned by Indians while Asian retailers, fewer in absolute numbers than their African competitors, controlled most of the retail trade as well.[28]

The social, economic, and religious exclusiveness of Uganda's Asian community, estimated at over 80,000 in 1970, and concentrated in urban centers or exposed as lone shopowners or traders in the countryside, attracted envy, mistrust, and hatred. Violent boycotts of Asian traders erupted in 1959, venting these dammed up feelings.[29] Though many Asians had been born in Uganda and considered it their home, and a growing number had entered specialized professions, staffing hospitals, clinics, and the civil service, the community was popularly viewed as engaged in mass hoarding, price gouging, and other commercial sharp practices, as split in its loyalties to Uganda, and as contributing to the country's growing outflow of private capital.

26. H. F. Morris, *The Indians in Uganda*; Dharam P. Ghai and Yash P. Ghai, eds., *Portrait of a Minority*; J. S. Mangat, *A History of the Asians in East Africa c. 1886 to 1945*.

27. Morris, *The Indians in Uganda*, p. 11.

28. See Jack D. Parson, "Africanizing Trade in Uganda," p. 62.

29. Dharam P. Ghai, "The Bugandan Trade Boycott."

The regime of Milton Obote tried to cope with popular frustration at the Asians' economic stranglehold by furthering the centralization and Africanization of the agricultural and marketing sectors. The collection, processing, and marketing of cotton, coffee, and tobacco, for example, were decreed to be fully under the control of African cooperatives and marketing boards. Obote also initiated legislation that encouraged the small Asian traders to emigrate, while at the same time he harnessed the expertise and capital of the wealthier Asians (such as the Mahdvani and Mehta families) in the development of secondary industry. In 1968 a government Commission on Africanization of Commerce and Industry urged a major program of Africanization. The commission's report deplored the situation in the private sector, where only 64 percent of positions were held by Africans, and in the professions, where only 20 percent of the top positions were staffed by nationals.[30] While the government did not accept all the recommendations, new restrictive and discriminatory legislation was introduced against commercial activities by noncitizens.[31] Obote's shift to the left with his *Common Man's Charter* and other pronouncements seemed to presage a major program of expropriation of Asian enterprises and gave the final impetus to the massive outflow of private capital that developed in 1970. (See table 5.7.) Inheriting the complex and multifaceted problem a year later, General Amin put an end to the "Asian problem" by ordering the mass expulsion of the entire Asian community. This simplistic "solution," its callousness notwithstanding, cogently reflected the pent up grievances, frustrations, and prejudices of the average Ugandan against Asian influence and economic power.

OBOTE AND THE POLITICS OF ETHNIC ALLIANCES

It has been said that in Uganda it was not nationalist agitation that led to independence, but rather the imminence of independence that gave birth to nationalist parties.[32] Regionalism, ethnic cleavages, and strong Bugandan cultural subnationalism worked

30. See *Uganda Argus*, October 4, 1968, and January 21, 1969.
31. Ibid., October 29, 1969.
32. Donald Rothchild and Michael Rogin, "Uganda," p. 351.

TABLE 5.7
Uganda: Direction of Flow of Private Capital, 1966–70
(in millions Ugandan shillings)

	Inflow	Outflow	Balance
1966	113.0	28.0	+ 85.0
1967	115.7	57.6	+ 58.1
1968	158.0	159.7	− 1.7
1969	174.0	193.7	− 17.6
1970	19.0	313.6	− 294.6

Source: *Bank of Uganda Quarterly Bulletin*, March 1971, p. 21, cited in
Selwyn Ryan, "Economic Nationalism and Socialism in Uganda,"
Journal of Commonwealth Political Studies, July 1973, p. 144.

against the early emergence of true nationalist leaders. The British
policy of indirect rule and later the emphasis upon local politics
entrenched the country's political divisiveness and assured lack of
popular concern or involvement with the central administration.[33]
Moreover, the intensity of Ganda exclusiveness and self-preoccu-
pation denied the nationalist movement the benefit of leadership
and mass support from the country's most politically advanced
segment.

The political evolution of Uganda is essentially the history of the
tug-of-war between Bugandan separatism and the idea of a
Ugandan nation; between modern political authority based upon
non-Baganda regional ethnic alliances and the concept of the
supremacy of the kabaka and traditional authority. Intertwined
with this struggle are center-periphery, Catholic-Protestant, civil-
military, and personality competitions. The 1965–66 constitutional
crisis and abolition of the kabakaship marked the ostensible
triumph of the "nationalist" alliance; the 1971 coup that raised
Amin to power and brought in both Nilotic and Moslem elements
underscored the weakness of the elite that won in 1966 and marked
the political assertion of the neglected periphery, societal as well as
geographical.

33. Kasfir, "Cultural Subnationalism," p. 73. See also R. C. Pratt, "Nationalism
in Uganda."

Ugandan parties have traditionally been decentralized cadres beholden to local interests, riveted to parochial issues, rent by internal lines of division along personality and regional/district lines, and popularly identified in terms of their religious denomination and pro- or anti-Buganda coloration.[34] Ganda politicians were grossly overrepresented in the higher echelons of political movements, including those that aspired to establish nationalist credentials. Yet because of ethnic, clan, or district pressures, local candidates constituted the vast majority of party slates at election time. Thus, for example, in 1961 fully 95 percent of the 185 African candidates for office had been born within the districts in which they were contesting an assembly seat.[35]

The preponderance of Ganda leadership in the postwar political parties worked against their mass acceptance outside Buganda, since they were invariably perceived as ill-disguised efforts to perpetuate or impose Ganda domination. At the same time political parties fared poorly within Buganda. For until the creation of the Kabaka Yekka (King Alone) movement in 1961, all parties operated without the blessing of the kabaka or his government (the Lukiiko) and were frequently headed either by Catholics or by members of minority clans who were viewed by the bulk of the population as inimical to the status of the kabaka. Indeed, the very concepts of direct election of national candidates (instead of their election or selection by the Lukiiko) and the replacement of British rule by the authority of an indigenous government composed of Ganda commoners and "second-class" ethnic groups were antithetical to the traditional concept of the supreme status of the kabakaship.[36]

Essentially because of these factors the Democratic party—the first major political formation that seriously embarked upon the quest for national power—failed to make a lasting impact on Ugandan politics. Founded in 1956 and composed primarily of

34. See Donald A. Low, *Political Parties in Uganda 1949–1962; David Apter, The Political Kingdom in Uganda*, especially chapter 14; Grace S. K. Ibingira, *The Forging of an African Nation*; and Cherry Gertzel, *Party and Locality in Northern Uganda, 1945–1962.*

35. Kasfir, "Cultural Subnationalism," p. 87.

36. See Lloyd A. Fallers, "Ideology and Culture in Uganda Nationalism."

Ganda Catholics with deep-seated personal and religious grievances against the establishment's historic discrimination against
Catholics,[37] the DP—supported by the powerful Catholic missions
—linked up with other Catholic elements in Acholi, Lango, and the
West Nile. The party also obtained some support in non-Ganda
southern districts (where it was seen as an antikabaka movement)
in exchange for promises of reciprocal support on divisive local
issues. Yet notwithstanding the numerical superiority of Catholics
in Buganda and festering resentments among descendants of chiefs
persecuted during religious wars, the DP was totally unsuccessful
in gaining support in its own home territory. The kabaka's call for a
boycott of the March 1961 elections was heeded by 98 percent of
the population who placed support for their king above religious
considerations and only 35,000 voters registered to vote. The
paradoxical outcome was that with insignificant support in Buganda the DP, led by Kampala lawyer Benedicto Kiwanuka,
carried twenty of Buganda's twenty-one seats and, with scattered
electoral victories elsewhere, was called upon to form Uganda's
first African government.[38]

With the Baganda abstaining from politics in the 1961 elections,
Kiwanuka's major competitor was the "Protestant," militant Uganda People's Congress of Milton Obote. (In the heated campaign
Catholic priests dubbed it communist and anti-Christ.) The UPC
was the end result of a series of opportunistic splits and mergers
from Uganda's oldest "national" party, the Uganda National
Congress,[39] in which personality and ethnic differences and competitions played a major role. Formed in 1960 by Obote (who is of
chiefly descent and was at the time the Lango representative to the
Legislative Council), the UPC was essentially the more militant

37. The DP's first president, a former Buganda government minister, barely failed
to become the first Catholic *katikiro* (premier) in 1955, allegedly following the
kabaka's intervention. See Apter, *The Political Kingdom*, p. 341. Low, *Political
Parties in Uganda*, p. 22, refers to the DP as "almost exclusively Roman Catholic in
inspiration and membership."

38. The DP gained forty-three seats, with 407,816 votes; Obote's UPC received
488,332 votes and thirty-five seats.

39. The UNC's lack on coherent programs and general procrastination led to its
internal decomposition and decline.

non-Ganda wing of the UNC and hence without support in Buganda. Decentralized and lacking strong organization or a true mass following despite its nationalist posture, the party's main electoral bases were in Lango, Acholi, Toro, and Busoga—traditionally anti-Buganda areas; later, advocating a referendum in the "Lost Counties" to settle the festering territorial dispute (between Buganda and Bunyoro) the UPC garnered important Bunyoro support.

The third political movement that played a dominant role in the immediate pre- and postindependence era was the Kabaka Yekka, formed after Buganda's pro forma January 1, 1961, independence declaration fizzled out[40] and its March 1961 electoral boycott failed to halt the country's constitutional evolution. Sparked by the spectacle of the detested DP representing Buganda and encouraged by feelers from the UPC for a tactical anti-DP alliance, the Kabaka Yekka was set up to protect the privileges of the monarchy and the status of Buganda.[41] The immediate goals of the KY were to capture Buganda's electoral seats and to obtain the best possible terms from the British in the rapidly approaching independence negotiations. Tapping the strong Ganda loyalties to the kabakaship the new party transformed Uganda's political array of power practically overnight. Less than a year after it was formed the Kabaka Yekka won sixty-five of the Lukiiko's sixty-eight seats and appointed all of the province's representatives in the April 1962 elections in an alliance with the UPC that became the ruling coalition of independent Uganda (see table 5.8).

The UPC-KY coalition provided major advantages to both partners despite the fact that it was an alliance of complete opposites. Since the DP had been proven to be an electoral straw man in Buganda though it was the UPC's major threat outside that province, and since the KY and DP were totally incompatible, the only possible parliamentary alliance in Uganda was that between

40. See the two pamphlets of the kabaka's government, *Buganda's Position* and *Buganda's Independence.*

41. See C. Gertzel, "How the Kabaka Yekka Came to Be"; I. R. Hancock, "Patriotism and Neo-Traditionalism in Buganda"; and Kasfir, "Cultural Subnationalism," pp. 89–94.

TABLE 5.8
Uganda: Composition of the National Assembly, 1962

Party	Regular seats	Special seats (elected by assembly)	Total
UPC	37	6	43
DP	24	—	24
KY	21	3	24
Total	82	9	91

Obote and the Kabaka Yekka. To the KY the coalition meant the elimination of DP government and major constitutional concessions—wrung from the British and the UPC—that gave Buganda internal autonomy within a quasi-federal system. The direct elections issue was also settled in favor of Buganda with the concession that the Lukiiko would continue to elect the region's National Assembly representatives. Finally, the kabaka, "Freddy" Mutesa II, was appointed nonexecutive president of Uganda "perpetuating" the tradition that no commoner could rise above the kabaka of Buganda.[42]

The coalition was, however, inherently unstable on many grounds, not least of which was the ideological incompatibility of the KY, which was traditionalist and inward-looking, and the UPC, which progressively developed a vocal socialist and pan-Africanist wing. The constitutional concessions granted Buganda's traditionalists irritated the colorless Obote, who aspired to make his mark on Africa by following the socialist footsteps of his mentor, Tanzania's Julius Nyerere. Moreover, the elimination of the DP, their common adversary, set loose disintegrative forces within both parties. The result of this process was on the one hand the internal UPC power challenge against Obote's leadership and on the other the kabaka's loss of control over his KY representatives in Kampala; and Buganda's third secessionist attempt in twelve years.

42. For a discussion of the constitutional provisions of the First Republic see Ibingira, *Forging of an African Nation*, pp. 212 ff., and Rothchild and Rogin, "Uganda," pp. 370–79. See also G. F. Engholm, "The Westminster Model in Uganda."

The Kabaka Yekka had never been a unified movement or a party machine but rather a structural umbrella for secessionist, moderate, and Bugandan expansionist factions linked by a common distaste for the DP.[43] The parliamentary coalition with the more nationalist and radical UPC in Kampala slowly drove a wedge between the moderate KY Bugandan nationalists and the die-hard "Buganda firsters." At the same time the policy of Michael Kintu, the Katikiro and executive committee head of the KY, to nominate only conservatives and ultraloyalists to the National Assembly alienated more progressive KY politicians. In 1963 nine KY National Assembly delegates crossed the aisle, incensed by the machinations at Mmengo Hill (the kabaka's palace) and enticed by UPC offers of patronage.

Yet simultaneously with the UPC's rapid acquisition of a parliamentary majority through KY and DP desertions, a similar internal decomposition and loss of authority was developing within the UPC itself. Never more than a coalition of power aspirants and district power brokers drawn from different parties and factions, the UPC was divided on a variety of ideological and ethnic lines and lacked a mass organizational base except in Acholi and Lango. Having temporarily papered over its internal schisms for purposes of gaining electoral victory and independence, the UPC began to disintegrate within a few years into its component factions under the pressure of opportunistic and personal rivalries. Moreover, the alliance with the Kabaka Yekka had forced the postponement of the UPC's "socialist" program, disenchanting militant elements who had their own electoral fiefdoms and power bases and could not be easily kept in line by Obote. Indeed Obote's own role in this fluid situation was to mediate between the various personalist formations and ideological groupings compressed into the UPC, utilizing his Lango-Acholi power base to retain his central position in the party.

That the various strains on the formal unity of the UPC could not be contained became transparent with the final resolution of the Lost Counties issue. Obote's decision to hold a popular referendum in the Lost Counties precipitated the collapse of the

---

43. Kasfir, "Cultural Subnationalism," pp. 89–97.

UPC-KY alliance in August 1964. And when the majority of the voters in the two counties opted in November to be reintegrated with Bunyoro, relations between the two former allies deteriorated to open hostility, with both sides preparing for the inevitable showdown.

The UPC-KY cleavage aggravated the internal tensions and rifts within the UPC and set in motion pressures for the removal of Obote from the leadership of the party. These were cultivated by KY leaders, who also made halfhearted coalition overtures to the DP. As Obote's grip over his own faction-ridden party appeared to be loosening, KY Secretary General Daudi Ocheng—utilizing Obote's prolonged trip to his Lango district—introduced a motion in the National Assembly calling for a full-scale investigation into the "gold and ivory" affair. At issue were charges of self-enrichment by Obote, Deputy Commander of the Army Colonel Idi Amin, Minister of Planning Adoko Nekyon (Obote's cousin), and Minister of Defense Felix Onama as a result of illicit gold, ivory, and coffee dealings with rebel leaders of the Soumaliot uprising in Congo/Kinshasa. In light of Obote's weak hold over the traditionally independent UPC rank and file and rumors regarding his imminent collapse, Daudi Ocheng's motion was passed with only one dissenting vote. When two weeks elapsed without any action on the part of the still absent Obote (who was, however, preparing a counterattack in consultation with key members of the army and police) a motion was passed for the resignation of the cited officials.[44] On February 4, 1966, Obote struck back by having five key ministers dragged out of a cabinet meeting dealing with his overthrow and placed in preventive detention in an army base in Lango. Among the ministers was Grace Ibingira, the moderate pro-Buganda UPC secretary-general, who had emerged as one of Obote's main challengers in the party.[45]

44. An independent commission of inquiry drawn from respected, non-Ugandan jurists investigated the affair; they exonerated the cited officials though some doubt was raised regarding the sharp increase in Amin's bank account. Amin apparently used his personal account for deposits and withdrawals in the name of the Congolese rebels.

45. The ministers languished in prison until the 1971 coup. Amin later appointed

The 1966 confrontation within the UPC was a direct result of the party's internal lack of cohesion, the clash between Obote's more militant faction and reconciliationist groups, and the emergence of alternate leaders. In the process Obote nearly lost control over both party and government. Having finally dislodged his opposition, however—and soon crushing Bugandan resistance—Obote was able to develop his socialist credo without being hampered by Bugandan traditionalists entrenched within a rigid federal system or conservatives within his own party. The 1966 confrontation also shifted the balance of power back from Buganda to the central government. On February 26, 1966, Obote assumed all powers, suspending the National Assembly and abrogating the 1962 Constitution. The president—Kabaka Mutesa II—was also suspended from office when he appealed for foreign military intervention against Obote's "coup." On April 15 the National Assembly was reconvened to hastily approve a new "revolutionary" constitution that established a unitary state, direct elections to the Assembly, purely symbolic and ritual powers to traditional leaders (including the kabaka), and an executive presidency.[46] Approved by fifty-five votes to four—with the opposition and four UPC members walking out in protest—the constitution was later upheld in Uganda's High Court.[47] The virtual elimination of Buganda's special privileges and the reduction of the kabaka's status to that of ceremonial leader inevitably sparked off a strong reaction in Buganda. On May 20 the Lukiiko "ordered" that the "illegal" central government remove its federal offices from Kampala by May 30. With this challenge the internal UPC struggle for power merged with the festering issue of Bugandan subnationalism. In this highly charged atmosphere Obote proclaimed martial law

Ibingira as Uganda's ambassador to the U.N. For details see M. C. Young, "The Obote Revolution," and A. de la Rue, "The Rise and Fall of Grace Ibingira."

46. See G. F. Engholm and Ali Mazrui, "Violent Constitutionalism in Uganda"; S. Ryan, "Electoral Engineering in Uganda"; Ali Picho, "The 1967 Republican Constitution of Uganda"; and Emory Bundy, "Uganda's New Constitution."

47. "Uganda v. Commissioner of Prisons, *ex parte* Matovu," p. 515. The final constitution was different in certain provisions from the 1966 document and was subject to relatively open and prolonged discussion by a Constituent Assembly.

throughout the country and the military was ordered to attack
Mmengo Hill, which was allegedly preparing for rebellion by
distributing arms to Bugandan veterans.[48] In the brief but sharp
fighting several hundred people lost their lives. The kabaka,
disguised as a commoner, escaped and went into exile in London,
where he was to die of alcohol poisoning in 1969. For all practical
purposes Obote seemed triumphant both within his party and in his
drive to speed up the modernization of Uganda.

Toward Ugandan "Socialism"

Freed from his cumbersome alliance with the Kabaka Yekka
and from the immediate challenge to his leadership in his own
party,[49] Obote moved to consolidate his personal powers in
Uganda and to leave his imprint on the African scene. Never a
"spell-binder, a martyr or a source of inspiration"[50] nor an
innovative thinker or intellectual,[51] Obote's position at the summit
of Ugandan politics was never secure nor was his prestige in
African circles very high until his victory over domestic traditionalist forces.[52] Dwarfed by Julius Nyerere's intellect and Jomo
Kenyatta's political acumen and charisma, Obote was very much
the odd man out in his East African peer group. At the same time
Obote's reliance upon Uganda's armed forces in crushing Buganda's resistance and the maintenance of tight martial law in the
province mortgaged his future to the loyalty of the increasingly

48. Colonel Amin, at the time Obote's ally, was placed in charge of the operation
since Chief of Staff Brigadier General Shaban Opolot (an Iteso with Bugandan
links) had allegedly rallied militarily to support the kabaka's cause. For the kabaka's
side of the conflict see Mutesa II, *Desecration of My Kingdom*; Obote's rather
different story is in his "The Footsteps of Uganda's Revolution." For a thorough
review of the events see the monthly issues of *Africa Research Bulletin*, Political,
Social and Cultural Series.

49. By 1969–70 a new faction had coalesced around Minister of Defense Felix
Onama, whose strength in several of the UPC's districts temporarily blocked UPC
adoption of some of Obote's proposals on delegate selection for the 1971 elections.

50. G. Glentworth and I. Hancock, "Obote and Amin," p. 239.

51. After attending Makerere College Obote worked in a variety of occupations
(e.g., salesman, clerk) until elected to the Legislative Council in 1957.

52. Ali Mazrui, "Leadership in Africa," and John D. Chick, "Uganda: The Quest
for Control."

autonomous and insubordinate group that had already shown its
dangerous potentialities in the 1964 mutiny.

An effort was made to transform the UPC into a broadly based
mass party that would not be beholden to district power wielders or
local interests. But the attempt to create an effective support/con-
trol mechanism, never zealously pursued, was resisted by threatened party factions and floundered in regions such as Buganda
where the UPC was anathema to the population. Again, though an
effort was made to maintain an ethnic and regional balance in the
cabinet and the National Assembly (see table 5.9)—in particular by

TABLE 5.9
Uganda: Ethnic Composition of Cabinets, 1959–67
(in percentages)

Language group	% of population, 1959	Sept. 1959 Exec. Council	Dec. 1961 DP	July 1963 UPC/KY	Aug. 1965 UPC	Mar. 1967 UPC
Bantu	65.7	100	75	80	68	61
Nilotic	14.5	0	19	10	18	19
Nilo-Hamitic	12.7	0	0	7	9	13
Sudanic	5.0	0	6	3	6	6
Other	2.1	0	0	0	0	0

Source: Part of table 3 in Kasfir, "Cultural Subnationalism," p. 123.
Note: Includes ministers, deputy ministers, parliamentary secretaries, and the
director of planning.

including Ganda representatives—a large number of politicians
and power aspirants had been swept aside by the 1965–66 events,
which bred frustrations, plots, and power gambits. The dismantlement of Uganda's federal system and the integration into the
central bureaucracy of former Buganda officials introduced yet
another source of hostility to Obote's attempts to transform the
country. Tensions within the bureaucracy (bloated with Ganda
personnel) were exacerbated by the regime's efforts to develop the
northern regions, diverting scarce resources that might have gone
into Buganda's economy.

Inevitably, Obote's regime began to rely more on coercive means to maintain itself, cracking down on freedom of the press[53] and using intimidation, preventive detention, and special security units to quell or hound opposition elements. Following the 1969 assassination attempt on Obote, the grip of the Special Forces and General Services details (a form of superpolice) dramatically tightened as opposition parties were banned and several non-UPC MPs and other politicians were arrested. As Obote, fearing for his life, became progressively more isolated from the masses the formulation of his long-expected "Move to the Left" [54] multiplied societal tensions and anxieties. For if followed through conscientiously, the "Move to the Left" signified a major rearrangement of the country's social and economic hierarchy.

The major ideological statement of Obote's vision of a better future was his *Common Man's Charter*, which attacked capitalism, neocolonialism, income inequalities, and expatriate control of the country's economy.[55] The suggested remedies for Uganda's ills included a wider role for collectives and state industry, state control over the import-export trade, government participation in private enterprises, and the inculcation of socialist values among youth through national service units. Though Obote had previously stated his preference for a militant "socialist" program for Uganda —and because of ambitious radicals such as former Secretary-General John Kikonge the UPC had gained a radical image—it is still not clear whether the *Common Man's Charter* was simply another example of radical rhetoric or a definite and concrete program for action.[56] While the import-export trade and some 85 companies

53. The classic case was the arrest and trial for sedition of Abu Mayanja (lawyer and MP), one of Obote's strongest critics, and Rajat Neogy, Kampala editor of one of East Africa's most sophisticated journals, *Transition* (since reestablished in Accra), for the publication of an article criticizing the government for employing "laws designed by the colonial regime to suppress freedom of association and expression." See *Transition*, October 18, 1968, p. 10. When the charges were thrown out of court by the Ugandan judge, the two were rearrested under the preventive detention regulations.

54. See A. G. G. Gingyera-Pinycwa, "On the Proposed Move to the Left in Uganda," and Selwyn Ryan, "Economic Nationalism and Socialism in Uganda."

55. Uganda, *The Common Man's Charter*. The latter includes a variety of other policy statements as well as Obote's major address of the same name.

56. Wallerstein, "Left and Right in Africa."

were officially nationalized on May 1, 1970 (Labor Day), with other projected takeovers interrupted and then shelved by the 1971 coup, some of the major stipulations of the charter appeared unrealistic, difficult to achieve given Uganda's economy and financial condition, or potentially inimical to the status and privileges of the UPC elite.[57] The "socialist" program of action, while stressing the "common man," essentially left most of the population in the countryside unaffected, nor did it seem to presage a crackdown on Uganda's prosperous and corrupt indigenous administrative and governmental elites.[58] Moreover, the "nationalization" of private companies frequently left the expatriate or Asian senior hierarchy in control under management contracts, which confused the man in the street while causing consternation among more militant elements. Also aggravating was the appointment of prominent capitalists to top positions of new quasi-public bodies; for example, Jayant Madhvani, Uganda's foremost Asian entrepreneur, was made head of the all-important Import-Export Corporation. Poor and hasty planning, idealistic goals, lack of attention to concrete details (as opposed to grand principles), ongoing intraministerial competitions and jealousies, and widespread cynicism regarding the government's efficiency contributed to the general impression that the various new programs would not change much in the economy.[59] At the same time, an array of factions and leaders within the UPC—including the hitherto loyal Adoke Nekyon, Obote's half-brother and minister of agriculture, and others in Obote's own Lango region—were maneuvering for power and utilizing the controversial nature of the Move to the Left to enhance their own positions.[60]

Obote's proclamation of the *Common Man's Charter* sparked a major outflow of private capital as both Asians (further restricted by the charter) and private companies fearing nationalization

57. For a good discussion of the provisions of the Charter and their implications see Irving Gershenberg, "Slouching Towards Socialism."

58. Ibid. Sam Adoka, minister of foreign affairs, noted that "[the Common Man's Charter] . . . does not stop a person building ten houses if he does it properly" (Uganda, *Parliamentary Debates*, vol. 95, p. 212).

59. Ryan, "Economic Nationalism and Socialism," pp. 146–48.

60. *Africa Contemporary Record* (1970–71), p. B187.

scrambled to repatriate their funds before currency exchange controls were imposed.[61] This heavy capital drain coincided with an expected sharp drop in coffee exports and a dramatic slowdown in the economy's rate of growth. (The fiscal repercussions of the Move to the Left were especially felt in 1971 after the military coup.) Conditions in the countryside had meanwhile independently deteriorated despite the significant material achievements of the regime in many domains, with social unrest reflected by a resurgence in *kondoism* (violent gangsterism) that affected even Kampala and the other main urban centers. Urban unemployment was rising, cash crop prices and money incomes were falling, and rising taxes were squeezing the "common man." Commerce in basic staples was either drying up or going on at inflated prices as Asians and other expatriates delayed stock replenishments so as to concentrate liquid assets in face of possible expropriation.[62] The bloated civil service felt threatened by projected salary and grading reforms with an emphasis on efficiency, austerity, and merit, while the "Mercedes Benz cult" and corruption in political circles went unchecked.[63] And though objectively there was no evidence that Obote was packing the government or civil service (but not the armed forces) with Langi, Acholi, and other northern personnel,[64] the feeling was that this was the case.

General social unrest was matched by civil-military tensions whose roots are traceable to the 1964 mutiny and its aftermath. Obote's problems with the armed forces, and in particular with his chief of staff, urgently required an unequivocal resolution. Paradoxically, at the time of the coup Obote seemed more concerned with democratizing and legitimating his regime than in assuring that his main threat, Amin, was effectively neutralized. Thus, the

61. The Bank of Uganda noted that this outflow was "a result of the cumulative effect of all the uncertainties connected with the absence of a clear policy statement about the role of the private sector in the economy since the publication of the "Common Man's Charter," and with the unclear and indecisive policy in regard to the position in this cojntry of the Asian community and, in general, of non-citizens" (Bank of Uganda, *Quarterly Bulletin*, p. 12).

62. For an excellent discussion of the economic conditions in the period prior to the coup see Tribe, "Uganda 1971."

63. Selwyn D. Ryan, "Uganda," p. 48.

64. Ibid., pp. 49–50. See also Kasfir, "Cultural Subnationalism," pp. 119–29.

elections scheduled for April 1971—the first since 1962—in light of their unique provisions,[65] might have brought about a partial reconciliation of most of Uganda's ethnic groups (especially the Baganda), while disencumbering Obote of a large number of incumbents whom he regarded as a hindrance to his "national" and modernization policies. However that might have worked out in reality Obote did not move early enough against his military protagonist and on January 25, 1971, General Idi Amin seized power and commenced to impose his brutal and highly idiosyncratic rule on the country.

THE UGANDAN ARMY: THE LION AT THE GATES

At independence Uganda's army was a small force of approximately 1,000 men, with little firepower, antiquated materiel and bases, and headed by some 50 British expatriates and 2 recently commissioned African officers. In accordance with British practice, personnel were recruited mostly from Acholi areas—where the population had more to offer of that unique colonial preference of alleged "martial qualities" and modest ambitions[66]—and military salaries and the army's general prestige and status were comparatively low. Barely five years later, in 1967, Uganda's armed forces were the seventh largest on the continent, having experienced the third highest rate of growth (an annual average of 48 percent);[67] thanks to a more than 400 percent increase in defense allocations (in itself the highest African rate of change),[68] it consumed 10.2 percent of the Ugandan budget.[69] Moreover, the greatly expanded

65. Three candidates (selected in a quasi-UPC primary) were to contest seats that would require electoral support from four essentially ethnic districts. Thus Buganda would have been given a measure of veto power over unacceptable non-Ganda candidates. See also Peter Willetts, "The Politics of Uganda as a One-Party State, 1969–1970."

66. See Lee, *African Armies and Civil Order*, p. 71, and First, *Power in Africa*, p. 77. The British also set height requirements that tended to discriminate against Bantu groups, many of which, however, were not attracted to a career that at the time offered few real prospects of upward mobility. See Kasfir, "Cultural Subnationalism," p. 80.

67. Morrison et al., *Black Africa*, p. 116.

68. Ibid., p. 119. Lee, *African armies and Civil Order*, p. 105.

69. While a 10.2 percent figure is high for a developing polity, Uganda's 1967 defense allocations were average when compared to the rest of Africa. Mali (21.2

armed forces had rapidly moved from the status of a weak and subservient structure mostly concerned with patrolling the borders[70] and maintaining order in the countryside[71] to a politicized control mechanism nominally at the disposal of Obote and the UPC but increasingly autonomous, unruly, and a source of societal tension.

Three basic factors underlie this shift in the civil-military balance in Uganda: the short-lived mutiny of 1964 and the manner in which the regime reacted to it; the politicization and manipulation of the armed forces by a variety of groups and politicians in the power struggles both within the UPC and vis-à-vis Buganda; and the 1969–70 tug-of-war between General Idi Amin and Obote, a struggle not promptly resolved by Obote because of his internally weak position and Amin's popularity in sections of the armed forces.[72]

In January 1964 classic pay strikes rocked the armed forces of East Africa. In Uganda elements of the First Infantry Battalion based in Jinja (fifty miles from Kampala) mutinied, demanding increased salaries, better working conditions, and more rapid Africanization of the officer corps. In the resultant negotiations, Minister of Interior (and shortly of Defense) Felix Onama was roughed up and imprisoned, and the mutiny appeared ready to spread to other units. The regime hastily responded by calling in 450 British soldiers who bloodlessly quelled the mutiny, while granting the mutineers (few of whom were disciplined) the bulk of their demands.[73] Pay revisions boosted salaries by up to 300

percent), Cameroun (19.5 percent), Somalia (18.1 percent), and Mauritania (17.9 percent) led the continent in military allocations as a percentage of national budgets (Morrison et al., *Black Africa*, p. 119.

70. Throughout the sixties two of Uganda's borders were extremely sensitive as civil wars and secession movements were taking place in Zaire and the Sudan.

71. Within Uganda there were several moderate secessionist efforts and localized rebellions such as the Ruwenzururu movements in the west, the Sebei-Bagisum struggle near Mount Elgin, and in the northeastern Karamojong and Turkana areas, still not fully under government control.

72. For a general discussion see A. G. G. Gingyera-Pinycwa, "A. M. Obote, the Baganda, and the Ugandan Army."

73. The basic pay of a private was raised, for example, from 105 to 265 shillings per month, with an additional 150-shilling rations allowance.

percent at an additional cost to the country of U£410,000 annually.[74] Overnight the formerly ill-paid profession became one of the most remunerative in the country, with rank and file salaries more than double those in neighboring Kenya and the second highest in anglophone Africa.[75] Obote's decision to virtually capitulate to the armed threat should be viewed within the context of his looming crisis with Buganda over the Lost Counties issue and the challenges to his authority from within the UPC.

The mutineers' demand for the Africanization of the officer corps met little opposition in the government, which merely hastened the appointment of its two senior African officers to command positions in Uganda's two battalions, while dispatching cadets, NCOs, and junior officers to crash officer training courses in Great Britain, Israel, and the Soviet Union. It was at this juncture that the Kakwa Idi Amin—until 1960 an effendi[76] in the Uganda African Rifles—rose to prominence as deputy commander of the army under the new Iteso chief of staff Colonel Shaban Opolot.

Thus, in a sense the 1964 mutiny achieved its goals, and the army witnessed the government's timidity under pressure. With higher pay scales came demands for better and more sophisticated materiel, further boosting defense costs and preparing the ground for pressure to expand the armed forces. Though the role of the armed forces in pacifying conflict in peripheral areas such as in

74. For a discussion of the 1964 mutinies in East Africa and the different ways in which the Kenya, Tanganyika, and Uganda governments reacted to them, see in particular Henry Bienen, "Public Order and the Military in Africa."

75. See the comparative data in table 5 in Lee, *African Armies and Civil Order*, p. 94.

76. Effendi, a unique rank midway between NCO and a Queen's Commission, was the highest rank most Africans could rise to until shortly before independence. British staff schools placed such emphasis upon quality—including formal education, "gentlemanly" attributes, and manners—that extremely few African officers graduated prior to the crash training program developed specifically for the former colonies. Essentially for this reason many African states in a hurry to develop an indigenous African corps dispatched their best candidates to countries such as Israel, which stressed other criteria for admission to staff colleges.

Karamojong and West Toro was quite limited, the prevalence in Uganda of very high rates of crime,[77] particularly *kondoism* and incursions into Ugandan territory of mercenary groups supporting Tshombé's second bid for power in the Congo and later southern Sudanese Anya Nya groups in conflict with Khartoum, all argued strongly for an expanded force equipped with more sophisticated weaponry.[78] Thus from very humble origins the Ugandan army mushroomed into a large and powerful pressure group.

The vast expansion of the armed forces provided opportunities for manipulation of recruitment patterns in favor of ethnic groups deemed more reliable. Thus, quite apart from the fact that in the north an army career became a very attractive vehicle for upward mobility, there was built in bias for recruitment from Obote's and related ethnic groups (Langi and Acholi), while Amin himself undertook strenuous campaigns to expand the recruitment of the Sudanic Kakwa. Inadequacies in training and socialization programs, in part caused by strains on existing structures due to sharply increased recruiting, resulted in poor integration of the various units and deepening cleavages and friction between ethnic groups.

At the same time the multinational offers of military assistance accepted by the government in order to churn out as fast as possible the indigenous officer corps necessary for the expanded army created a multitude of strains and competitions among returning officers, between them and their units, and between the "crash-trained," "Sandhurst" officers and those promoted from the ranks in 1964.[79] All these factors generated internal factionalism and explosive situations in which officers were rejected by their

77. See Colin Leys, "Violence in Africa." Uganda has traditionally had the highest incidence of violent crime in East Africa, with one murder per 10,000 people.

78. Gingyera-Pinycwa, "A. M. Obote," p. 39.

79. Such friction was especially intense between officers returning from training in different countries. Obote's reliance upon a multitude of foreign resident military training missions also complicated materiel standardization, particularly acute in the small air force, part of which was trained in French Mirages by Israel, the rest in Migs by the Soviet Union. A similar situation existed in the Ghanaian air force in 1959 and 1964.

units when they tried to assume command.[80] Obote himself, still smarting from the 1964 mutiny and sensitive to the spread of coups throughout Africa, actively encouraged factionalism in the army. Using classic "divide and rule" tactics he appointed different foreign military missions to each battalion, scrambled operational channels of command, played off the police against the army (and later set up two elite paramilitary structures), encouraged personal infighting between his main military "protégés," and removed from operational control of troops officers who appeared unreliable or too authoritative. (This was done with Brigadier Opolot prior to his purge and was later repeated in 1970 with Amin.) In the final analysis these tactics produced mixed results: certainly when Amin finally moved against Obote he was able to do so only with a small fraction of the army, but at the same time the army's fragmentation prevented the considerable pro-Obote support from deflecting the power grab.

Factionalism, ethnic cleavages, and intercommand jealousies were also manipulated by a variety of opportunist political cliques in their quest for advancement. So intense was this scramble for civil-military linkages (especially during the period preceding the Ibingira-Obote confrontation) that the main entrance to Army Headquarters at Mbuya carried a sign, "Politicians Not Allowed." [81] Ibingira himself tried to swing several officers from his own district behind his power drive while Obote from the outset had cultivated close relations with key police and military officers such as Amin, who served him well during the UPC power struggle and the confrontation with the kabaka.[82] The kabaka in turn was linked with the Iteso chief of staff, Brigadier Shaban Opolot, who was favorably inclined toward the Buganda cause and uneasy with the heavy predominance of Langi and Acholi in the officer corps. Indeed, just before the assault on Mmengo Hill it was rumored in Kampala that the kabaka had convinced Opolot to stage an anti-Obote coup; consequently, Opolot was arrested and his Teso

80. Ruth First, "Uganda: The Latest Coup d'Etat in Africa," p. 133.

81. Gingyera-Pinycwa, "A. M. Obote," p. 39.

82. First, "Uganda." See also the kabaka's account of Amin's role in his *Desecration of My Kingdom*, p. 53 inter alia.

group purged, and Amin, made de facto chief of staff, directed the army in the 1966 clash. Following the battle of Mmengo Hill, a more thorough purge in the army officer corps sanitized it of pro-Opolot and pro-Buganda supporters and strengthened those elements loyal to Amin and Obote. Indeed, so intertwined were civil and military power in Uganda and so important were ethnic loyalties within the army that one of the earliest indications of a falling out of Amin and Obote was the clash between them over the promotion of several of Obote's new protégés, notably Lieutenant Colonels Oyite Ojok and Masuseru Arach.

The involvement of segments of the armed forces with the Congolese rebels in 1964–65 (out of which grew the gold and ivory affair), its utilization to bulldoze political opposition (as during the arrest of the five ministers), and the free license for intimidation given the army during the attack on Mmengo Hill and during the debates at the National Assembly on the new constitution,[83] all deeply politicized the army, aggravating split loyalties and internal tensions and promoting the feeling that the armed forces were a quasi-coequal partner of the government. Yet the largely northern army remained basically loyal to Obote because of ethnic consider- ations, preferential fiscal treatment, and the "hands off" policy Obote usually adopted with respect to its internal affairs.[84] Even so, at least six plots from within the army—most barely or indirectly reported in the press—underscored the fact that opposition to the regime was not absent.[85]

The manner in which the 1964 mutiny was resolved (contrary to press reports, few of the mutineers were cashiered) gave the army its first taste of influence on the civilian elite. Its politicization, manipulation, and role in later events rapidly transformed it into Obote's principal prop against multifaceted challenges to his authority—a prop, however, with corporate interests of its own that could not be denied without inviting rebellion. Thus the army's demands for better pay, materiel, and logistic and tactical support could not easily be rejected. The regime turned a blind eye to

83. See Ryan, "Uganda," p. 54.
84. Gingyera-Pinycwa, "A. M. Obote," pp. 40–42.
85. From personal fieldwork in 1971 and 1972. See also First, "Uganda," p. 134.

perennial overexpenditures of millions of shillings by the Defense Ministry, making an issue of it only in 1970 when the Amin-Obote estrangement was at its height.[86] In the countryside, particularly in garrison or barracks towns, the army moved as though in feudal domains. Corruption, embezzlement, petty theft, smuggling, and general rowdiness by army elements remained outside the scope of action of the government or the police.

Partly because of the unruliness of the army and the inability of the police to cope with rising societal violence and political opposition, Obote authorized the creation of two elite forces: a paramilitary Special Force and an elite 1,000-man General Service Unit, a presidential bodyguard that also gathered intelligence about the armed forces. The command of the latter was entrusted to Obote's cousin, Akena Adoko. As has already been noted, military hierarchies deeply resent and suspect armed structures outside their control that impinge upon their corporate hegemony over the use of force, provide alternate channels to political influence, and siphon off funds that might otherwise have been allocated to them. Such was indeed the case in Uganda, as Amin frankly stated in justifying his coup,[87] and after the collapse of Obote's regime the Special Force was absorbed into the army, while personnel of the General Service Unit, overwhelmingly Langi from Obote's and Adoko's Akokoro District, were hunted down and eliminated.

But the coup that finally dislodged Obote cannot be viewed as essentially springing from the military's historic volatility, from societal tensions percolating into the officer hierarchy, or from the latter's distaste for Obote's paramilitary units. Without minimizing the precariousness of power in Uganda in 1969–70, the prevalence of power aspirants and political intrigues, or the host of problems

86. See, for example, Uganda, *The Public Accounts of the Republic of Uganda for the Year Ended 30th June, 1969*, pp. 3, 26.

87. Uganda, *The Birth of the Second Republic*, p. 28. Lofchie, "The Uganda Coup," inordinately stresses the corporate and economic threat to the armed forces in several of Obote's policies just prior to his overthrow. While these were definitely there, Lofchie greatly minimizes the *personal* threat to Amin, completely misinterpreting the causes for the coup and hence misjudging the nature of the regime that followed Obote's overthrow.

the regime had either failed to solve satisfactorily or had not moved resolutely against, it would seem that a rapprochement with Buganda, the electoral legitimation of the regime, and the resolution of several thorny problems were but a few months away when Amin's armor moved into Kampala. Though the state of emergency declared at the time of the 1966 disturbances was still in effect in Buganda, a number of political detainees had been released in the spirit of reconciliation, and old KY politicians were timidly joining the UPC in anticipation of the scheduled April 1971 elections. The elections could have given birth to a somewhat less ethnically polarized National Assembly. For under the somewhat complicated rules (which Amin later claimed were incomprehensible to the majority of the people) candidates could succeed in winning seats only if they had support in ethnically diverse constituencies. (Whether these provisions would have been properly implemented is obviously speculative.)

The armed forces were not especially restless in the months prior to the coup, though Obote, trying to cope with the fiscal outlays necessitated by the 1969–70 partial nationalizations, had been equivocating on requests for new defense appropriations. Moreover, at the time of his overthrow Obote still retained significant support in the army, as was clearly manifest when several units resisted Amin's forces for several weeks and later joined the attempted invasion from Tanzania. Indeed, the bulk of the force that Amin mobilized was composed of Kakwa, Lugbara, and Madi elements which were at the time a small segment of the armed forces.

Rather, the impetus for the 1971 coup has to be traced to the personal estrangement between Obote and Amin, which began over a year before January 25, 1971. The close alliance between the two men became a burden and then a threat to Obote, after a series of incidents and policy disputes. For instance, Amin made frequent personal recruiting campaigns in the West Nile districts in an effort to augment his following in the army, whereas Obote was interested in further recruitment from Lango areas. The two disagreed over Uganda's policy toward the Anya Nya efforts to secede from Khartoum's Moslem government, and Amin deeply resented the quasi-secret bases along the border staffed by Adoko's staff. More important, a major dispute developed between Amin and Obote over military promotions. In this instance Amin blocked the promotion of several (mostly Langi and Acholi) officers on the ground that while they possessed formal training they had little experience. (Amin's stress upon the value of leadership qualities and experience as opposed to formal training and education is a direct outcome of his own military background and was vividly attested to after the coup when he promoted to top command positions a large number of former NCOs.) In the background, however, was Amin's deepening suspicion that he was being asked to groom and promote his potential replacements.[88]

Further tensions developed between Amin and Obote over the creation of the two paramilitary structures, especially the General Service Unit, and Obote's close links with several other Langi officers including Lieutenant Colonel Oyite-Ojok, the latter discussed in Kampala as Amin's probable replacement. Amin was notoriously critical of Adoko, with whom he could not get along and whom he correctly suspected of planting spies in the armed forces while protecting (together with Obote) senior Langi officers who allegedly passed petitions against Amin to discredit him in the army.[89] In the highly volatile, rumor-prone, and fluid factional struggle for supremacy in the army insignificant incidents were distorted beyond recognition, minor slights were magnified into power plays, and rumors were touted as fact.

Then on January 25, 1970, occurred the still unsolved murder of Brigadier Pierino Yere Okoya, the army's deputy commander and a strong supporter of Obote as well as former friend of Amin.[90] The killers allegedly implicated several junior officers, who in turn, under torture, implicated Amin, though they later rescinded their confessions. In September 1970 the army was reorganized; Amin, "promoted" to army commander, was in effect deprived of operational control of troops by the creation of two new opera-

---

88. From interviews in Nairobi, June 1971.

89. *Africa Contemporary Record* (1970–71), p. B188.

90. According to one report Okoya strongly criticized Amin's roughly handled witchhunt following the Obote assassination attempt three weeks previously. Ibid.

tional commands, chief of staff of the army (filled by Brigadier Hussein Suleiman) and chief of staff of the air force (Lieutenant Colonel Juma Mussa), both northerners. The ratification of a series on promotions Amin had fought against also angered the former chief of staff.

Amin was obviously being squeezed out of his control over the army. To prevent the excitable and volatile general from retaliating, the reorganization was planned while he was representing the government at Nasser's funeral in Cairo, a trip extended to include a pilgrimage to Mecca. (There he caused a flutter by urging unification of Uganda's Moslems behind Prince Badru Kakungulu, Mutesa's uncle and head of the Uganda Muslim Congress, which was not in favor in Obote circles because they were supporting a rival association.) Rumors of Amin's imminent arrest were so prevalent in Kampala that a fully armed complement of NCOs and junior officers came to the airport to protect him, with loyal units in the countryside placed on alert in case of an actual clash.[91]

The showdown was finally precipitated by the auditor-general's report of gross unauthorized defense expenditures and possible embezzlements to the tune of 35–40 million shillings.[92] Leaving for the Singapore Commonwealth Conference Obote issued an ultimatum to Amin and Onama (the Madi minister of defense and a new challenger to Obote in the UPC) to account for the expenditures[93] and to clear up the Okoya murder. There are at least two versions of what happened next. Amin's version is that Obote had left orders for a takeover of the army by Hussein and Ojok in order to establish a total Langi-Acholi hegemony, a plot that was nipped in the bud by officers loyal to Amin.[94] The second account, Obote's (in several variations), is that the police uncovered a plot to assassinate him immediately upon his return to Kampala and, while he was making up his mind as to his course of action vis-à-vis

91. From interviews in Nairobi, June 1971.

92. Uganda, *The Public Accounts of the Republic of Uganda*, pp. 26–28.

93. As recounted by Obote after the coup. See the *B.B.C. News Monitoring Service*, January 26, 1971.

94. *Uganda Argus*, January 27, 1971.

Amin, the latter seized power.[95] A variation cited by Listowel is that Obote finally made up his mind, on the advice of colleagues in Singapore, and called Oyite-Ojok to have Amin arrested for the plot, for Okoya's murder, and for grand larceny, but the call was intercepted by the Kakwa Signals orderly Sergeant Major Mussa (later generously promoted), who loyally reported it to Amin, sparking the latter's preemptive takeover.[96] While any one of these scenarios is feasible, it has also been argued that, within the context of paranoid tension surrounding the Amin-Obote tug-of-war and factional competition, misapprehension of the actions and intentions of each side played a major role. Hence, as one scholar has argued, it is possible that neither of the two contestants truly desired a showdown but both misunderstood their adversary's intentions. And since the stakes were much higher for him (his life could have been in jeopardy) Amin struck first.[97] Whatever version is the correct one—and Obote's is corroborated more amply—January 25, 1971, forcibly wrenched Uganda onto a radically different developmental path, catapulting to power one of Africa's most unpredictable and violent leaders.

AMIN'S PRESIDENCY: PERSONALIST RULE AND "FINAL SOLUTIONS"

Consolidation of Power and Decay of Military Discipline

Amin's power grab was a personal takeover supported by a minority of the armed forces and facilitated by Obote's policy of keeping the army weak through command and factional fragmentation. Hence, the initial success of the coup did not mark Amin's rise to preeminence in the armed forces, but rather heralded the beginning of a tortuous and eventually brutal consolidation of power by the clique that had engineered the takeover. Fratricidal intergarrison battles, interethnic massacres, the liquidation of

95. *Africa Contemporary Record* (1970–71), pp. B188–90, and more fully expanded in *The Observer* (London), January 31, 1971.

96. Listowel, *Amin*, pp. 70–71, relying apparently on an interview in *Sunday Nation* (Nairobi), February 14, 1971.

97. Michael Twaddle, "The Amin Coup."

Adoko's General Service force, and an uncontrolled reign of terror was necessary before Amin could feel even moderately secure in Kampala. Despite wide international publicity the intensity, venom, and brutality with which the army devoured itself and liquidated Obote's supporters has been underreported. Loyalist forces held out in isolation of Moroto barracks for a few weeks before being massacred by Amin forces. Extermination squads composed largely of Nilotic and Sudanic personnel purged the various army camps of suspected Obote loyalist officers and soldiers. Langi and Acholi officers were sequestered and individually murdered both before and after the attempted 1972 pro-Obote invasion from Tanzania.[98] Protracted manhunts were mounted for civilians and officers who might rally forces for an internal countercoup. The 1971 decree empowering the military to arrest any individual on the suspicion of any crime gave the armed forces license for a major, free-for-all settling of accounts throughout the country, which merged with the eruption of interethnic clashes and fighting between pro-kabaka and pro-Obote elements in Buganda and between other antagonistic ethnic groups elsewhere.

Within a few months after the coup Uganda's prisons were full and as military terrorism entrenched itself hundreds of prominent Ugandans of all ethnic groups began "disappearing" (the local euphemism for murder). Karume Falls Bridge, spanning the Nile, became popularly known as the Bridge of Blood, since it provided a convenient disposal point for massacre victims.[99] By the end of 1971 as many as 10,000 people, civilian as well as military, had been liquidated throughout the country, with the emphasis in Langi and Acholi districts or military units;[100] in Kampala alone five

98. An attempt by an American journalist and a scholar (Siedle and Stroh, respectively) to verify a massacre in the Mbarara barracks led to their brutal murder there. The Jones Commission report of the incident, which blamed Amin's recently appointed commanding officers of the camp, was mailed from Nairobi by the presiding British justice, who feared for his life. See "The Report of the Commission of Inquiry in the Case of Two Missing Americans in Uganda," pp. 23–30.

99. See *The Observer*, March 14, 1971.

100. According to Amin himself 70 officers and 1,600 men died in the intra-army slaughter of June and July 1971 alone. See "Uganda under Military Rule," p. 14. Total deaths by mid-1973 could have reached 85,000.

months after the coup there were an estimated 1,500 political detainees in the jails.[101] The purge of the military resulted in thousands of desertions across the borders to Kenya and Tanzania. Slow international recognition of the coup,[102] Nyerere's unequivocal hostility to the new regime, and Tanzanian support for a pro-Obote invasion force (headed by Oyite-Ojok) caused further jitters in Kampala and a renewed attempt to purge the army of all potential subversive or disloyal elements. In mid-1974 the International Commission of Jurists estimated that as many as 250,000 Ugandans may have been arbitrarily executed, though more conservative figures place the number around 100,000.[103]

The immense gaps in the army's hierarchy and rank and file caused by the liquidation of Langi and Acholi members opened the door for massive recruitment and promotion of Nilotic elements personally loyal to Amin. Powerful recruitment drives were mounted among Uganda's Nubians, Southern Sudanese, Nilotics, and Zairien refugees,[104] and by 1972 the Ugandan armed forces— augmented to over 20,000 in the process—resembled a mercenary occupation force differentiated from much of the population in terms of ethnicity, language, customs, religion (many were Moslem), and regional origin. Since less than one-third of the original army remained intact,[105] in a sense the entire army—Amin's major power prop, though he has encountered difficulties in controlling it—was rebuilt from the ground up as a force committed to the hegemony of one region, the far north, and loyal to one individual, Amin.

Vacancies in the command hierarchy were filled by a series of bizarre promotions from the ranks that completely bypassed the few middle-level non-Langi/Acholi officers who were not purged. Virtually all ranks above that of major had to be filled, and most of the officers emerged from the small group of NCOs and orderlies who initially rallied behind Amin. Many were from the Malire

101. *Africa Contemporary Record* (1971–72), p. B228.

102. "Reacting to the Coup" and "Who Keeps Africa's Conscience?"

103. For a summary of their report see *Africa Research Bulletin*, July 1974, and *Transition*, July-September 1975.

104. See "Uganda: Nubians and Southern Sudanese."

105. "Inside Amin's Uganda: More Africans Murdered," p. 14.

(Kampala) Mechanized Regiment—composed mostly of Lugbara, Madi, and Kakwa—and from the Paratroop Regiment, both of which had formerly been commanded by Amin. In accordance with Amin's bias in favor of experience and loyalty, as opposed to formal military training (though there were limitations because of the absence of trained Nilotic officers), a completely new officer corps emerged from the ashes of the old.

The April 1971 promotions saw, for example, the advancement of Regimental Sergeant Major Waris Ali to Lieutenant colonel and commanding officer of the Mbarara battalion (where he was later implicated in the Stroh/Siedle murders); Sergeant Major Beka, one of Amin's loyal Signals NCOs, became major and chief Signals officer; Private Ismail, one of Amin's orderlies and former driver, was promoted directly to captain; Signals Sergeant Major Mussa, an old crony of Amin and a key figure in the coup (later also involved in the Stroh/Siedle murders), became a company commander; Captain Guwedeko, in jail at the time of the coup because of his implication in Brigadier Okoya's murder, was promoted within two years to brigadier general and commanding officer of the air force; and Lieutenant Malera, who headed special Langi extermination squads after the coup, rapidly became major, colonel and commanding officer of the Military Police and in January 1974 brigadier general and acting chief of staff.

Rapid promotions frequently led to equally rapid demotions as heightened personal ambitions clashed with Amin's fear of the development of competitive foci of loyalties in the army. Thus Captain Charles Arube, a Christian Kakwa who in April 1971 was promoted to lieutenant colonel, in May 1972 to colonel, and in June 1973 to brigadier general and chief of staff, was liquidated and dumped in the Nile in March 1974 following a plot to depose Amin. A similar fate awaited the Alur Captain Valentine Ochima, promoted by Amin to lieutenant colonel and chief of staff and then murdered, again on the ground of conspiracy. Lieutenant Colonel Mussa was removed from operational command in mid-1973 when he joined other officers in requesting that Amin step down, and the equally rapidly promoted Major General Francis Nyangweso (an easterner who served Amin as minister of defense and chief of staff) was "promoted" in 1973 to minister of culture because, in Amin's words, "he knows sports well."

Paradoxically, Amin commenced his rule—the military purges notwithstanding—with a measure of popular support.[106] His role in the 1966 assault on Mmengo Hill conveniently forgotten, Amin's gestures of conciliation to Buganda (which included permission to fly Mutesa's coffin from England for ceremonial reburial in Buganda) raised expectations of a reversal of Obote's abolition of the kingdoms and drastic restrictions on traditional rulers. Amin also assiduously courted support from other southern ethnic groups, paying his respects to elders and traditional leaders and continuously stressing the end of Langi-Acholi domination of Uganda.

Uganda's Asian community—extremely tense and rife with rumors during Obote's last year in office—also warmly greeted the coup and the cancellation of the latter's Move to the Left policies. Anti-Obote politicians purged from the UPC and former KY and DP leaders shunted from political life by the establishment of a uniparty system in Uganda also rejoiced at Amin's rise to power, taking seriously his pledge to bring about a rapid transition to civilian rule and competitive politics. Yet all these conciliatory gestures and promises were but a phase in the consolidation of Amin's personal powers.[107] As soon as he felt secure enough, his erratic policies and decrees did not spare any of the groups that had rallied behind him during the first critical months after the coup.

Amin soon began to alienate—at times it appeared deliberate—every one of Uganda's ethnic, religious, economic, and social groups, civil as well as military. The Langi and Acholi, prime losers in the 1971 power shuffle, were completely alienated from the outset by the purge and murder of their leaders, military officers, and intellectuals. The Karamoja, never fully under central control, were driven to the point of quasirebellion by the army's inability (preoccupied as it was with internal problems) to provide security

106. See Jeffrey T. Strate, "Post-Military Coup Strategy in Uganda: Amin's Early Attempts to Consolidate Political Support."

107. Ibid.

from ethnic marauders from Kenya while it brutally enforced Amin's decree that they clothe themselves more fully. The southern Bantu groupings were rapidly disenchanted with the rise to preeminence in the army and government of northern Nilotics and Nubians and the mass arrest or disappearance of prominent intellectuals, professionals, and politicians. Amin's strongly pro-Moslem orientation—both his domestic financial and political support for a religious minority that at best amounts to 6 percent of the population and his foreign linkages with Libya, Saudi Arabia, and Kuwait—deeply disturbed Christian communities. Intellectuals scorned Amin's populist style, crass mannerisms, and violent purges of their ranks. Salaried workers and unemployed labor grew bitter at declining employment prospects, the virtual collapse of several sectors of the economy (due to the expulsion of the Asian community), the total halt of tourism (formerly Uganda's second most important cash earner), and the sharp rise in consumer prices and austerity taxes. The Asians were shortly to discover the depth of Amin's anti-Indian prejudices; their expulsion and the confiscation and public auction of their property tended to disproportionately benefit enterprising Nilotic officers, who had first choice at auction time, rather than aspiring Bantu entrepreneurs.

Indeed, as one observer has remarked, Amin, starting with a measure of popular support, turned out to be his own worst enemy.[108] Originally setting loose the already unruly army to brutalize the country into submission, Amin found it increasingly difficult to arrest the process and impose discipline on his troops. While he did not hesitate to purge the police force, which he had long despised, or the civil service, his handling of flagrant abuses of authority by the armed forces has been timid and forgiving except when he felt he had to set stern examples. Amin's loss of firm control over the military aided the decay of discipline and cohesiveness and contributed to military praetorianism within the army.

The ambitions of former NCOs and junior officers who almost overnight acquired rank, regimental command, and the taste of absolute power over life and property were whetted for more

108. B. L. Jacobs, "Uganda's Second Republic," p. 53.

power. Officer cliques and secondary power apexes mushroomed outside Amin's direct control and without his knowledge. Military factions cemented together by ethnic and personal bonds moved to promote their own interests in the armed forces. It would not be too great an exaggeration to conceptualize Uganda in 1971–74 as only nominally ruled by Amin from Kampala with his Public Safety Units (allegedly set up to eradicate *kondoism*) carrying out assassinations and "disappearances"; the countryside became essentially a series of peripheral zones of operation for local military garrisons, under the command of functional war lords having power over life, death, and property in their territorial spheres. Within the context of a fully developed praetorian military system, factions clashed in their scramble for a larger share of the spoils of office—looted property, payoffs, promotions, and patronage.

At least four, and probably six, assassination attempts were made against Amin, the success of which might have propelled the country into a bloodbath unparalleled in past experience. As Amin grappled to assert his grip through purges of ethnic groups and the liquidation of power formations, his sources of support in the army and in the country at large further plummeted.

By 1972 the Nilotic-Nubian alliance in the armed forces had begun to crumble. Amin's idiosyncratic pro-Nubian, pro-Moslem promotions and the spread of the purge into West Nile officer cliques, combined with heightened ethnic tensions, began to cause increased unrest in the army. Non-Nubian officers and their ethnic followings in the rank and file chafed at being skipped over in the allocation of operational commands and assigned instead to sinecure positions in staff headquarters that did not offer control over troops. In July 1972 Amin had to cut short his trip to North Africa because of dissidence among the Alur and Lugbara in the army (after the murder of several of their members) and the spread of the military's terror tactics into the far north, including Amin's own West Nile district. As a result of the decline in military discipline and the ossification of lines of control, schisms began to widen between the Christian (and animist) Lugbara and Madi—a major component of the army that had been among Amin's earliest supporters—and the more Moslemized Kakwa and Nubians, internally within the Kakwa group (also along Christian-Moslem lines), and between the Nubians, Amin's ultimate prop, and the rest of the northern groups. These internal cleavages and jostling for supremacy within the original alliance finally led to the 1974 liquidation of key Lugbara officers such as Lieutenant Colonel Michael Ondoga (Amin's foreign minister and later ambassador to the USSR), whose body was found floating in the Nile.

The elimination of Ondoga was one in a series of "disappearances" of Alur, Madi, and Lugbara officers that brought warnings to Amin from chiefs and elders of their ethnic groups of a massive retaliation if the murders of their tribal members did not cease.[109] With Ondoga's liquidation, however, the last tenuous bonds holding the northern alliance together broke and a major uprising occurred in the armed forces, news of which could not be suppressed as was information about previous mutinies. Involved this time was the elite—formerly Amin's own—Malire Mechanized Regiment. The rebellion was crushed by Nubian troops with an estimated 500 casualties. It is noteworthy that Kakwa troops joined the uprising, led by the Christian Brigadier General Charles Arube, a former chief of staff and captain until Amin's rise to power.[110] After this latest phase in the army's self-mutilation Amin's ethnic support was so weak that a generally reliable source has noted that he has been extremely hesitant to visit Arua, district headquarters of the West Nile and his own regional home base.[111] His major remaining military power base is the Nubian component of the army (and the strong Nubian presidential bodyguard units); fear of the consequences of failure, along with the patronage largesse of the regime (mostly shops and enterprises previously owned by the expelled Asian community), keeps potential power aspirants in line.

The Era of Final Solutions

Possibly no other African regime, certainly no African head of state, has received as much foreign press attention as Idi Amin.

109. *Africa Contemporary Record* (1972–73), p. B273.

110. "Uganda Purge." See also the analysis of Martin Meredith in *Sunday Times* (London), March 30, 1974.

111. "Uganda: Nubians and Southern Sudanese," p. 1.

World headlines announced Uganda's expulsion of the Asians, the disgrace of foreign minister and United Nations ambassador Elizabeth Bagaya, and the Denis Hills fiasco, Amin's crude messages to Nixon and to Golda Meir received thorough coverage as have his marital problems, which have resulted in the murder of at least one of his wives and the brutalization of a second.[112] Indeed, hardly a week passes without some news item or tidbit of gossip in respectable newspapers regarding the state of the regime in Uganda. Undoubtedly much of this press attention is attributable to the bizarreness of events and policies in Kampala and Amin's colorful style and language. (The uniformly bad press that Amin has received has led to the expulsion of various reporters from Kampala—tourists were barred in mid-1971—and the threat to expel all British and French expatriates in the country.)[113] Moreover, Uganda is no backwater state (such as Equatorial Guinea or even Dahomey) that can safely be ignored except at times of coups or elections. Since all important policies in Kampala are forged and announced by Amin and Amin represents the rare African example of a personal dictatorship, journalists and scholars have attempted to understand his motivations, biases, and traits, which are such an important ingredient in the formulation of Uganda's erratic domestic and foreign policy.

One need not go into the various speculations based on psychological insights[114] to gain an understanding of the current ruler in Kampala. Culturally very much a marginal man, a product

112. *The Observer*, February 23, 1975. For the fiasco see, for example, Denis Hills, "The Jailer as Seen by His Ex-prisoner."

113. Over the BBC's coverage of the report of the International Commission of Jurists on the massacres in Uganda and a mocking documentary film made by a French team (and approved by Amin) that became the rage in Paris. The film's title is "Idi Amin Dada: No One Can Run Faster than a Bullet."

114. It has been suggested—and there appears to be considerable supporting evidence—that Amin suffers from hypomania, a nervous disorder characterized by alternating periods of heightened physical and mental activity, flurries of optimism and disconnected thought processes, and total nervous exhaustion and gloom. In this context Amin's flights of heavenly inspiration, visions of grand solutions to complex problems, and erratic policies certainly appear much more comprehensible. See *The Times* (London), October 25, 1972, and *Africa Contemporary Record* (1972–73), p. B270.

of the harsh, backward, and isolated environment of the West Nile periphery, Amin acquired only a partial primary education before joining the Fourth Battalion of the King's African Rifles in 1946. Despite his lack of formal education and only elementary English, Amin's initiative, gregariousness, prowess, abject servility to British authority (which according to observers camouflages a love-hate relationship), and excellence in sports allowed him to move up the hierarchy to effendi, the highest rank obtainable by Africans, by 1959. Amin's ruthlessness when on military patrols in Kenya, Somalia, and Uganda twice nearly wrecked his military career, though he relishes recounting (as to an OAU heads of state meeting) his expertise in strangling prisoners.[115]

"Not even semi-Westernized . . . at most sub-Westernized," [116] Amin has the feelings, biases, instincts, and political naiveté of Uganda's "common man," combined with the shrewdness, ruthlessness, and monomania that enabled him to reach the pinnacle of both military and civilian power. His world outlook is largely colored by simplistic moral imperatives; complex social and economic problems are reduced to their essential and smaller than life characteristics and crude and final solutions are proposed: "Economic welfare comes from working hard, obeying the government and trusting God; decisions for happiness become effective once orders have been issued." [117]

Inherently combative, volatile, and uninhibited by intellectual or administrative limitations, Amin has ruthlessly bulldozed problems aside. With a deep-rooted suspicion of intellectuals and an odd preference for particularistic, parochial issues over matters of state, he has indelibly stamped Uganda's foreign and domestic policies with his outlook. He has utilized his position to create a world in his own image, ruling like an imperial potentate unlimited by economic or political imperatives. He is, according to one observer,

115. *Africa Contemporary Record* (1972–73). See also Christopher Munnion, "If Idi Amin of Uganda is a Madman, he's a Ruthless and Cunning One."

116. Ali Mazrui, "Racial Self-Reliance and Cultural Dependency," p. 114. See also idem, "The Social Origins of Ugandan Presidents"; and idem, "Resurrection of the Warrior Tradition in African Political Culture."

117. Glentworth and Hancock, "Obote and Amin," p. 254.

"the embodiment of a man who has made it big from humble, peasant beginnings without having to submit himself to the frustration of formal education's acculturation process." [118] Paradoxically, were he not a member of a numerically insignificant, fringe ethnic group (and hence, within the context of political reality in Uganda, forced to rely extensively on force and his narrow regional base of support), Amin's presidency—with all its intellectual aridness, earthiness, reliance on soothsayers,[119] inspiration from God, diplomatic crudity, and charisma of "political masculinity" [120]—might have developed greater permanence and popularity notwithstanding the revulsion and horror of domestic and foreign intellectuals. For as an African diplomat in Nairobi so aptly remarked, "The common man in Africa looks up to him as fearless, as a great man, because he goes around saying what he thinks." [121] Yet, as has also been observed, the inherent instability of his regime and the continuous purges, "disappearances," and unruliness of the army give Amin greater popularity abroad than at home.

Amin commenced his era in office with pledges of an interim military administration and speedy return to competitive politics. His first cabinet was largely composed of politically neutral and ethnically balanced technocrats with only one military officer—Lieutenant Colonel E. Obitre-Gama. (He was the former Lugbara head of the Paratroop School who was dismissed in October 1973 after embarrassing the government with his brazen self-enrichment.) Among the other ministers were Amin's young brother-in-law Wanume Kibedi, who later defected to Kenya, the veteran KY politician Abu Mayanja (several times imprisoned by Obote), who was also eventually dismissed, and the former commissioner of prisons (promoted to the cabinet to allow Colonel Malera unhampered freedom in the prisons), who later became a victim of the wave of "disappearances."

118. Strate, "Post-Military Coup Strategy," p. 51. See also A. Southall, "General Amin and the Coup: Great Man or Historical Inevitability?"

119. *Africa Contemporary Record* (1972–73), p. B269.

120. Ali Mazrui, "Phallic Symbols in Politics and War," p. 59.

121. *The Washington Post*, May 5, 1974.

That Amin was incapable of either delegating authority or listening to expert advice from his handpicked cabinet ministers rapidly became clear. The cabinet was forced to enroll as cadets in the armed forces and submit to military discipline. Their authority was further undermined by Amin's constant public reference to the fact that even the lowliest private in the army was empowered to arrest ministers on suspicion of subversive activities. Intolerant of contrary opinions, bad news, or reminders on the subtleties of diplomatic protocol and international niceties, Amin tended to brutalize his cabinet, hand-whipping several of his ministers when they cautiously suggested alternatives to his aggressive and impulsive approach to most matters or pointed out his lack of concern for the repercussions of his policies. Amin's physical outbursts and lack of consultation with the cabinet prior to major policy speeches setting forth controversial and contradictory programs reduced the membership of the cabinet as several members escaped the country.[122] After the desertion of his own brother-in-law, Foreign Minister Kibedi (who had tried and failed to rein in Amin's temper in foreign affairs), the entire cabinet was given three months of "vacation" and then reassigned to other duties on the ground that their ministries were running perfectly without their presence. And in April 1972 the civil service and police were purged of their highest and most competent personnel, their replacements frequently being hand picked Amin appointees.

Both before and after the dismissal of the cabinet, many of Amin's policies evoked support among sectors of Ugandan opinion, though the negative repercussions were not slow in arriving. In May 1, 1971, Amin had lashed out against Obote's "ill-conceived ideas" and "politically motivated" Move to the Left programs. Commodities previously monopolized by state bodies were decontrolled, and much to the satisfaction of foreign interests the government reduced its partnership in foreign companies from 60 percent to 49 percent.[123] Theoretically this reduced the govern-

122. In January 1975 Finance Minister Emmanuel Wakhweya escaped to London, bringing to eleven the number of ministers or senior diplomats who have defected since 1971. *The Observer*, January 19, 1975. See also former foreign minister Kibedi's open letter to Amin from exile, in *Transition*, July-September 1975.

123. *Uganda Argus*, May 3, 1971, and *New York Times*, May 2, 1971.

ment's compensation obligations to foreign enterprises, lightening Uganda's financial load. The funds thus "saved" were, however, essentially nonexistent paper commitments that were promptly converted by Amin into hard currency, short-term debts through heavy procurements of materiel for the armed forces and contracts (later defaulted on) for the construction of military barracks, airfields, and officers' housing.[124] The massive uncontrolled expenditures on the armed forces sharply reduced the fiscal reserves of the Central Bank. The latter's warnings, however, together with international pressure deflected Amin's inclination to solve the economic dilemma by printing more paper currency. Consequently, with the country in the midst of a major liquidity and credit crisis, at the brink of bankruptcy, and lacking even a semblance of economic policy for over a year, a variety of taxes were introduced that mostly affected the "common man." Despite skyrocketing prices for staples and a general austerity budget, defense appropriations continued to consume one-third of recurrent expenditures and three-fourths of the development fund.[125]

In general, Amin has shown a tendency to involve himself more with parochial or local matters rather than with the paramount issues facing Uganda. In the words of the state radio itself, Amin's record after two years in office (apart from having "expelled" the Asians, British, and Israelis) was that he had "resolved all religious differences . . . reduced excessive drinking . . . abolished minidresses." [126] Amin has harangued gatherings of students about the high incidence of venereal disease and warned officers not to pursue each other's wives in light of the abundance of other women, and he has not hesitated to divorce three of his own wives (he has four and is extramaritally promiscuous) in connection with the ethnic purges in the army.[127] Until the 1973–74 disintegration of

124. The intricacies of the current budgetary allocations allow for only estimates of the percentage of the defense share (between 25 and 33 percent). See *Africa Contemporary Record* (1972–73), p. B281, and Timothy Shaw, "Uganda under Amin," p. 41.

125. "Behind the Rhetoric in Uganda—The Expulsion of the Asians," p. 41.

126. *Voice of Uganda*, January 27, 1973, p. 1.

127. See *The Observer* (London), April 14, 1974.

the Nilotic alliance, Amin relished touring the countryside to hold impromptu lectures in wayside villages on the benefits of hard work, trust in God, and obedience to the government. In Kampala, too, he has convened numerous "functional" gatherings (of taxi drivers, Catholics, shopowners, students) to air his thoughts on matters of concern to them. His capacity to deliver long off-the-cuff speeches—an average of twenty a week—has been remarked upon: they have usually been rambling and disconnected, parochial and particularistic, and have offered bush medicine solutions to issues bothering his audiences.

Amin's aggressive and impulsive style has been especially noticeable in the foreign arena, where he has antagonized or embarrassed most states, nearly wrecking the East African Economic Community as a result of his dispute with Tanzania and his inability to safeguard the community's Kenyan and Tanzanian officials in Kampala. Barely months after he came to power he discussed with the incredulous Israeli government (then his ally) the occupation of Tanzania's port of Tanga, in order to gain an outlet to the sea. He has alternately threatened to destroy Kigali within minutes because of Rwanda's maintenance of diplomatic relations with Israel,[128] to occupy part of Tanzania because of Obote's presence there, and to "drastically" retaliate against France over a documentary film about him (which he had prescreened and found outstanding), drawing packed and hilarious audiences in Paris. He has complained that the Arab states would not listen to his master plan to defeat Israel in twenty-four hours, defended Hitler's genocide policies and the 1972 Munich Olympics massacre, set up a banana and vegetable collection for a Save Britain Fund (from its current economic difficulties),[129] and sent crude diplomatic messages calculated to personally offend President Nixon (on the Watergate affair), Nyerere, and Premier Meir. He refused to attend the 1973 Ottawa commonwealth meeting after being rebuffed in his request for a British "loan" with which to compensate the Asians expelled in 1972 and after both Premier

128. *Uganda Argus*, August 17, 1972.
129. *Los Angeles Times*, January 20, 1974.

Trudeau and Zimbabwe's Ian Smith (as well as Queen Elizabeth) rejected his request for a private jet to the conference. He had previously sent a cable to Prime Minister Heath suggesting a "radical solution" to the Ulster problem, which was ignored as was his request of Ian Smith for assistance in locating size thirteen shoes for himself. After two years of berating China for allegedly assisting Obote's invasion plans Amin cabled an invitation to Chairman Mao Tse-tung to visit Uganda and participate in the celebrations marking his third anniversary in power. He offered to help in the "dialogue" with South Africa and when rebuffed announced he had the strategy to militarily defeat the racist republic. And when on November 8, 1973, the United States recalled its diplomatic staff from Kampala, Amin retaliated by appointing an army private as representative to Washington, vowing the appointment would be rescinded only after the United States had a new president and "government." [130] And these examples are but a few illustrations of Amin's bizarre international conduct.

Many of Amin's impulsive "policies" have been applauded both in Uganda and elsewhere in Africa. Acclaim for his bravery and "nationalism" was loudest when he decreed the hasty expulsion of Uganda's long-established Asian community despite warnings from several of his advisers of the potential negative repercussions of such a policy. In October 1971 Amin ordered a special census of Uganda's Asians, having in his characteristic style assembled their "leaders" several times to accuse the entire community bluntly of a host of sins, including failure to intermarry and be culturally assimilated into the African population. [131] In December some 12,000 applications for Ugandan citizenship were canceled, sparking an exodus that culminated in Amin's August 9, 1972, decree that all noncitizens would be expelled within three months. Some 50,000 Asians were involved in the forced removal, which was punctuated by the ill-fated invasion of pro-Obote forces trying to take advantage of the crisis. Amin's handling of the Asian issue placed intolerable strains on his relationship with Great Britain

130. *Africa Research Bulletin*, December 1973.
131. For the text of this harangue see *Uganda Argus*, December 9, 1971.

and when the British retaliated by ending subsidies and financial aid, Amin ordered the January 4, 1973, takeover of many British firms in the country.

The decision to expel Uganda's Asian community was less a function of divine inspiration—as Amin claimed—than a cunning attempt to shore up the regime's sagging support in the country through a cruel though immensely popular move. An additional consideration that could not have escaped Amin was the prospect of creating a class of Ugandans beholden to him by the confiscation and reallocation of abandoned Asian enterprises, residences, and household goods. The expulsion decree indeed turned out to be a move close to the hearts of many Ugandans who, like Amin, tended to view Asians as the source of most of their economic hardships. And in a sense the expulsion did alleviate certain short-term economic problems: the heavy outflow of private capital was stopped, though the inflow also practically dried up. Moreover, as a privileged economic strata Asians had, after Europeans, contributed much to the heavy demand (and hence hard currency outflow) for luxury consumption items, which declined with their expulsion. Finally, the surgical removal of the Asian community "Africanized" Uganda's economy as none of Obote's more moderate policies ever could have done.[132]

Yet the long-run negative repercussions of the expulsion have been quite devastating. For along with traders Uganda also lost a major pool of trained manpower, professionals, intellectuals, and civil servants. Many of the reallocated firms promptly collapsed because of lack of working capital, depleted (or looted) inventories, restrictive import policies, and/or inefficiency. The vast Madhvani $60 million plantation and industrial empire (as well as the Mehta estates) were still not operating at even half capacity two years after they were taken over by the government, forcing Uganda to rely on sugar and other commodity imports previously produced locally. (By 1975 the sugar industry was barely operating at 20 percent of capacity, the textile industry, at 50 percent.) Hospitals,

132. See Shaw, "Uganda under Amin"; H. Patel, "General Amin and the Indian Exodus from Uganda"; Justin O'Brien, "General Amin and the Ugandan Asians."

schools, and repair shops found their skilled manpower cut by up to 75 percent causing an irreparable strain, decline, and inefficiency in services throughout the country.[133] The distributive sector has also not yet recovered from the elimination of the ubiquitous Indian trader, with scarcities in basic commodities cropping up everywhere. And while it has been argued that these may be but temporary dislocations, evidence indicates that the short term has blurred into the long run in the context of Amin's erratic handling of the economy and the fiscal strains caused by a voracious military.

Government tax revenues have also sizably declined, denied their former prime source—the high taxable earning power of the Asian community. As Parson has suggested,[134] as much as 38 percent of the government's recurrent revenue may have been forfeited. Urban unemployment has spurted with the departure of the Asian community, which had utilized African manpower in its residences and enterprises and had sustained a sizable service sector catering to its needs. The expropriation of thirty-six British enterprises, the closing of another eighty-seven and the early departure of many British expatriates further aggravated these trends, as did the exodus from Uganda of most missions of technical assistance, some at their own initiative, others, such as the Israeli, after Amin's diplomatic shift to the Arab states for fiscal support.[135] By 1975 the government was forced to reimpose the 5 percent development levy that was abolished following the coup and to announce a series of new taxes, including a 10 percent increase in the sales tax. (In mid-1975 the regime expropriated the property of all those who had gone into exile—including those murdered—since the government had run out of plundered goods or enterprises to distribute to its cohorts.) Foreign trade was proceeding at a snail's pace with all shippers requesting prepayment in hard currency, and the uncertainties of commerce under such conditions had created immense shortages of certain commodities throughout the country.

133. Philip Short, "Uganda," p. 37.
134. Parson, "Africanizing Trade," p. 70.
135. J. Gueriviere, "Ouganda"; Israel, Ministry for Foreign Affairs, Information Division, *Israel and Uganda*; *Uganda Argus*, March 27 and 31, 1972.

The Asian community left behind some 3,500 enterprises as well as residences and household goods estimated at around $400 million in value; they were allocated to Africans by committees that included representatives of the armed forces.[136] In many instances the army was given first choice in the redistribution, creating a new class of military entrepreneurs with a stake in the survival of military rule. Cases of abuses of authority in the reallocation of property have been many, with officers and their families, and Nilotics in general, acquiring some of the more valuable properties, which were treated by the government for accounting purposes as repayable state loans with rents payable directly to the treasury. By refusing immediate compensation for expropriated property and by preventing Asians from leaving with or liquidating their possessions, the regime created new sources of revenue and patronage that were supposed to allay military and urban dissatisfaction for some time to come. On the other hand, the government has been unable to collect most of the rents owed by the new owners of the Asian shops, tax payments have been low from deteriorating enterprises, and many of the officers who won the choice firms promptly liquidated their holdings for cash. By 1975 the regime was faced with a wave of bankruptcies of unsalvageable and cannibalized former Asian enterprises and with a further reduction of economic activity in the country. Since the economic morass affected some vitally important industries a second wave of "expropriations" began late in 1974 as Africans were dispossessed of the looted Asian enterprises in favor of Pakistanis, Indians, and Arabs who had been brought into the country to staff the paralyzed social services sector. In short, the circle has been completed; from the expulsion of indigenous Asians to the reintegration of expatriate Asian nationals. More importantly, however, the widely acclaimed "populist" expropriations have done little for the masses in the countryside, who now find themselves economically exploited by indigenous African traders charging as much as six times the official price for scarce staples, and up to ten times what the former Asian traders used to charge. Since many of the expelled Asians were Moslem, Amin's

136. Short, "Uganda" and "Amin's Uganda."

anti-Asian drive stands in contrast to his avid espousal of Moslem causes, and his transnational links with the Arab Middle East. It is somewhat problematic whether Amin's religious fervor is truly deeply ingrained or whether he utilizes religious "inspiration" (albeit Islamic, a minority faith in Uganda) as a means of communication and legitimation vis-à-vis the masses in the countryside, where such appeals tap strong feelings. While it might be easy to comprehend the internationally isolated Amin paying religious homage to the fundamentalist Qaddafi (and receiving in return developmental funds and prompt military assistance during the 1972 invasion attempt) much of the trivial pro-Moslem bias in Uganda is not simply an attempt to promote and reward elements potentially loyal to Amin. Historically, religion and politics have been intertwined in factional struggles for supremacy in Uganda, and Amin's religious policies may be seen against this background; but the vehemence with which Moslem causes have been espoused probably stems more from Amin's aggressive zero-sum mentality and from his early feelings of inferiority as the unschooled, semi-Westernized, Moslem representative of the peripheral Nilotics. At the same time his crude populist religious prescriptions for happiness, economic welfare, and success are probably extensions of his generally simplistic (peasant, according to many observers) outlook on life.

Completely isolated from most ethnic groups in Uganda, essentially relying upon alternating purges and populist appeals, his Nubian troops and bodyguard, a highly factionalized army, and the cementing effect of patronage, state allocations, and plundered expatriate possessions, Amin's regime may be toppled tomorrow or survive for years. In light of the fully developed praetorian system in Uganda the former may appear a more likely possibility except that futurists have continuously been wrong about Amin's survival powers. What is safe to conclude, however, is that in light of Amin's limited bases of support and his decimation of the leadership of Uganda, political power will not be released voluntarily. The collective guilt of the entire military hierarchy in the various atrocities committed in Uganda and the growth of a ruling military-economic elite argue against any optimistic expectation of a return to civilian rule or meaningful economic development. The law of averages and the experience of Uganda strongly suggest an eventual assassination or military overthrow followed by yet another bloodbath as a new military clique either consolidates power over the other military factions and society or triggers a civil war.

6 Modalities of Military Rule in Africa

The previous four chapters outlined the socioeconomic setting and political evolution of Dahomey, Togo, Congo, and Uganda, and the origins, composition, and internal dynamics of their armed forces. Though the four states obviously differ in many respects, systemically they share a common background of intraelite strife, sharp and politicized ethnic cleavages, and weak economies. In all four the original armed forces were small, ill-equipped, and not overly professional. The following analysis will summarize some of the conclusions and suggest a tentative typology of military style in political office.

Of the eleven coups surveyed, two—the 1963 upheavals in Dahomey and Congo/Brazzaville—were classic "arbitration" actions in which minuscule armies, still led by former colonial officers, presided over extralegal reshuffles of civilian elites against the background of societal turmoil. In these cases, Presidents Maga and Youlou had practically lost control of events, though they were still popular in their respective electoral fiefdoms. Urban dissatisfaction and unrest caused by profligate spending, corruption, and lack of emphasis on economic priorities on the part of highly autocratic regimes set the societal upheaval into motion. From a functional point of view and armed forces merely assured a peaceful (or bloodless) collapse of the ruling groups.

In the remaining nine coups (five of which occurred in Dahomey) military intervention was directly or indirectly linked to the personal ambitions or fears of specific key officers, though societal tensions may have abetted and other civilian groups may have supported the destruction of civilian authority. In Dahomey one important impetus for the twin coups of 1965 (which though part of the same civil-military clash were nevertheless separate events) was General Soglo's humiliation, loss of prestige, and apprehension regarding his possible purge. Societal tensions created a situation favorable to a takeover by Soglo, since the governmental deadlock and popular urban demonstrations were somewhat reminiscent of the 1963 events. The 1967 and 1970 coups by Colonel Kouandété were clearcut personalist takeovers.[1] Colonel Kerekou's 1972 coup d'état was also in part a result of personal ambitions, though by that time civilian authority had totally eroded and Dahomey had become classically praetorian.

The 1963 upheaval in Togo was caused by a linkup of indigenous ambitions for professional advancement in an enlarged army with similar demands by the returning veterans of the French colonial armies. In 1967 the possibility of an Ewe regime was a direct personal threat to Eyadema and other former NCOs who had been involved in Olympio's 1963 murder, and hence the coup can be seen as a defensive reaction against this threat. Amin's coup in Uganda was similarly a reaction against his imminent purge, while Ngouabi's takeover in Brazzaville followed personal and corporate threats to Ngouabi's control of the armed forces.

Thus, except for the 1963 coups in Dahomey and Congo, personal factors have played an important, and at times dominant, role in propelling the armed forces into the political arena. Notwithstanding enduring structural, ethnic, and economic factors also conducive to the breakdown of political order (and present in all African systems), the interpersonal dynamics of the officer corps and interpersonal clashes between civil and military elites have been primary causes of political intervention by the armed forces. Though largely neglected in studies of the African military, the "personal variable" was either the primary factor (as in Togo in 1963 and 1967, Dahomey in 1967, and Uganda in 1970) or a major secondary motive for the coup d'état (twice in Dahomey in 1965 and 1972 and once in Congo/Brazzaville in 1968). In two instances (Uganda 1971 and Togo 1967) a personal threat to the leader of the coup was involved; personal ambitions played a role in three instances (Togo, 1963; twice in Dahomey in 1967 and 1970); and a

1. Colonel Kouandété, in an interview in July 1971, forcefully argued that a military regime was needed in Dahomey (with himself at its head), though when pressed he could not specify any particular policy innovations such a regime might introduce to solve Dahomey's socioeconomic problems. The consensus in foreign circles in Cotonou at the time was also that Kouandété, who wished to be president, had no clearcut program to enact if he came to power.

combination of threats and ambitions was evident in the remaining cases (Congo, 1968; twice in Dahomey in 1965 and once in 1972).

Nor are the four case studies selected for analysis unique. Detailed empirical research into the internal dynamics of other armed forces and civil-military relations elsewhere in Africa reveal personal tensions and ambitions that were directly instrumental in sparking off attempted takeovers. Rich untapped data is available, for example, for a better reconstruction of events leading to the coups in Ghana, Chad, Sierra Leone, and Mali. On the other hand, military intrusion in politics has not been solely or even mostly the result of civil-military tensions or personalist ambitions in the officer corps in all instances. The prevalence and importance of the idiosyncratic variable in military upheavals can be correctly assessed only after more empirical work has been done and the data evaluated. Studies to date have been quite inadequate, and the literature on military coups in Africa is cluttered with unfounded theories on the corporate integrity, professionalism, and nationalist credentials of armed forces.

Turning to the systemic results of military rule, the analysis of the case studies support the contentions outlined in the first chapter. Army rule has not been necessarily more free of corruption or conducive to economic and political development than civilian rule. Corruption remained a fact of life in all four countries. If anything it increased in both Uganda and Congo/Brazzaville, striking deeper roots among officers-turned-administrators. In Uganda it has been Amin's policy to build up a class of officer-entrepreneurs beholden to him alone, while Ngouabi's frequent pleas, admonitions, and warnings against the self-enrichment of officers provide official testimonials to the intensity and intractability of the problem in Brazzaville. The weaker Dahomean and Togolese economies have allowed fewer opportunities for sizable embezzlement or corruption. Still, self-enrichment of officers while in political office has continued, warnings by both General Eyadema and Colonel Kerekou notwithstanding. In most instances military officers have engaged in commerce, petty larceny, or smuggling and have obtained free or preferential state services and exemptions from various taxes and duties. The more prominent cases of military enrichment while in office have been treated gently; the previously noted example of Major Adewui in Togo is a case in point, and more recently Dahomey's Major Barthelemy Ohouens, head of the *gendarmerie* and minister of justice in 1974, was dropped from the Political Bureau of Kerekou's National Council of the Revolution because of his accumulated wealth.[2] Such mild measures in regimes avowedly socialist and contemplating death penalties for petty crimes argue against the thesis that army rule is more strict with misuse of state resources.

It has already been illustrated with regard to economic development that upswings are frequently not directly attributable to the military clique in power. Such, indeed, has been the case in the countries selected for analysis. Uganda has been brought to the brink of bankruptcy and economic decay under Amin. This has been in part a consequence of the international reaction to the expulsion of the Asian community and the various confiscations and nationalizations of property since the coup; but a significant degree of economic decay has been caused by maladministration, the lack of economic priorities, and the renunciation of fiscal accountability by the armed forces. In Dahomey the successive military administrations had neither the length of time in office nor the resources to achieve anything worthwhile in the economy. The current Kerekou administration has opted for a "Marxist-Leninist" approach.[3] Rhetoric aside, this has resulted in the 1973–74 nationalization of private schools and gas stations. The takeover of educational facilities may prove to be merely a change in nomenclature, since the state has no resources to assume larger fiscal and personnel responsibilities in this area; and the petroleum distribution network in Dahomey is so small that its nationalization is merely symbolic. The government has announced that these are just the harbingers of total nationalization of all productive sectors of the economy (which indeed commenced in 1974–75), but there are few truly profitable ones to take over and nationalization in itself will not necessarily create conditions more favorable to economic growth. Congo's economic "growth" has been essentially

2. *West Africa*, December 9, 1974.

3. For a long extract of Colonel Kerekou's "Socialist Doctrine" see *Africa Research Bulletin*, January 1975, pp. 3457–58.

in the form of proliferation of an unviable and uneconomic state sector of sinecure industries that have drained the treasury of increased revenues from mineral exports. Though the country has widely diversified its external sources of support, the French connection has remained virtually intact while embezzlement in state-owned industries has turned them into hindrances to development. Purely external factors (the quadrupling of world oil prices), and not any of the economic policies formulated by Ngouabi or his cabinet, are behind Congo's recent fiscal strength that has allowed for the retirement of part of the national debt, major subsidies for the state sector and ambitious development budgets. Only in Togo has modest economic progress taken place under military rule, though the infrastructure for this had been created long before Eyadema came to power. It should also be noted that as a consequence of Eyadema's still precarious political position in the midst of a large Ewe-dominated social and economic elite he has given considerable attention to popular economic policies.

Political development, defined narrowly as the bridging of mass-elite gaps through the institutionalization of politics and political structures,[4] has also not been the prime achievement of military regimes in the case studies analyzed. In Uganda what may indeed be in the process of institutionalization is the politics of force and terror as means of social control. The collective guilt of much of the officer corps in the wave of massacres since the coup has probably firmly shut the door to any possible return to civilian politics with its inevitable retributions. In like manner Amin's narrow base of support praxeologically argues against any liberalization of the regime (even if this were possible), and his wholesale tinkering with military promotions and demotions has destroyed whatever military legitimacy rank may have previously had. The constitutional provisions of Congo and attention to the structural outlines of the PCT do not stand up under even cursory examination, since by 1972 the party's membership had been reduced to 160 (though it has been augmented since) and the constitution has been a statement more of ideals than of objective reality. In Dahomey the current Kerekou administration seems concerned

4. See Huntington, "Political Development and Political Decay."

with the institutionalization of a variety of "decentralized" regional and local "revolutionary committees" and other structures. Eyewitnesses report stress, however, that the outcome has been lifeless paper structures or changes only in the names of previously existing organs and administrative units.[5] In Togo, it is true, there have been cautious efforts to legitimate Eyadema's regime by the creation of a "national" party and other ancillary structures in which Ewe leaders have been given a role. Even here, though, the established political machinery is very tightly controlled at the center, which expends considerable effort to give the appearance of popular participation and of closer rapport between the elite and the masses, while in reality much of the party activity (even in Kabré areas) is intermittent and illusory. Nevertheless there appear to be grounds for suggesting that the regime is slowly forging some form of political consensus, fragile as it may be. In all four countries, however, civilian participation in the decision-making process is tolerated only as long as certain basic military prerogatives are respected, and it is, in any case, extremely limited.

Finally, stability—the ultimate argument for military rule—has not been the hallmark of the current administrations in Uganda, Congo/Brazzaville, Dahomey, or Togo. In Uganda perpetual instability has been the norm with purges, "disappearances," mutinies, and attempted assassinations and countercoups regularly punctuating life in Kampala. For reasons already outlined, this may be expected to continue in the future. While prediction is obviously foolhardy, it is not impossible that the decay of lines of command in the Ugandan army—already well advanced—may lead to a "secession" of territorial units dominated by the military, the ultimate in political decay. Political instability has also been the norm rather than the exception in Congo/Brazzaville, exacerbated by external support and/or interference (by either Zaire or U.S. agencies), though Ngouabi's regime has been remarkably lenient with unsuccessful efforts by the opposition to dislodge it. Neither has stability finally settled on Cotonou now that the triumvirate and senior military hierarchy have been purged. Intense interper-

5. Michael Wolfers, "Letter from Cotonou." See also the gloomy analysis of the regime's performance in the Nairobi *Daily Nation*, January 27, 1975, in part reprinted in *Africa Research Bulletin*, February 1975, p. 3497.

sonal friction within the ruling hierarchy has already erupted several times, and the still mysterious January 1975 attempted coup of Captain Janvier Assogba and March 1975 murder of Captain Aikpé underscores the precariousness of command authority in Dahomey's armed forces.[6] Togo, on the other hand, has been somewhat more stable under military rule. Noë Kutuklui's various unsuccessful plots aside, there have been two minor mutinies in the armed forces. (Details and reliable information are nonexistent, but it appears that the mutinies were linked with Bodjollé's purge from the army.) The ease with which the regime has been able to ward off these assaults and the recent signs that wide segments of the urban population are disinclined to join any anti-Eyadema upheaval indicates that the regime has accumulated some staying power and a measure of legitimacy.

Thus, in three of our four case studies military rule has not brought about a significant decline in social tensions and political strife or improved a situation of economic stagnation. Only in Togo has the experience been different. (Togo's military regime is best compared with the military administration in Upper Volta, another rather unusual case of significantly positive advances under military rule.) The success of Eyadema's administration has not been a function of Togo's economic superiority (both Uganda and Congo have more developed and viable economics) or significantly lower levels of intraelite or interethnic strife. Rather, stability and a modicum of economic development have stemmed from the cohesion of the officer corps[7] (a result of ethnic homogeneity *and* routinization of promotions and allocation of commands) and the satisfaction of societal group demands (mostly economic) within the setting of a largely unobtrusive administration. A comparison of the internal dynamics and style of rule of the Togolese and Voltaic armies may be highly significant in pinpointing the characteristics of stable and successful military rule in Africa. There are few other unequivocal examples on the continent.

6. *Africa Research Bulletin*, February 1975, p. 3497.

7. The analysis of military rule in the four countries studied and preliminary data from armed forces and military rule elsewhere seem to underscore the importance of the ethnic cohesiveness of the officer corps for systemic stability in military regimes even if the regime is ruling a political system where other ethnic groups predominate.

This rarity of successful military rule does not necessarily warrant a blanket indictment. Only if one starts off with unduly optimistic and/or erroneous assumptions about the integrity, unity, or modernity of African armed forces will one be disappointed with their performance in office. Similarly, only if one's criteria for military success in office include *rapid* socioeconomic change and political development will military rule usually fall short of ideals. In most states in Africa, meaningful socioeconomic change has to be conceived of as a long and arduous process punctuated by discontinuities; with few exceptions, it has to span several generations and, perforce, a variety of civil and military administrations. Thus even in the case of resource-poor Dahomey the first fifteen years of civil and military musical chairs does not necessarily consign the country to the oblivion of political and economic decay, though Togo (systemically so similar to Dahomey) may be building toward more rapid future advances. In light of the huge systemic loads all African governments must sustain, the success or failure of a military regime should always be compared with the performance of previous civilian administrations. There is nothing unique about the abilities or characteristics of "colonels in command cars" [8] that should incline us to expect them to hurdle the universal obstacles in the road to socioeconomic and political development. Indeed, as has previously been argued, a proper evaluation of the characteristics of African armed forces in power should find that they fare as poorly, or as well, as civilian regimes. Any deviations from this expectation—in other words, any marked success of military rule compared to preceding civilian rule— should be viewed as unique and merits especially close attention and analysis.

It should also be borne in mind that in some cases there are no viable alternatives to military rule even if the latter is ushered in through the interplay of personal or group ambitions within the officer corps. Dahomey's abysmal record of military rule should not cloud the fact that once the triumvirate was shunted from the political arena in 1965 (by Soglo's first coup of that year) there was no viable leader who could have taken charge of the splintered

8. Samuel Decalo, "The Colonel in Command Car: Towards a Re-examination of Motives for Military Intervention in Africa," pp. 765–81.

society and calmed the interethnic strife that had just erupted. Also, even though military administration may not be systemically any different from civilian rule the extra-constitutionality of the regime allows it to perform certain actions no civilian regime may dare attempt. As Kirk-Greene has recently argued, the beneficial aspects of these "surgical" decrees may in some instances far outweigh the possible lack of originality, imagination, or efficiency of the army in day-to-day administration.[9] The best example of this surgical action is General Gowon's decree abolishing Nigeria's cumbersome four regions and setting up twelve states in their stead. In Kirk-Greene's words, "What in 1957 was argued before the Minorities Commission as the dreaded opening of Pandora's Box was realized in 1967 as the welcome cutting of the Gordian knot." [10] In like manner—though it is more controversial—bringing to an end Nkrumah's regime in Ghana might have been impossible without a coup d'état (which inevitably set the stage for a second one) and may have been well worth the consequent lackluster administration of Ankrah. Depending upon one's ideological coloration, the recent surgical elimination of the Ethiopian monarchy and feudal system may prove to be the benchmark of an army that has so far brought the country to the brink of disintegration and civil war.

However, the purpose of this study is not to evaluate the merits of military over civilian rule. Rather, its attempts to underscore the weaknesses in a number of theoretical constructs about African armies by applying them to the empirical realities. Quite apart from the fact that theoretical generalizations about African armed forces simply do not hold true when superimposed on specific armed hierarchies in Africa, an idiosyncratic variable was found to be operative in many cases. The weakness of theory together with the presence of the "random" variable make generalization and prediction hazardous. If African armies are no longer viewed as modern corporate hierarchies under a single command but are instead seen as autonomous, only quasi-modern, tenuously interlinked, personalist pyramids clashing over the allocation of promo-

9. A. H. M. Kirk-Greene, "The Soldiers and the Second Chance Syndrome: An Enquiry into the Remedial Imperative of Military Regimes in Black Africa."
10. Ibid., p. 789.

tions, commands, and patronage, theoretical generalizations about motivations for coups must come to an abrupt standstill. Only when these supplementary variables have been taken into account, codified into the equation if you will, can theory building proceed on a sure footing. In short, the objective reality has turned out to be much more complex than previously described. And because current theory has been so inadequate in explaining the motivations for coups, scholars have been turning to analysis of the systemic outcomes of military rule. This research orientation is fully justified, for in the long run the manner in which military regimes rule is a proper object of scholarly research and is rich in theoretical significance. But analysis of the characteristics of military rule cannot be completely divorced from an accurate assessment of the motivations for coups d'état.

It has already been stressed that an empirical analysis of military rule in the four case studies indicates that the army has not performed well in its self-imposed tasks and that from the systemic point of view (subject to certain qualifications) military rule has not proved to be significantly different from civilian rule. This does not mean that military regimes cannot be differentiated from one another. Significant differences have already been abserved in the manner in which military leaders in Dahomey, Togo, Congo/Brazzaville, and Uganda have attempted to cope with the various problems confronting their countries and the systemic effects of military rule on the armed forces and political development. The sum total of these general approaches and orientations toward political issues, power, and the role of the army in society may be called the military style in office. In order to differentiate military style more sharply from the somewhat similar concept of political style one can also talk of *modalities of military rule.* This refers to the principal systemically relevant features of military behavior in office. Of interest are not the specific policies of military regimes, their particular ideological hues, or their sources of societal support; but rather whether their approach to issues and problems is combative or reconciliatory, whether policies are formulated in a decentralized or autocratic manner and whether the demands of nonmilitary groups are met with attention or lack of concern. If national differences between the systemic outcomes of military rule tend to fade into insignificance (at least statistically) as recent research seems to indicate, one remaining dimension along which such regimes may be comparable is their styles of rule. One can also note that none of the early typologies of civilian rule in Africa has stood the test of time and the empirical research of scholars, precisely because they mixed myth with reality, accepting structural characteristics that were often only paper diagrams as differentiating criteria for civilian regimes. The only typology that still has some heuristic value is the one developed by Coleman and Rosberg[11] and then only if the rubrics are modified (contrary to the authors' intentions) to refer to styles and not to policy.

To serve its purpose a typology should be capable of differentiating between political systems that share secondary characteristics. To have heuristic utility the criteria must be systemically important and the typology categories (or rubrics) neither too all-encompassing nor too narrow. Moreover, since what is desired is a typology of *style,* at best a hazy and somewhat subjective concept, the differentiating dimensions should be empirically verifiable or at least not subject to significantly diverse interpretations or assessments. There are a large number of components that make up an elite's peculiar style of rule, and diverse modalities of military rule may be constructed along several of these dimensions. Since this is but a preliminary and exploratory step toward the creation of such a typology and since concrete examples of modalities of military rule will be anchored in data presented in the four studies, no attempt will be made here to specify the relative importance of the suggested typology criteria. A great deal of further empirical research will be necessary in order to arrive at a proper assessment of relative significance. Neat two-dimensional typologies already clutter up the literature without significantly furthering either theoretical knowledge or empirical research.

Of the various characteristics of military rule, the following six may be suggested as having prime importance: the corporate status

11. See the introduction and conclusion of Coleman and Rosberg, *Political Parties and National Integration.*

of the armed forces, the permeability of civil-military boundaries, the degree of personalist concentration of decision-making authority and coercive power, the satisfaction or nonsatisfaction of nonmilitary group demands, the relative immunity of the regime from personality cleavages leading to praetorian assaults, and the active-combative or passive-reconciliationist approach of the regime to societal issues. (Such a typology would benefit, of course, from a culturally modified "attitude toward authority" or a precise active-passive indicator of the kind increasingly used in other areas of research,[12] but the possibility of extending these concepts to African studies currently appears slim.) One aspect of military rule that might appear to be important but is not included in this list is the prospect of a return to civilian rule. Quite apart from the fact that military cliques frequently promise but do not deliver a return to civilian rule (thus complicating analytic distinctions that might be based on this eventuality) the prospect of a return to civilian rule is to some extent subsumed under other characteristics of military rule. Thus, for example, the modality of Amin's rule in Uganda, Qaddafi's in Libya, the Ethiopian clique's in Addis Ababa, or Ngouabi's in Brazzaville is conditioned by an assumption that the army will remain in power for the foreseeable future. In certain instances where there exists a concrete possibility of withdrawal of the military from the political arena this will similarly affect the regime's modality of rule, as will be noted shortly.

The six suggested variables are all quite explicit in terms of the characteristics of military rule they define. Also, they should not offer any insurmountable difficulties to the empirical researcher wishing to operationalize them in order to set up preliminary ordinal scales against which all military regimes may be scored. It is true that the active-combative/passive-reconciliationist dimension would be somewhat difficult to apply in some instances, but

12. See, for example, the work of Barber and George in James D. Barber, "Classifying and Predicting Presidential Styles," *Journal of Social Issues* 24, no. 3 (1969); idem, *The Presidential Character* (Englewood Cliffs: Prentice Hall, 1972); Alexander L. George, "Assessing Presidential Character," *World Politics*, January 1974; idem, "Power as a Compensatory Value for Political Leaders," *Journal of Social Issues* 24, no. 3 (1969).

this may be in part a function of our lack of familiarity with the political style of military leaders in some of the lesser-known African countries. Also, in assessing the regime's satisfaction of nonmilitary group demands it should be clear that the criteria are concrete and do not refer to symbolic policies or rhetoric, though the latter may be to some extent functionally equivalent. The recent structural reorganizations undertaken by Kerekou's regime in Dahomey and Bokassa's various "popular mobilization drives" cannot be described as satisfying group demands even though they were announced to be for the benefit of "the people" or are theoretically capable of satisfying group demands. With these qualifications, the analysis of the experience of Dahomey, Togo, Congo/Brazzaville, and Uganda with military rule can be seen to illustrate three distinct modalities of military rule.

The dominant features of Dahomean military rule under Kerekou and under previous military regimes have been the low concentration of power at the center and the inability of the regime to satisfy group demands. The army's corporate status has been relatively high, and there has been a significant interpenetration of civil-military elites. Praetorian assaults on the weak authority core have been frequent, and the military have been as incapable of governing the country as civilian elites. Withdrawal from the political arena has been a function of the military's lack of cohesiveness rather than a commitment to civilian rule. Both under Kerekou and under Kouandété the government has exhibited an active-combative posture vis-à-vis societal issues and groups even though the prime systemic output has been symbolic rhetoric of different ideological hues and/or mechanical juggling of structural reorganizations of little systemic consequence. The underlying feature of military rule in Dahomey has been the instability of the weak central core of authority resulting from acute societal and military factionalism, which has led to armed assaults on the power hierarchy. The political system may be classified as exhibiting the *praetorian* modality of rule.

A praetorian system is typified by intense intra- and interelite strife, the presence of continuous plotting and jockeying for supremacy within the ruling junta, and a perennial tug-of-war for influence and power between various groups and military factions.

The mushrooming of alternate apexes of allegiance in the army and society and the weak authority of the de facto center of power tend to result in governmental paralysis and the dissipation of considerable time and effort on merely maintaining the regime in power. Consensus in society is nonexistent, and no particular group is able to completely impose its leadership or supremacy over the others. Since the clique in power cannot assure either societal control or leadership within the army, rhetoric and symbolic decrees frequently abound, further eroding the credibility of the regime. Thus the distinguishing feature of a praetorian modality of rule is usually acute instability coupled with high permeability of civil-military boundaries in the context of low achievements in the socioeconomic and political arenas.

The praetorian modality is also clearly visible in Brazzaville, where since 1963 a fully developed praetorian system has developed. Congo's civil-military boundaries are highly permeable (indeed the regime has insisted upon elimination of the boundaries) and the corporate status of the army is high. Political power—seemingly concentrated in Ngouabi's hands—has until recently been diffused among several civilian and military cliques that have periodically mounted assaults on authority. The regime has had a strong active-combative posture on all domestic and international issues, though in order to even minimally satisfy economic group demands its symbolic rhetoric has been tempered by quite conservative policies. In terms of modalities of rule Congo/Brazzaville is similar to Dahomey despite the latter's (until recently) different ideological coloration. The prime characteristics of Ngouabi's military regime are its symbolic output, weak authority core, susceptibility to power grabs, and lack of economic and political development.

At first sight Uganda may appear to be yet another praetorian system, with Amin's regime manifesting the praetorian modality of rule. Certainly civil-military boundaries are thoroughly permeable, the army's corporate status is high, there is little satisfaction of nonmilitary group demands, and the regime has been highly unstable, Amin's staying power notwithstanding. Yet on two dimensions Uganda's regime differs significantly from that of Kerekou or Ngouabi: in the concentration of power in Amin's hands and in the nonsymbolic outcome of his highly active-combative political stance. Amin's personal power in Uganda—despite the internal mutinies and general unruliness of the armed forces—is of a completely different dimension from that of either Ngouabi or Kerekou. Though Amin is not secure in power, as can be seen by the various mutinies in the armed forces, this reflects upon his authority; Amin's personal power—to coerce, punish, purge or liquidate officer cliques or even entire army strata, and to enforce decrees decided upon by his immediate clique—is considerable and is not comparable to that of either Kerekou or Ngouabi. Moreover, Amin's nationalization of industries, expulsion of the Asian community, and international and religious positions can scarcely be called symbolic nor are they in the same class as the policies emanating from Brazzaville and Cotonou. Since the distinctive style of Uganda's military regime is Amin's own and all decisions flow essentially from him, the modality of rule in Kampala may be referred to as *personal dictatorship* or *personalist.*

Personal dictatorship systems are frequently also praetorian polities in which an essentially weak, beleaguered regime is willing and able to use the ultimate weapon of brute force to quell real or potential threats to its supremacy. In a personal military dictatorship (just as in praetorian systems there may also be personal civilian dictatorships, for example, Equatorial Guinea) power becomes centralized in the hands of one leader, who uses selective terror and purges to maintain himself in office. Ruling more or less in an "imperial style," [13] with all benefits, patronage, largesse, and authority flowing directly from the "throne," personal dictatorships are the ultimate in political decay. This is so not only because of the pulverization of all preexisting structures and the concentration of all systemic functions in the hands of the leader. More importantly, since such a modality of rule often involves terror and bloodshed and leaders fear retribution if they lose power, a return to civilian rule or the legitimation of the regime through the creation of political institutions is highly unlikely. Also, since handouts from the state coffers tend to keep the system going, prospects of economic development are poor. The stakes are

13. See Decalo, "The 'Imperial Style' in Africa."

high—absolute power—so competition for the "throne" tends to be intense. This holds true for Uganda as well as for the military regimes of the Central African Republic and Burundi, which may also be seen to manifest the personalist modality of rule. In the Central African Republic and to a lesser extent in Burundi, some of the secondary systemic and rule modality characteristics are different from those in Uganda, but in both instances active-combative military rulers have acquired preponderant power and have used it to impress their particular outlooks on their societies in an unmistakable and unilateral manner.

Togo, the last case study, scores quite differently on the six suggested dimensions. The corporate status of the army is not as high as in Dahomey, Congo/Brazzaville, or Uganda while civil-military boundaries are only moderately permeable, official doctrine aside. Thus, while in Dahomey, Uganda, and Congo/Brazzaville military officers are scattered throughout the state-run industries and civil service (in what are referred to as "supervisory" positions, which also tend to be lucrative sinecures), this is not the case in Togo. The 1972 appointment of a military engineer as director of the local electric company (following a fiasco prior to the Lomé OCAM meeting) was regarded in Togolese civilian circles as highly unusual.[14] In Togo, too, the satisfaction of economic demands has been given high priority (though not ahead of the military's needs), and the only moderate permeability of civil-military boundaries has allowed modest advances on the economic front. In terms of style the regime has been essentially reconciliationist and passive on societal issues and international affairs. Apart from the rather inept plots by Noë Kutuklui there have not been praetorian assaults on the center of political power. Though there is little doubt that the army is in control of the country and that Eyadema has a sure grip over the armed forces, there is a significant devolution of decision-making authority; the Ewe Joachim Hunlédé, for example, has had a virtual monopoly over setting the country's foreign policy. Routinization of promotions and allocation of command positions have worked against the growth of personal grudges and aspirations in the armed forces.

14. From interviews in Lomé, July-August 1972.

The army has also taken care of its own, as when James Assila was retained in both the cabinet and his important command position despite his terminal illness. Major Adewui retained both rank and military status when "purged" of operational command for commercial activities that were contrary to Eyadema's new edict on the role of the army in commerce. Military cohesiveness has thus been maintained, allowing Eyadema a measure of security while he attempts to legitimize his rule via political institutions. The distinctive modality of rule of the Togolese regime can thus be said to be one of *managerial brokerage.*

The distinctive feature of the brokerage modality of rule is its attention to competing group demands; the regime is the ultimate broker in the decision-making process. Since this interest arbitration approach requires that no group (including the army) gain a stranglehold over patronage, largesse, or state resources, managerial brokerage systems are able to build a modicum of popular support and consensus in the absence of other systemic disruptions. Army control may be unobtrusive (as in Togo) or quite visible (as in Zaire) and other secondary characteristics of such regimes may be different, but their prime feature is the interest-group brokerage role of the army.

Managerial brokerage systems tend to be relatively stable regimes that actively cater to the satisfaction of group demands outside the armed forces. Such regimes may show limited positive achievements. Their stability is enhanced by their economic brokerage and by their tendency to set up alternate political control mechanisms such as political parties and other structures that allow for some popular (nonmilitary) participation in the decision-making process. The limitations this approach places upon the tendency of some military leaders to concentrate power too much in their own hands is especially visible in Mobutu's Zaire. That the latter system has been referred to as "Caesarist" [15] reflects on Mobutu's recent active-combative style and his tendency to accumulate power. These proclivities, however, are reined in—or channeled into symbolic activities—by the other imperatives of military rule in Zaire. Thus military rule in Kinshasa (Mobutu's

15. Willame, *Patrimonialism and Political Change.*

idiosyncrasies and Zaire's secondary characteristics notwithstanding)[16] can be best understood if the regime is squarely placed in the managerial brokerage category of modalities of rule.

Dahomey, Togo, Uganda, and Congo/Brazzaville thus exhibit three distinct modalities of military rule, which are also shared by several other military regimes. Some of the comparative data for the four case studies are summarized in table 6.1. There appear to be, however, two additional forms of military style in office that are quite similar to each other but, at least for analytic purposes, should be separated. One may be called the *bureaucratic* modality and the other the *holding operation* modality; the criterion for distinguishing between them is the apparent permanence of military rule.

Military regimes whose credentials as transitional or temporary administrations are relatively valid may be seen to be performing essentially holding operations. Such administrations tend to be quite stable, civil-military boundaries are not overly destroyed by their intrusion into the political arena (though future coups may lead to different modalities of rule, and the corporate status of the military is high. Self-aggrandizement by officers in political office tends to be of modest proportions, and the corporate unity of the army is not usually significantly threatened.[17] The regime also avoids a strong active-combative posture even though it may be engaged in "cleaning up the mess" of the preceding civilian or military administration. Ankrah's military regime in Ghana and Lamizana's first Voltaic administration are good illustrations of the holding operation modality of rule. Moderation while in office and the correction of the previous government's abuses of fiscal responsibility may alleviate some economic problems (as the Voltaic example cogently shows), though this is definitely not a common characteristic of all such military regimes.

The bureaucratic modality of rule is by contrast exhibited by less efficient or less successful managerial brokerages (such as Acheampong's current administration in Ghana), by as yet undetermined

16. See, for example, Decalo, "The 'Imperial Style' in Africa."
17. Indeed, some evidence indicates corporate unity may be enhanced in the short run.

TABLE 6.1

Societal and Military Characteristics of Dahomey, Togo, Congo/Brazzaville, and Uganda

	Societal characteristics				Military characteristics				
	Economic	Ethnic	Political	Impetus for coup	Corporate fragmentation	Personal strife in officer corps	Instability of rule	Modality of rule	Typology category
Dahomey	acute unviability	sharp cleavages	intraelite strife	1963—arbitration 1965a—personal 1965b—personal 1967—personal 1970—personal 1972—personal	high	high	high	symbolic decrees	praetorian
Togo	acute unviability	moderate cleavages	intraelite strife	1963—personal 1967—personal	low	low	low	economic brokerage	managerial brokerage
Congo	acute unviability	sharp cleavages	intraelite strife	1963—arbitration 1968—personal	high	high	high	symbolic decrees	praetorian
Uganda	temporary stress	sharp cleavages	intraelite strife	1971—personal	high	high	high	terror	personal dictatorship

holding operations (as Niger may turn out to be), or by regimes midway between the two (for example, Mali). In such administrations the status of the armed forces is not especially high and civil-military boundaries are quasi-permeable though not as blurred as in praetorian or personalist systems. Concentration of power at the center is low and diffused and satisfaction of group demands is less evident than in brokerage systems. Moreover, occasional rhetoric aside, the distinctive feature of such military regimes is their status quo bureaucratic approach to socioeconomic and political issues, which is usually marked by a passive-reconciliationist political style.[18] Sharing some of the characteristics of both managerial brokerages and holding operations, while not completely free of either cleavages or praetorian assaults, the bureaucratic modality of rule is only moderately stable.

The five modalities of military rule and their relative scores along the suggested six analytic criteria are presented in summary form in table 6.2. The degree to which these modalities are conducive to political stability or economic development is illustrated in diagrams 6.1 and 6.2. Similar diagrammatic comparisons may be made along the other dimensions. If the variables are operationalized and made more precise a rank ordering of specific military administrations within each modality is feasible, as well as more precise cross-category comparisons. Theoretically also, composite (multidimensional) scores could be developed for each military regime for purposes of correlational or factor analysis involving a variety of other socioeconomic variables.

More importantly, however, this regrouping of African military regimes under new rubrics suggests potentially fruitful areas for future research. Thus, for example, the praetorian syndrome might be usefully studied in the context of a comparison of Congo/Brazzaville and Dahomey. To date these two countries have not been analytically linked [19] largely because of their formerly radically

18. With some obvious qualifications, the bureaucratic modality of rule most closely resembles Edward Feit's overencompassing model of military rule. The bureaucratic style is to some extent found in every military regime but can hardly be said to be the dominant characteristic of all. See Edward Feit, *The Amred Bureaucrats*, chapter 1, and his "Military, Coups and Political Development."

19. Except for one study of their 1963 coups. See Terray, "Les Revolutions Congolaise et Dahoméenne."

TABLE 6.2
Modalities of Military Rule

	Praetorian	Personalist	Brokerage	Bureaucratic	Holding operations
Corporate status of army	high	high	moderate	moderate	high
Permeability of civil-military boundaries	high	high	moderate	moderate	low
Personalist concentration of power	low	high	low	low	low
Satisfaction of group demands	low	low	high	moderate	moderate
Immunity to praetorian assaults	low	low	high	moderate	high
Active-combative approach	high	high	low	low	low
Typical examples	Congo/Brazzaville Dahomey	Uganda Burundi Central African Republic	Togo Zaire	Mali Ghana Malagasy Somalia	Nigeria (?) Upper Volta Niger (?) Rwanda

DIAGRAM 6.1: Economic Development under Military Rule

Conducive to Development						*Not Conducive to Development*
1	2	3	4	5	6	7
	Brokerage		Bureaucratic, Holding Operations		Personalist, Praetorian	

DIAGRAM 6.2: Stability of Military Rule

Stable						*Unstable*
1	2	3	4	5	6	7
	Holding Operations	Brokerages	Bureaucratic	Personalist		Praetorian

different ideological positions and socioeconomic characteristics. Yet while it is true that Dahomey and Congo/Brazzaville are quite different on a multitude of dimensions, their prime systemic characteristic—a praetorian modality—should allow very significant comparisons for purposes of better understanding the specific nature of the evolution of praetorianism and the role played by a variety of factors in this process. In like manner Uganda, which manifests both the personalist and praetorian modalities, might be compared with Burundi and the Central African Republic for insights into the specific parameters of personalist concentration of power and the development of personalist dictatorships. This again would require a radical shift in analytic perspective. Though Uganda has been viewed as a praetorian system (which, however, is not sufficiently precise because of Amin's personalist role) all three countries have more often than not been regarded as sui generis examples of military rule. Yet the rulership style and systemic effects of Micombero, Amin, and Bokassa in their respective "imperial fiefdoms" are directly comparable and both analytically and theoretically rewarding.

Again, a detailed comparison of Togo's military brokerage with Zaire's and Upper Volta's[20]—rather than with the other Entente states as has been the practice to date—might provide insights into the role of certain systemic factors in producing some military stability in office that could be transferred to the study of civilian regimes in Africa. Further research along these lines may also indicate that the analytic distinction between brokerage and bureaucratic modalities of rule is unnecessary, and the regimes seem to be separated into these two categories only because they are more or less successful in their efforts to accommodate group demands and to prevent the growth of personal ambitions within the armed forces. However that may be, a composite model of stable military rule would emphasize the interpersonal cohesiveness

20. In many respects Upper Volta exhibits a classical brokerage modality except for the army's pledge to turn power over to civilian elites, which has somewhat limited its scope of action and style. It is quite possible that since the 1974 events in Ouagadougou the regime should be reclassified in the brokerage modality.

of the officer corps within the context of relatively impermeable civil-military boundaries, the high corporate unity and status of the entire army, and the nondiscriminatory satisfaction of societal group demands. Such a regime's specific economic performance in office appears to be of secondary importance insofar as stability is concerned, as both Mali and Upper Volta illustrate, though the existence of some exploitable resources, properly administered (as in Togo), can create support, which enhances stability. The mere existence of a more viable or developed economy, however, is not sufficient and indeed appears irrelevant as far as military stability in office is concerned in the absence of the other conditions suggested.

Apart from the nondiscriminatory satisfaction of group demands, stability is specifically enhanced by the routinization within the army of promotions and allocations of operational commands. The striking feature of the Togolese army is the manner in which Bodjollé, Dadjo, and Assila were kept in top (though increasingly symbolic) positions even though the first officer's role in the 1963 coup was somewhat questionable; the second was different in training, temperament, and outlook from the former NCO's; and the third was on medical leave of absence for several years. Such policies have been very rare in African military hierarchies, and their absence has exacerbated ethnic and personality divisions in the armed forces both before and after military upheavals. Thus, though many military administrations govern economies far more resilient than Togo's, their internal dynamics preclude stable military rule. While the suggested typology cannot be regarded as more than a first step toward the development of a cross-national comparative framework—and indeed typologies are essentially tautological—the somewhat different analytic perspective suggested may make a modest contribution to the theoretical reconceptualization needed for the more realistic analysis of the characteristics of military rule, the motivations for coups, and the prospects for stability in Africa.

Selected Bibliography

Africa Contemporary Record. Volumes 1–5 (1968–74).

Africa Research Bulletin. Political, Social and Cultural Series, 1966–74.

Akinjogbin, I. A. *Dahomey and Its Neighbors.* Cambridge: Cambridge University Press, 1967.

Amenumey, D. E. K. "German Administration in Southern Togo." *Journal of African History* 10 (1969): 623–39.

————. "The Pre-1947 Background to the Ewe Unification Question." *Transactions of the Historical Society of Ghana* 10 (1969): 65–85.

Amin, Samir. *L'Afrique de l'ouest bloquée: l'économie politique de la colonisation 1880–1970.* Paris: Editions Minuit, 1971.

———— and Catherine Coquery-Vidrovitch. *Histoire économique du Congo 1880–1968.* Paris: Editions Anthropos, 1969.

"Amin's Uganda." *Transition,* December 1971.

Andersson, E. *Churches at the Grass-Roots. A Study in Congo-Brazzaville.* London: Lutterworth, 1968.

————. *Messianic Popular Movements in the Lower Congo.* New York: W. S. Heinman, 1958.

Andreski, Stanislav. *The African Predicament: A Study in the Pathology of Modernization.* New York: Atherton Press, 1968.

L'Année Politique Africaine, 1970.

Apter, David. *The Political Kingdom in Uganda.* Princeton, N.J.: Princeton University Press, 1961.

————. "The Role of Traditionalism in the Political Modernization of Ghana and Uganda." *World Politics,* October 1960.

Argyle, W. J. *The Fon of Dahomey.* Oxford: Clarendon Press, 1966.

Austin, Dennis. "The Army and Politics in Ghana." *West Africa,* March 24, 1972.

————. "The Coup in Togo." *The World Today,* February 1963.

————. "The Underlying Problem of the Army Coup d'Etat in Africa." *Optima,* June 1966.

"Back to the Land: The Campaign against Unemployment in Dahomey." *International Labour Review,* January 1966.

Balandier, Georges. *The Sociology of Black Africa: Social Dynamics in Central Africa.* New York: Praeger, 1970.

Ballard, John A. "Four Equatorial States." In Gwendolen Carter, ed., *National Unity and Regionalism in Eight African States*, Ithaca, N.Y.: Cornell University Press, 1966.

Bank of Uganda. *Quarterly Bulletin*, December 1970.

Banque Centrale des Etats de l'Afrique de l'Ouest. *Le Commerce exterieur du Togo*, May 1964.

————. *Commerce du Togo*, March 1965.

————. *L'Economie Dahoméenne en 1964*, May 1965.

————. *L'Economie Togolaise*, July 1965.

————. *L'Exécution du premier plan du developpement économique et sociale du Togo*, March 1969.

————. *Indicateurs économiques dahoméens*, July 1970, February 1973, April 1975.

————. *Indicateurs économiques togolais*, January 1971, May 1972, January 1974, February 1975.

Bazola, Etienne. "Le Kimbanguisme."*Cahiers des Religions Africaines* (Kinshasa), July, 1968.

Beattie, J. H. M. "Bunyoro: An African Feudality?" *Journal of African History* 5, no. 1 (1964).

————. *Bunyoro: An African Kingdom.* New York: Holt, Rinehart and Winston, 1960.

Bebler, Anton. "Military Rule in Africa." Ph.D. dissertation, University of Pennsylvania, 1971.

"Behind the Rhetoric in Uganda—the Expulsion of the Asians." *International Perspectives*, January-February 1973.

"Behind the Togo Coup." *West Africa*, August 22, 1970.

Bennett, Valerie P. "The Intransferability of Patterns of Civil-Military Relations: The Case of Ghana." Special Studies no. 20, Council on International Studies. Buffalo: State University of New York, 1972.

————. "The Military under the Busia Government." *West Africa*, February 15, 1972.

————. "The Non-politicians Take Over." *Africa Report*, April 1972.

Bienen, Henry. "Public Order and the Military in Africa: Mutinies in Kenya, Uganda and Tanganyika." In Henry Bienen, ed., *The Military Intervenes*, New York: Russell Sage Foundation, 1968.

————. "The Background to Contemporary Studies of Militaries and Modernization." In Henry Bienen, ed., *The Military and Modernization*, Chicago: Aldine-Atherton, 1971.

Bonnafé, Pierre. "Une Classe d'age politique: La JMNR de la Republique du Congo-Brazzaville." *Cahiers d'Etudes Africaines* 31, no. 3 (1968).

"Brazzaville: Ten Years of Revolution." Part 1, *West Africa*, August 13, 1973; part 2, *West Africa*, August 20, 1973.

Brunschwig, Henri. *French Colonialism 1871–1914: Myth and Reality*. New York: Praeger, 1966.

Buganda's Independence. Mmengo: Information Department of Kabaka's Government, 1960.

Buganda's Position. Mmengo: Information Department of Kabaka's Government, 1960.

Bundy, Emory. "Uganda's New Constitution." *East African Journal* (Nairobi), June 1966.

Chick, John D. "Uganda: The Quest for Control." *The World Today*, January 1970.

Chronologie Politique Africaine, January-February 1970; March-April 1970.

Civilisations (Brussels), vol. 17 (1967).

Clark, P. "Development Strategy in Early Stage Economy: Uganda." *The Journal of Modern African Studies*, May 1966.

Cohen, William B. *Rulers of Empire*. Stanford, California: Hoover Institution Press, 1971.

Coleman, James S. *Togoland*. New York: International Conciliation, 1956.

——— and Carl G. Rosberg, Jr., eds. *Political Parties and National Integration in Tropical Africa*. Berkeley: University of California Press, 1966.

Comte, Gilbert. "Dahomey: Une election pour rien." *Revue Française d'Etudes Politiques Africaines*, May 1968.

———. "Les Européens inquiets mais prosperes." *Le Monde Hebdomadaire*, April 2–8, 1970.

———. "Le Socialisme de la parole." *Le Monde Hebdomadaire*, March 26–April 1, 1970.

Constantin, F. "Fulbert Youlou 1917–1972." *Revue Française d'Etudes Politiques Africaines*, June 1972.

Coquery-Vidrovitch, Catherine. *Le Congo au temps du grandes compagnies concessionaires*. Paris: Mouton, 1974.

Cornevin, Robert. *Les Bassari du nord Togo*. Paris: Berger-Levrault, 1962.

———. *Le Dahomey*. Paris: Presses Universitaires de France, 1965.

———. *Histoire du Dahomey*. Paris: Berger-Levrault, 1962.

———. *Histoire du Togo*. Paris; Berger-Levrault, 1959.

———. "Les militaires au Dahomey et au Togo." *Revue Française d'Etudes Politiques Africaines*, December 1968.

———. *Le Togo*. Paris: Presses Universitaires de France, 1967.

———. *Le Togo: Nation-Pilote*. Paris: Nouvelles Editions Latines, 1963.

Croce-Spinelli, Michel. *Les Enfants de Poto-Poto*. Paris: B. Grasset, 1967.

"Dahomey: Reglement des comptes entre officers superieurs." *Revue Française d'Etudes Politiques Africaines*, November 1969.

Davies, James. "Towards a Theory of Revolution." *The American Sociological Review*, February 1962.

Davis, David H. *The Economic Development of Uganda*. Baltimore: The Johns Hopkins Press, 1962.

Decalo, Samuel. "The Colonel in Command Car: Towards a Re-examination of Motives for Military Intervention in Africa." *Cultures et Developpement*, January 1974.

———. "The Development of a Praetorian System in Congo/Brazzaville." Forthcoming.

———. "Full Circle in Dahomey." *African Studies Review*, December 1970.

———. *Historical Dictionary of Dahomey*. Metuchen, N.J.: Scarecrow Press, 1976.

———. *Historical Dictionary of Togo*. Metuchen, N.J.: Scarecrow Press, 1976.

———. "The 'Imperial Style' in Africa: Personalist Rule under Bokassa and Amin." Forthcoming.

———. "The Politics of Instability in Dahomey." *Geneva-Africa* 7, no. 2 (1968).

———. "The Politics of Military Rule in Togo." *Geneva-Africa* 12, no. 2 (1973).

———. "Regionalism, Politics and the Military in Dahomey." *The Journal of Developing Areas*, April 1973.

De Chardon, Théophile. "Togo's Liberal General." *Africa Report*, January 1970.

De la Gueriviere, Jean. "Ouganda: Traversée du dessert pour Israel." *Revue Française d'Etudes Politiques Africaines*, April 1972.

———. "République populaire du Congo: 'Socialisme scientifique' contre 'gauche anarchiste.' " *Revue Française d'Etudes Politiques Africaines*, March 1972.

De la Rue, A. "The Rise and Fall of Grace Ibingira." *New African*, March 1967.

Devauges, Roland. *Le Chômage à Brazzaville: Etude Sociologique*. Paris: ORSTOM, 1959.

Dowse, Robert E. "The Military and Political Development." In Colin Leys, ed., *Politics and Change in Developing Nations*, Cambridge: Cambridge University Press, 1969.

Dunbar, A. R. *A History of Bunyoro-Kitara*. Nairobi: Oxford University Press, 1969.

East African Statistical Department. *Uganda General African Census*. Entebbe, 1959.

Edel, May. "African Tribalism: Some Reflections on Uganda." *Political Science Quarterly*, September 1965.

Eleazu, Uma O. "The Role of the Army in African Politics: A Reconsideration of Existing Theories and Practices." *The Journal of Developing Areas*, April 1973.

Engholm, G. F. "The Westminster Model in Uganda." *International Journal*, Autumn 1963.

——— and Ali Mazrui. "Violent Constitutionalism in Uganda." *Government and Opposition*, July 1967.

Enjalbert, H. "Paysans noirs, les Kabres du nord Togo." *Cahiers d'Outre Mer,* no. 34 (April-June 1956).

Erny, P. "Parole et travail chez les jeunes d'Afrique centrale." *Projet*, September-October 1966.

———. "The White Man as seen through the eyes of Congolese (Brazzaville) children." In *Psychologie des Peuples*, July-September 1966. Joint Publications Research Service, *Translations on Africa*, no. 475, 1966.

Etudes Dahoméennes, nos. 10 and 11 (1968).

Fallers, Lloyd A. *Bantu Bureaucracy: A Century of Political Evolution among the Basoga of Uganda.* Chicago: University of Chicago Press, 1965.

———. "Ideology and Culture in Uganda Nationalism." *American Anthropologist* 63, no. 4 (August 1961).

———. *Inequality: Social Stratification Reconsidered.* Chicago: University of Chicago Press, 1973.

———. *The King's Men: Leadership and Status in Buganda on the Eve of Independence.* London: Oxford University Press, 1964.

———. *Law Without Precedent: Legal Ideas in Action in the Courts of Colonial Busoga.* Chicago: University of Chicago Press, 1969.

Fanon, Franz. *Black Skin, White Masks.* New York: Grove Press, 1967.

Feheran, H. W. "Kimbanguism Prophetic Christianity in the Congo." *Practical Anthropology*, July-August 1962.

Feiraband, Ivo and R. "Aggressive Behavior Within Polities." *The Journal of Conflict Resolution*, July 1966.

Feit, Edward. *The Armed Bureaucrats.* Boston: Houghton Mifflin, 1973.

———. "Military Coups and Political Development." *World Politics*, January 1969.

———. "The Rule of the Iron Surgeons: Military Government in Spain and Ghana." *Comparative Politics*, July 1969.

Finer, Samuel. *The Man on Horseback: The Role of the Military in Politics.* London: Pall Mall, 1962.

————. "The One-Party Systems in Africa: Reconsiderations."*Government and Opposition*, July-October 1967.

First, Ruth. *Power in Africa.* New York: Pantheon Books, 1970.

————. "Uganda: The Latest Coup d'etat in Africa." *The World Today*, March 1971.

Fisher, Humphrey J. "Elections and Coups in Sierra Leone 1967." *The Journal of Modern African Studies*, December 1969.

Fortes, Meyer and E. E. Evans-Pritchard. *African Political Systems.* London: Oxford University Press, 1940.

Friedland, W. H. "Paradoxes of African Trade Unionism." *Africa Report*, June 1965.

Froelich, J. C. *L'Année Africaine.* Paris: Pedone, 1965.

————. *Les Konkomba.* Paris: IFAN, 1952.

————, P. Alexandre and Robert Cornevin. *Les Populations du nord Togo.* Paris: Presses Universitaires de France, 1963.

Garin, Claude. *Africa Report*, January 1970.

Gershenberg, Irving. "Slouching Towards Socialism: Obote's Uganda." *African Studies Review*, April 1972.

Gertzel, Cherry. "How the Kabaka Yekka Came to Be." *Africa Report*, October 1964.

————. *Party and Locality in Northern Uganda, 1945–1962.* London: The Athlone Press, 1974.

Ghai, Dharam P. "The Bugandan Trade Boycott." In Robert Rotberg and Ali Mazrui, eds., *Protest and Power in Black Africa*, New York: Oxford University Press, 1970.

Ghai, Dharam P. and Yash P., eds. *Portrait of a Minority: Asians in East Africa.* Nairobi: Oxford University Press, 1970.

Gide, André, *Voyage au Congo.* Paris: Gallimard, 1927.

Gingyera-Pinycwa, A. G. G. "A. M. Obote, the Baganda, and the Ugandan Army." *Mawazo* 3, no. 2 (December 1971).

————. "On the Proposed Move to the Left in Uganda." *East Africa Journal*, February 1970.

Glélé, Maurice A. *Naissance d'un état noir.* Paris: Pichon and Durand-Auzias, 1969.

Glentworth, G. and I. Hancock. "Obote and Amin: Change and Continuity in Modern Uganda Politics." *African Affairs*, July 1973.

Gray, Richard and David Birmingham, eds. *Pre-Colonial African Trade: Essays in Central and Eastern Africa Before 1900.* London: Oxford University Press, 1970.

Grundy, Kenneth W. *Conflicting Images of the Military in Africa.* Nairobi: East Africa Publishing House, 1968.

Gurr, Ted. "Psychological Factors in Civil Violence." *World Politics*, January 1968.

Hancock, I. R. "Patriotism and Neo-Traditionalism in Buganda: The Kabaka Yekka 'The King Alone' Movement 1961–62." *The Journal of African History* 11, no. 3 (1970).

Hardy, Georges. *Le Reverend Père F. F. Aupiais.* Paris: Larose, 1949.

Herskovits, Melville J. *Dahomey.* 2 vols. Evanston, Ill.: Northwestern University Press, 1938.

Hills, Denis. "The Jailer as Seen by His Ex-prisoner." *New York Times Magazine*, September 7, 1975.

House, Arthur H. "Brazzaville: Revolution or Rhetoric?" *Africa Report*, April 1971.

Howe, Russell. "Togo: Four Years of Military Rule." *Africa Report*, May 1967.

Hughes, A. J. *East Africa: The Search for Unity.* Harmondsworth, Great Britain: Penguin Books, 1963.

Huntington, Samuel. "Political Development and Political Decay." *World Politics*, April 1965.

———. *Political Order in Changing Societies.* New Haven: Yale University Press, 1968.

———. *The Soldier and the State.* New York: Random House, 1964.

Ibingira, Grace S. K. *The Forging of an African Nation.* New York: Viking Press, 1973.

Ingham, Kenneth. *The Kingdom of Toro in Uganda.* London: Methuen, 1975.

———. *The Making of Modern Uganda.* London: Allen & Unwin, 1958.

"Inside Amin's Uganda: More Africans Murdered." *Munger Africana Library Notes*, no. 18 (March 1973).

Israel. Ministry for Foreign Affairs. Information Division. *Israel and Uganda.* Jerusalem, 1972.

Jacobs, B. L. "Uganda's Second Republic: The First Two Years." *Africa Today*, Spring 1973.

Janowitz, Morris. *The Military in the Political Development of New Nations.* Chicago: University of Chicago Press, 1964.

Janzen, John M. "Kongo Religious Renewal: Iconoclastic and Iconorthostic." *Canadian Journal of African Studies*, Spring 1971.

Joachim, Paulin. "Le Général Soglo, ou le provisoire qui dure." *Europe France-outre-mer*, no. 453 (1967).

Johnson, John J., ed. *The Role of the Military in Underdeveloped Countries.* Princeton, N.J.: Princeton University Press, 1962.

Kalck, Pierre. *Central African Republic: A Failure in De-colonization.* New York: Praeger, 1971.

Kasfir, Nelson. "Cultural Subnationalism in Uganda." In Victor A. Olorunsola, ed., *The Politics of Cultural Subnationalism in Africa*, New York: Anchor Books, 1972.

Kiba, Simon. "Le Régime militaire au Togo II." *Afrique Nouvelle*, Nov. 4, 1971.

Kirk-Greene, A. H. M. "The Soldiers and the Second Chance Syndrome: An Enquiry into the Remedial Imperative of Military Regimes in Black Africa." *Cultures et Developpement*, January 1974.

Kitchen, Helen. "Filling the Togo Vacuum." *Africa Report*, February, 1963.

Kiwanuku, M. S. M. "Bunyoro and the British: A Reappraisal of the Causes for the Fall of an African Kingdom." *Journal of African History* 9, no. 4 (1968).

———. *A History of Buganda to 1900.* London: Longmans, 1971.

Kottak, C. "Ecological Variables in the Origin and Evolution of African States: The Buganda Example." *Comparative Studies in Society and History*, June 1972.

Kouandété, Lt. Colonel I. M. *Kaba: Un Aspect de l'insurrection nationaliste au Dahomey.* Cotonou: Editions Silva, 1971.

Kraus, Jon. "Arms and Politics in Ghana." In Claude E. Welch, ed., *Soldier and State in Africa*, Evanston, Ill.: Northwestern University Press, 1970.

Lacroix, J. L. "Evolution de l'économie et transformation des structures au Congo depuis 1960." *Revue Française d'Etudes Politiques Africaines*, October 1972.

Lee, J. M. *African Armies and Civil Order.* New York: Praeger, 1969.

———. "Clan Loyalties and Socialist Doctrine in the People's Republic of the Congo." *The World Today*, January 1971.

Lemarchand, René. "Dahomey: Coup Within a Coup." *Africa Report*, June 1968.

———. "Political Clientelism and Ethnicity in Tropical Africa." *American Political Science Review*, March 1972.

——— and Keith Legg. "Political Clientelism and Development." *Comparative Politics,* January 1972.

"Letter from Kluoto." *West Africa*, May 25, 1972.

Levy, Marion J. *Modernization and the Structure of Societies.* Princeton, N.J.: Princeton University Press, 1966.

Leys, Colin. "Violence in Africa." *Transition* 5, no. 21 (1965).

Lijphart, Arend. "Consociational Democracy." *World Politics*, January 1969.

———. *The Politics of Accommodation.* Berkeley: University of California Press, 1968.

Listowel, Judith. *Amin*. Dublin: Irish University Press, 1973.

Lockard, K. G. "Church-State Relations in Uganda 1962–1971." Ph.D. dissertation, University of Wisconsin, 1973.

Lofchie, Michael. "The Uganda Coup—Class Action by the Military." *The Journal of Modern African Studies*, May 1972.

Lombard, Jacques. *Structures du type "feodal" en Afrique Noire*. Paris and the Hague: Mouton, 1965.

Lorwin, Val R. "Segmented Pluralism: Ideological Cleavages in the Smaller European Democracies." *Comparative Politics*, January 1971.

Low, A. "The British and the Baganda." *International Affairs*, July 1956.

Low, Donald A. *Buganda in Modern History*. Berkeley: University of California Press, 1971.

———. *The Mind of Buganda: Documents of the Modern History of an African Kingdom*. Berkeley: University of California Press, 1971.

———. *Political Parties in Uganda 1949–1962*. London: Oxford University Press, 1962.

——— and R. Cranford Pratt. *Buganda and British Over-rule 1900–1955*. London: Oxford University Press, 1960.

Makedonsky, E. "Nouvelle tentatives de creation d'un parti unique au Dahomey." *Revue Française d'Etudes Politiques Africaines*, September 1969.

Mangat, J. S. *A History of the Asians in East Africa c. 1886 to 1945*. London: Oxford University Press, 1969.

Mannoni, O. *Prospero and Caliban: The Psychology of Colonization*. New York: Praeger, 1956.

Mapp, Roberta Koplin. "Domestic Correlates of Military Intervention in African Politics." Paper presented at the Canadian Political Science Association, Winnipeg, Canada, 1970.

Matthews, Ronald. *African Powder Keg*. London: Bodley Head. 1966.

Mazrui, Ali. "Leadership in Africa: Obote of Uganda." *International Journal*, Summer 1970.

———. "Phallic Symbols in Politics and War: An African Perspective." *Journal of African Studies* 1, no. 1 (Spring 1974).

———. "Racial Self-Reliance and Cultural Dependency: Nyerere and Amin in Comparative Perspective." *Journal of International Affairs* 27, no. 1 (1973).

———. "Resurrection of the Warrior Tradition in African Political Culture." *Journal of Modern African Studies*, March 1975.

———. "The Social Origins of Ugandan Presidents: From King to Peasant Warrior." *Canadian Journal of African Studies*, November 1973.

Memmi, Albert. *The Colonized and Colonizer*. Boston: Beacon Press, 1965.

Middleton, J. *The Lugbara of Uganda.* New York: Holt, Rinehart and Winston, 1965.

Milcent, E. "Tribalisme et vie politique dans les états du Benin: Togo a l'ombre d'Olympio." *Revue Française de Sciences Politiques Africaines,* June 1967.

Morris, H. F. "Buganda and Tribalism." In P. H. Gulliver, ed., *Tradition and Transition in East Africa,* Berkeley: University of California Press, 1965.

————. *The Indians in Uganda: Caste and Sect in a Plural Society.* London: Weidenfeld and Nicolson, 1968.

Morrison, Donald G. et al. *Black Africa: A Comparative Handbook.* New York: The Free Press, 1972.

———— and H. M. Stevenson. "Political Instability in Independent Black Africa: More Dimensions of Conflict Behavior within Nations." *The Journal of Conflict Resolution,* September 1971.

Moseley, K. P. "Rural Resistance in Southern Dahomey 1900–1919." Paper presented at the African Studies Association, 1972.

Munnion, Christopher. "If Idi Amin of Uganda Is a Madman, He's a Ruthless and Cunning One." *The New York Times Magazine,* November 12, 1972.

Mutesa II. *Desecration of My Kingdom.* London: Constable, 1967.

Nelkin, Dorothy. "The Economic and Social Setting of Military Takeovers in Africa." *Journal of Asian and African Studies* 2 (1967).

Nesvold, Betty. "Scalogram Analysis of Political Violence." *Comparative Political Studies,* July 1969.

Nettle, J. P. *Political Mobilization.* New York: Basic Books, 1967.

Nordlinger, Eric. "Soldier in Mufti." *The American Political Science Review,* December 1970.

Oberk, K. "The Kingdom of Ankole in Uganda." In Meyer Fortes and E. E. Evans-Pritchard, eds., *African Political Systems,* London: Oxford University Press, 1940.

Obote, Milton. "The Footsteps of Uganda's Revolution." *East Africa Journal,* October 1968.

O'Brien, Justin. "General Amin and the Ugandan Asians." *Round Table,* January 1973.

O'Connell, James. "The Inevitability of Instability." *Journal of Modern African Studies,* September 1967.

Oké, Finagnon M. "Des Comités electoraux aux partis dahoméens." *Revue Française d'Etudes Politiques Africaines,* August 1969.

————. "Survivance tribale ou problematique nationale en Afrique noire." *Etudes Dahoméennes,* no. 2 (1967).

Olatundji, S. "Pourquoi le président Zinsou a ecarte Alley de l'état major?" *Afrique Nouvelle*, September 19, 1968.

Parson, Jack D. "Africanizing Trade in Uganda: The Final Solution." *Africa Today* 20, no. 1 (1973).

Patel, H. "General Amin and the Indian Exodus from Uganda." *Issue*, Winter 1972.

Pauvert, J. C. "L'évolution politique des Ewe." *Cahiers d'Etudes Africain*, vol. 2 (1960).

Perlmutter, Amos. "The Praetorian State and the Praetorian Army." *Comparative Politics*, April 1969.

Picho, Ali. "The 1967 Republican Constitution of Uganda." *Transition* (Kampala), December 1967–January 1968.

Powell, John D. "Peasant Society and Clientelist Politics." *The American Political Science Review*, June 1970.

Pratt, R. C. "Nationalism in Uganda." *Political Studies*, June 1961.

Price, Robert M. "Military Officers and Political Leadership: The Ghanaian Case." *Comparative Politics*, April 1971.

———. "A Theoretical Approach to Military Rule in New Staes: Reference Group Theory and the Ghanaian Case." *World Politics*, April 1971.

Pye, Lucian. "Armies in the Process of Political Modernization." In John J. Johnson, ed., *The Role of the Military in Underdeveloped Countries*, Princeton, N.J.: Princeton University Press, 1962.

———. *Aspects of Political Development*. Boston: Little, Brown, 1969.

Rapoport, David C. "A Comparative Theory of Military and Political Types." In Samuel Huntington, ed., *Changing Patterns of Military Politics*, New York: The Free Press, 1962.

"Reacting to the Coup." *West Africa*, February 6, 1971.

Renwick, Allan. "Makerere and Uganda's Elite." *Africa Today*, December 1963.

"The Report of the Commission of Inquiry in the Case of Two Missing Americans in Uganda." *Transition*, no. 42 (1973).

Rey, Pierre Philippe. *Colonialisme, neo-colonialsme et transition au capitalisme: Exemple de la "comilog" au Congo-Brazzaville*. Paris: Maspero, 1971.

Riggs, Fred. "Bureaucrats and Political Development: A Paradoxical View." In J. LaPalombara, ed., *Bureaucracy and Political Development*, Princeton, N.J.: Princeton University Press, 1963.

Roberts, A. D. "The Sub-Imperialism of the Buganda." *The Journal of African History* 3, no. 3 (1962).

Ronen, Dov. "Preliminary Notes on the Concept of Regionalism in Dahomey." *Etudes Dahoméennes*, no. 2 (1967).

————. "The Two Dahomeys." *Africa Report*, June 1968.

Ross, David. "Dahomey." In Michael Crowder, ed., *West African Resistance*, New York: Africana Publishing Co., 1971.

Roth, G. "Personal Rulership, Patrimonialism and Empire-Building." *World Politics*, January 1968.

Rothchild, Donald and Michael Rogin. "Uganda." In Gwendolen Carter, ed., *National Unity and Regionalism in Eight African States*, Ithaca, N.Y.: Cornell University Press, 1966.

Ryan, Selwyn. "Economic Nationalism and Socialism in Uganda." *Journal of Commonwealth Political Studies*, July 1973.

————. "Electoral Engineering in Uganda." *Mawazo*, December 1970.

————. "Uganda: A Balance Sheet of the Revolution." *Mawazo*, June 1971.

Saintoyant, Jules. *L'Affaire du Congo, 1905*. Paris: Editions de l'Epi, 1960.

Sandbrook, Richard. "Patrons, Clients and Factions: New Dimensions of Conflict Analysis in Africa." *Canadian Journal of African Studies*, March 1972.

Shaw, Timothy. "Uganda under Amin: The Costs of Confronting Dependence." *Africa Today*, Spring 1973.

Shepherd, George W., Jr. "Modernization in Uganda: The Struggle for Unity." In Stanley Diamond and Fred W. Burke, eds., *The Transformation of East Africa*, New York: Basic Books, 1966.

Short, Philip. "Uganda: Putting It in Perspective." *Africa Report*, March-April 1973.

Sigisbert, G. "L'Enseignement vise a former les hommes qu'exige le developpement du pays." *Europe-France-outre-mer*, November 1971.

Sinda, Martial. *Le Messianisme Congolaise*. Paris: Payot, 1972.

Skurnik, W. A. E. "The Military and Politics: Dahomey and Upper Volta." In Claude E. Welch, ed., *Soldier and State in Africa*, Evanston, Ill.: Northwestern University Press, 1970.

Southall, A. "General Amin and the Coup: Great Man or Historical Inevitability?" *Journal of Modern African Studies*, March 1975.

Staniland, Martin. "The Three-Party System in Dahomey." *Journal of African History* 14, nos. 2 and 3 (1973).

Strate, Jeffrey T. "Post-Military Coup Strategy in Uganda: Amin's Early Attempts to Consolidate Political Support." Papers in International Studies: African Series, no. 18. Athens, Ohio: Ohio University Center for International Studies, 1973.

Taylor, J. *The Growth of the Church in Buganda*. London: SCM Press, 1958.

Terray, Emmanuel. "Les Révolutions congolaise et Dahoméenne." *Revue Française de Science Politique*, October 1964.

Terrell, Louis. "Societal Stress, Political Instability and Levels of Military Effort." *The Journal of Conflict Resolution*, September 1971.

Thompson, Virginia. "Dahomey." In Gwendolen Carter, ed., *Five African States*, Ithaca, N.Y.: Cornell University Press, 1963.

────── and Richard Adloff. *The Emerging States of French Equatorial Africa*. Stanford, Calif.: Stanford University Press, 1960.

──────. *Historical Dictionary of the Republic of the Congo (Congo-Brazzaville)*. Metuchen, N.J.: The Scarecrow Press, 1974.

"Togo." Special issue of *Europe-France-outre-mer*, November 1971.

"Togo Coup?" *Africa Report*, November 1970.

"Togo: une rémarquable stabilité." *L'Année Politique Africaine*, 1970.

Tribe, Michael. "Uganda 1971: An Economic Background." *Mawazo*, June 1971.

Twaddle, Michael. "The Amin Coup." *The Journal of Commonwealth Studies*, July 1972.

Uganda. *The Birth of the Second Republic*. Entebbe, 1971.

Uganda. *The Common Man's Charter*. Entebbe, 1969.

Uganda. *Parliamentary Debates*, vol. 95.

Uganda. *The Public Accounts of the Republic of Uganda for the Year Ended 30th June, 1969*. Entebbe, 1970.

Uganda. *Report of the Uganda Cotton Commission*. Entebbe, 1968.

"Uganda v. Commissioner of Prisons, *ex parte* Matovu." *East African Law Reports*, 1966, pp. 514–46.

"Uganda 1972 Economic Survey." *African Development*, June 1972.

"Uganda: Nubians and Southern Sudanese." *Africa Confidential*, May 3, 1974.

"Uganda Purge." *Africa Confidential*, April 5, 1974.

"Uganda under Military Rule." *Africa Today* 20, no. 2 (Spring 1973).

United States. *Area Handbook for People's Republic of the Congo*. Washington, D.C.: U.S. Government Printing Office, 1971.

United States. Arms Control and Disarmament Agency. *World Military Expenditures, 1970*. Washington, D.C.: U.S. Government Printing Office, 1971.

Wagret, J. M. *Histoire et sociologie politiques de la République du Congo Brazzaville*. Paris: R. Pichon and R. Durand-Auzias, 1964.

Wallerstein, Immanuel. "Left and Right in Africa." *Journal of Modern African Studies*, May 1971.

Welbourn, F. B. *Religion and Politics in Uganda 1952–1972*. Nairobi: East Africa Publishing House, 1967.

Welch, Claude E., Jr. *Dream of Unity: Pan Africanism and Political Unification in West Africa*. Ithaca, N.Y.: Cornell University Press, 1966.

———. "Praetorianism in Commonwealth West Africa." *Journal of Modern African Studies*, July 1972.

———. "Soldier and State in Africa." *Journal of Modern African Studies*, November 1967.

———. *Soldier and State in Africa*. Evanston, Ill.: Northwestern University Press, 1970.

"Who Keeps Africa's Conscience?" *West Africa*, February 19, 1971.

Willame, Jean Claude. *Patrimonialism and Political Change in the Congo*. Stanford, Calif.: Stanford University Press, 1972.

Willetts, Peter. "The Politics of Uganda as a One-Party State, 1969–1970." *African Affairs*, July 1975.

Wolfers, Michael. "Letter from Cotonou." *West Africa*, December 19, 1974.

Wood, David. *The Armed Forces of African States*. Adelphi Papers No. 27. London: Institute for Strategic Studies, 1966.

Wrigley, C. C. *Buganda: An Outline of Economic History,* Reprint Series No. 1. London: Institute of Commonwealth Studies, 1962.

Young, M. C. "The Obote Revolution." *Africa Report*, June 1966.

Zolberg, Aristide. *Creating Political Order: The Party-States of West Africa*. Chicago: Rand McNally, 1966.

———. "Military Intervention in the New States of Africa." In Henry Bienen, ed., *The Military Intervenes*, New York: Russell Sage Foundation, 1968.

Index